Act of Love

Radically Reprogram Your Mind

Kino MacGregor

BALBOA.PRESS

A DIVISION OF HAY HOUSE

Balboa Press books may be ordered through booksellers or by contacting:

Balboa Press
A Division of Hay House
1663 Liberty Drive
Bloomington, IN 47403
www.balboapress.com
844-682-1282

Because of the dynamic nature of the Internet, any web addresses or links contained in this book may have changed since publication and may no longer be valid. The views expressed in this work are solely those of the author and do not necessarily reflect the views of the publisher, and the publisher hereby disclaims any responsibility for them.

The author of this book does not dispense medical advice or prescribe the use of any technique as a form of treatment for physical, emotional, or medical problems without the advice of a physician, either directly or indirectly. The intent of the author is only to offer information of a general nature to help you in your quest for emotional and spiritual well-being. In the event you use any of the information in this book for yourself, which is your constitutional right, the author and the publisher assume no responsibility for your actions.

Any people depicted in stock imagery provided by Getty Images are models, and such images are being used for illustrative purposes only. Certain stock imagery © Getty Images.

Print information available on the last page.

THE HOLY BIBLE, NEW INTERNATIONAL VERSION®, NIV® Copyright © 1973, 1978, 1984, 2011 by Biblica, Inc.® Used by permission. All rights reserved worldwide.

Scriptures taken from the New King James Version®. Copyright © 1982 by Thomas Nelson. Used by permission. All rights reserved.

The ESV® Bible (The Holy Bible, English Standard Version®). ESV® Text Edition: 2016. Copyright © 2001 by Crossway, a publishing ministry of Good News Publishers. The ESV® text has been reproduced in cooperation with and by permission of Good News Publishers. Unauthorized reproduction of this publication is prohibited. All rights reserved.

ISBN: 978-1-9822-7872-4 (sc)
ISBN: 978-1-9822-7873-1 (hc)
ISBN: 978-1-9822-7871-7 (e)

Library of Congress Control Number: 2022900162

Balboa Press rev. date: 11/17/2022

For all who wander,

For the seekers of the world,

And all born with an inexplicable yearning,

May the path ahead be well lit for the journey back home.

Special thanks to Lashanna Small, Melanie Klein, Beth Frankl, and Barri DeFrancisci for believing in this project, for encouraging me, for rounds of edits, and for sharing the path.

All stories shared with permission. Names changed for privacy.

Contents

Introduction

This is a book about finding love and true happiness, even if you're brokenhearted. It's about making the courageous decision to reset your mind and choose your outlook. The promise is simple, but the work is deceptively hard. I know from my own experience that the innate ability to feel joy can never be destroyed, even if it sometimes seems like it's gone for good. There is nothing any one of us could ever do that would make us unworthy of feeling the gift of love. No authority sits as judge and jury and convicts us of a misdeed so terrible that our happiness is put in chains. Our hearts remain eternally free: free to search for the smile in simple things, free to forgive ourselves and others, free to fall in love with life all over again. And I present a new paradigm that has the potential to radically reprogram your mind with one simple shift—learn how to make everything an act of love.

Maybe you, like me, have spent your life searching for answers to the deepest questions of life. Maybe you, like me, have felt infinitely dissatisfied with the answers presented to you by conventional religion and spiritual self-help. I've always seen hypocrisy in the madness of organized religion, delusion in fundamentalism of any type, and superficiality in the culture of positivity around most self-help communities. I was starving for something real, deep, and profound when I discovered the principles that I share with you in this book. And now, I invite you to shift your willfulness to willingness and begin what will be an adventure of the spirit.

The Lotus Thrives in Muddy Waters

It would be fair to wonder who I am to have the audacity to offer something so radical as a change in the very foundation of the nature of the mind. Well, let me clearly state what I'm not. I'm not an Ivy League neuroscientist, but I do draw upon leading-edge neuroscience. I'm not an incarnate lama, guru, or lineage holder of a spiritual tradition, yet the teaching presented here is informed by the legacy teachings of the East. I'm not an ordained pastor, minister, or prophet, although I have a deeply personal connection to Jesus Christ. I have no formal training in the science of the brain or body, other than my lifelong devotion to yoga and meditation. In other words, I'm no one special. Why, at this point, should anyone keep reading; why devote one's precious hours of life to the ramblings of an unqualified fool? Truthfully, maybe I am just that. But maybe I've also found something through a deep, thorough, personal quest that could help you too. Maybe the very fact that I have no formal higher education on the subjects on which I write will make what I'm sharing accessible and directly applicable. Think of me as a hacker, except instead of deconstructing the programming of a computer, I hacked into the brain and deconstructed the core principles of the software that defined my life. I set my brain and the thoughts it thinks free, and I know anyone can do it too.

I had great motivation to perform such an operation of the mind. For me, it was a matter of existential urgency. I have struggled with depression since I was nine years old. Over twenty years ago, when I was nineteen, I began a spiritual quest that has defined my life. Through yoga, meditation, prayer, and personal-growth work, I developed what I thought was a firm foundation in a life of inner peace. But then, a series of major events challenged the glass-house spirituality I'd built.

To say it was a difficult period would be an understatement. My father passed away after nearly three years of medical issues, including multiple strokes, congestive heart failure, cancer, dementia, and aspiration pneumonia. His loss opened a chasm of grief and uncertainty within me that I am still processing. A series of personal and professional betrayals resulted in lawsuits, social media wars, cancel culture bullying, and an explosion of vitriol. Physically, I was in pain from injuries sustained while teaching and a second-degree burn from my husband's motorcycle. My cat and my parents' dog both had to be put down. I was heartbroken and filled with a rage that would overflow like a volcanic eruption.

Until that point, I was comfortable with sadness, but I was not comfortable with anger. If someone raised their voice or got angry, I would be uncomfortable. I felt it was a personal failure if I raised my voice, yet there I was, lashing out at others, throwing a temper tantrum on a broad public platform. The collateral damage of my actions is a bill that's still being paid. I walked away from this period of my life with a resurgence of debilitating depression, and all the tools I had previously used were inadequate to address the depth of my anguish. Now, in hindsight, I can see how the universe gave me the exact situation I needed to wake up from the dream. But in the moment, I was miserable, desperate, and lost. There was an urgency to my spiritual searching that had not been present before. Old thoughts of suicidal ideation reappeared, and there were days when I felt the only answer to life's quandary was to press the restart button and begin again. I'm so grateful that I got the help I needed and found the way out of my misery. Now, I'm here today to share the road map, to offer up a small piece of the wisdom that I've acquired in the hope that someone else might find the way out of suffering too.

After the dust had settled from the onslaught of difficulties, I felt like I stood in the midst of a scorched-earth landscape. The devastation was overwhelming, and to make matters worse, I felt responsible for the devastation. I saw myself and my failures as the cause of the misery, and no matter where I turned, I was always there. While I continued my yoga practice and sought the help of healers, spiritual counselors, and therapists, I needed a major system reset. Meditation has always been an integral part of my spiritual path, and I decided to sign up for a three-day silent meditation retreat. I had completed three ten-day silent meditation retreats before, and I knew the power of a complete and total unplugging of the mind. Whenever I mention a silent retreat, I find that people are simultaneously intrigued and terrified. (Don't worry; the teachings presented here do not require anyone to join a silent retreat. But if the desire to join a silent retreat is there, follow it.)

After three days of silent meditation, a shift happened that I can only describe as an awakening. I picked up my toothbrush and looked in the mirror. I heard—or perhaps felt—a voice that penetrated my soul, saying, "Let everything you do be an act of love." The quality of the light in the room shifted, and golden embers seemed to bloom from the air. Everything was vibrating and had a hint of musicality, as though the rhythm of the soul was being played off in the distance. The words hung in the air and in my heart and touched every fiber of my being as a presence engaged in an act that I can only describe as a reprogramming.

This seemingly mundane task was transformed into a magical act, an act of love. It may sound exceedingly simple, but it changed my entire world. Instead of brushing my teeth to remove plaque or to get the job done, I brushed my teeth out of love and respect for the gift of my physical body. To brush the teeth as an act of love is to be mindful, caring, present, and nurturing. I realized that the way I had been thinking of life up until that moment operated from a paradigm of fear. I took action to avoid pain or perhaps to produce pleasure, but nothing was really an act of love. I thought that if I truly let everything I did be an act of love, it might change my whole world. Whether brushing my teeth, eating, speaking with another human being, writing, traveling, or living, this simple thought—let everything you do be an act of love—would be a revolution. And just like that, the seed of a new world was planted. It took me years to fully reboot my mind's operating system and integrate this simple yet truly life-changing principle.

This Is for You

You are reading this book for a reason. It is not mere coincidence. There is something within you that is hungry for a spiritual rebirth.

There is an unspoken acquiescence to the status quo that happens merely by living life. Few people may think that they have sublimated their personal desires and said no to the true self, but in many more ways than we realize, many people have done just that. In some ways, we all have had to do just that. There is no way that any human being could go to school, get a job, drive a car, or exist within the paradigm of modernity without a subtle acquiescence to the status quo. The price each of us pays for subservience to a system of deeply entrenched thoughts is quite steep. When the operating system of the collective subconscious is the paradigm that governs the inner workings of the mind, it can feel like each being is a cog in a giant system created by someone else. Even if we think we are doing well or that we are good persons, the systemic patterns of the subconscious mind often subvert even the best of intentions. Without a conscious deconstruction of the system, whereby awareness of hidden inner workings of the mind are brought to light, even the best acts of kindness can sometimes be mere masks for the status quo—or worse, further entrench cycles of oppression and suffering.

There is something inside of me that yearned for a full-throated revelation against the powerful forces of inertia held within systemic structures of power. When I spent my time questioning what I could do to change "the world," I only tied myself deeper into the paradigm that I hoped to change. It was only when I began to assess what I could do to change "my world" that things started to shift. It wasn't enough for me to sit in my bubble of personal goodness and look out at the world as something separate from my own struggle, something in need of redemption and help. The seed of separation was woven into the fabric of my thinking, and if I was going to break free of the paradigm, I would have to start with reprogramming my own mind. It just wasn't enough to think I was a good person with a good heart and stop the work there. There was an unmanifest potential that needed to be activated, and while I didn't realize it at the time, all the struggle and difficulty of my life was just the catalyst I needed to trigger a process of awakening. And now, I share that process here, in the hope that perhaps others might find what is needed to ignite a bright spiritual fire.

This book is an initiation to an entirely different way of living and being; it is a complete reboot for the operating system. And it will have a dramatic effect on how we see ourselves and our places in the world. Think of it as an unlearning of the conditioned and limited definition of humanity up until now. I know it sounds like a lot, and it is. In some ways, we have all been asleep, and it is our time to awaken. Our awakening is crucial to the evolution of the human race and the health of the planet. We do not need to engage in public acts of heroism and charity in order to do the important work of making the world a better place (but we can, if we are called to). All we really need is to put all our hearts and souls into the very real process of awakening. Everything else will shift from that pivotal choice, with a bit of patience, persistence, and hard work. Start here, with the mind, and then let the impact radiate outward like a wave that emanates from the heart.

Radical Change

This book is the crystallization of the work that I put in to actualize this radical change in my life. I share anecdotal stories of students of mine and fellow spiritual practitioners who also walk the path of awakening. It might seem incredulous that one's entire life will change from one simple teaching. While apparently simple, the teaching is profound. To get the most out of this time we have together, focus on receptivity to the teaching. Changing the paradigm of our most deeply held thoughts requires courage, strength, and determination. Going against the grain of the known stirs the pot of society, family, and the past. Struggles, doubt, and difficulty inevitably will arise. But if these teachings are taken to heart, sooner or later there will be a shift that liberates the mind. What it feels like on a good day is heaven right here on earth.

Here's how to use this book: The first three chapters set up the parameters of love, action, and the paradigm shift. Like learning a new language, learning how to truly act from love requires the redefinition of what we may think we already know. As we define what it means to love and to act, we will create a new diction and syntax that express the logic of the new paradigm. Think of the first three chapters as a recalibration of the code language on which your life relies to function. Before a new software can be installed, sometimes we need to adjust the wire frame of the hardware of our thinking. The remaining nine chapters apply this new paradigm to a key segment of life—think of each core area of life like an app on a personal device that interfaces with key metrics, data, and community. After the update to the operating system is firmly established, each application needs to be adjusted to the new parameters so that it can flourish within the updated ecosystem. Each chapter ends with a short review, as well as meditation and reflection points.

What I present to you in this book is a distillation of the spiritual journey work that I've done over the past twenty years of my life. It is by no means the end, for I am not an enlightened master, not Jesus or Buddha. But I am someone who has perhaps taken a few more steps along the spiritual path than others—or at least in a unique direction. I share the best road map of the journey that I can offer so far. My hope is that others won't get lost in the places where I did and that future travelers will tread more lightly and with more grace than I did. Let's get started.

Chapter 1

What Is Love?

A deep sense of love and belonging is an irreducible need of all men, women, and children. We are biologically, cognitively, physically, and spiritually wired to love, to be loved, and to belong.

—Brené Brown

Love is one of the most overused phrases and clichés in the English language, yet in many ways, we have no idea what love is. The very fact that we have to define what love is proves how far we are from the state of our maximum potential. We must ask: what, really, is love?

The frequency with which the concept of love is tossed around is staggering. Love gets sprinkled over things, like a condiment used to mask the unappealing flavor of the main dish of life. Yet love is real—so real that every single human being who exists, has ever existed, or will ever exist can be said to be defined entirely on the basis of the love that they contain, express, and live.

The word *love* is cheapened by our perfunctory usage. Its magnitude is lessened by association with mere preferences that shift over time, sometimes with such great rapidity that it is impossible to keep track of what we claim to love. We love chocolate—but not in the morning. We love pizza—but not too much of it. We love travel—but want to go home. We love our family—but cannot stand them. We love nature—but check in with social media as soon as there's reception. Is this really love? I would wager that it isn't real love but that our usage of the word *love* has come to denote the much-more-common framework of strong personal likes. And in a contemporary culture increasingly defined by the accumulation of "likes" on various social media networks, the equation of like with love has important implications for our sense of self-worth, identity, and, ultimately, real love.

Most of what we know as love in the world is not the deep, pervasive feeling of unconditional love that is a mystical state of being. Most of what we know of love is transactional. We say we love a certain thing because it makes us feel good. Whether that thing is a food item, an electronic device, a job, or another person, the root of the relationship is based in a kind of exchange for services rendered. Love, in this context, is a form of capital, and, as is fitting of any form of payment, it is monetized and commodified.

Part of the transactional equation of love includes vying for attention. Attention is not love, but it sure does feel like it sometimes. Attention temporarily fills a void located at the center of self-worth. When someone or something appears to be paying attention to you, it triggers a kind of dopamine hit in the brain that seems to tell a story of worthiness. The problem is that attention is a placebo for true love. Attention shifts faster than the wind. And although what you pay attention to can signify what you place value on, attention itself is not love. In a generation where attention-seeking behavior displayed on social media garners increasing likes, the downward spiral of a lack of love leads to increasingly extreme maneuvering to grab the attention of would-be viewers and generate likes. What we are all saying when we post and share things meant to grab attention is the child's cry that says, "Look at me; pay attention to me; love me."

Love is something totally other than a cycle of attention-seeking meant to satisfy a temporary feeling of emptiness. My hope in this book is to first establish the parameters of love by refreshing the definition, deepening the understanding, and encouraging a radical new application of the concept of love in our lives. We cannot act in love if we do not fully understand the revolutionary concept of love as a state of being. Love is not the most powerful force in the universe when it is relegated to a conditional existence.

Live in Love

Most people have at least once had the intoxicating feeling of being in love with another person. It is, perhaps, the best high in the world. There is no drug that can even come close to the overwhelming, life-changing experience of falling in love. Knees get weak around that special person. We can hardly breathe for the feeling of bliss that comes when we stand in close proximity to our love interest. The feeling of being in love affects everything. We whistle and sing while walking down the street, and everything appears through rose-colored glasses. We are happy—so happy that we want that high to last forever. The mistake so many of us make when we have the amazing blessing of falling in love is to think that the key to that state of love lies in the other person. The destination of the other person as the source of love begins a cycle of unhealthy codependency that eats away at the heart of love. The true source of love, even when we feel we have fallen head over heels in love with another person, is always within ourselves.

Once we understand that love is our nature, then our capacity to love grows. Imagine if we could live every day in love, not with another person but with everything in life. We can. What's more, living in love is inherent to who we are. We were meant to fall in love with the world, ourselves, and everyone and everything in it. Every act can be an act of love, once we commit to changing our paradigm about life. And when we make this small shift, everything changes.

I discovered this view primarily because I needed a big change in my own life. After years of hard work and goal-oriented thinking, I was operating from a place of fear, scarcity, and aggression. I often saw people as my enemies and felt intense jealousy and defensiveness. After my father passed away and I suffered a series of personal losses, I was drowning in a stream of hate. I was far from living in love. I will describe in detail what the root of that hate was really about, but at that time, I had no idea. I naively thought that by directing my energy toward perceived threats in the material world that I could affect positive change in my life and the lives of others. Little did I know that I was not truly acting in love. I was fueled by hate and anger so deeply held within my subconscious mind that I was utterly oblivious to it.

On certain occasions, most frequently in the comment section of social media, anonymous people would point out that they felt I had repressed anger or that my anger made them uncomfortable. While I did recognize that I was upset, I felt at that time that my anger was righteous and justified. I thought I knew what it was about and that since my anger appeared, on the surface, to be valid and just, it was still rooted in love. Little did I know the true source of my frustrations was actually a tightly held knot within my own consciousness. I had a lot to learn about what love actually is.

No matter where I looked, I could not find a definition of love that could teach me what I needed to learn. I was not able to connect with any definition of love expressed by an organized faith-based community—this is more of a reflection of me as a person than a statement against organized religion. Many people find great solace, depth, and meaning in connecting with religious communities. Regardless of whether or not there is a sectarian tradition with which you connect, I am suggesting that it might be useful to expand your definition of love. My own previous understanding of what love is was too restrictive to be beneficial. Rarely do we, as humans, allow for a truly inclusive expansion of consciousness, unless prompted to seek it. Pain was a catalyst for me, and I am writing this book in the hope that my words will serve as a catalyst for others.

Love, as I have come to understand it, is not restricted by race, gender, age, size, shape, religious affiliation, or any other human destination of difference. Love is not bound by body, materiality, or circumstance, nor is love an experience that happens only between human beings. We love our cherished pets, wild animals, plants, nature, and sometimes inanimate objects; sometimes, we feel in love with the whole universe. Love is all things, in all time, and in all ways. Love is more than a declaration of the mind. It is a heart held in action over many years. There are people who eschew traditional religious designation and claim love to be their religion. Yet there is perhaps no greater example of universal love than Jesus Christ giving his life on the cross as atonement for every human being. Perhaps wherever love is present, the divine is manifest. First John 4:7–8 (NIV) says, "Everyone who loves has been born of God and knows God. Whoever does not love does not know God, because God is love." Could it be that love and love alone signifies the presence of God? Imagine if no religious doctrine held the sole proprietorship of love and that all we needed to do in order to connect with the Universal Presence was to act in love, to let every action be born of love, and to become love at the very core of our beings. Well, then, love would be a revolution. And perhaps it is.

To live in love is harder than it sounds. Judgment, hierarchical thinking, separation, anger, fear, bitterness, and so many other habitual patterns get in the way. To live in love might very well be spiritual enlightenment, the magic key that opens the doors to the kingdom of God here on earth. But even if the door is opened, the journey is not finished. Or at least, it isn't finished for me. I am in process, like most of us, and I hope that we will awaken together and support one another as we walk down the path of love.

What is of the universe could be seen as a kind of law, much like gravity is a law that governs the earthly plane. Perhaps love is a universal law, a principle of self-realization that makes good on the promise of liberation for all beings. Love is incarnate in all human beings and in all living beings. The realization of that incarnation is the essence of the spiritual path. There is matter, the material world that is divisible and identifiable by modern science. There is spirit, which is the realm of the supernatural, the mystical, and the inexplicable. Without a bridge between these worlds, rooted in the tactile subjective experience of each person, there will forever be a divide between the thinking and reasoning and the devout and faithful. But the promise of the human being is to bridge that gap, to be both human and divine, to be at once dualistic, mired in the ordinary, and eternal, lifted up with grace.

To be human is to sit at the intersection of the flow of love. We have the capacity to give love, to receive love, and to be in the flow of the love of the universe. To be whole means to be fully immersed in the capacity to give, receive, and flow—with love. If one side of this energy exchange is blocked, the energy is blocked. I have spent and continue to spend many moments blocking the flow of love. The process, for me, is not about perfection but about understanding where and when I'm blocking love and then returning to love, over and over again. For example, if a person is only able to give love but not receive love, then there is an aspect within the person that is not functioning at full capacity. If a person has a hard time in the other direction—that is, if that person is a kind of love-taker but withholds their love from others—they also end up restricting the natural movement of love within their own heart. Lastly, if a person feels comfortable, on a personal level, with giving and receiving love but somehow fails to tap into the vast greatness of the love of the universe, God's love, then an aspect of their inner being will always feel lost and disconnected from the infinite.

Spiritual teacher Ram Dass describes the qualities of conscious love as being broken up into three types: biochemical love or lust, romantic love that exists between two beings, and conscious love, which is defined by embodiment. We all have experiences with regard to the lust that is often equated with love. We will explore that connection in depth in a later chapter. Similarly, the polarity that often pulls one person toward another in a relationship is an ever-present and often dominant narrative in most people's lives. Love based exclusively on this interpersonal dynamic is often rooted in a lack of a true sense of self. It is easy to lose oneself to the power dynamic of this interpersonal love and generate boundary problems and codependency. This will be explored in greater depth in a later chapter as well. Lastly, conscious love, as defined by Ram Dass, is a state akin to deep spiritual realization, a self-transcendent state to which ancient yogis aspired. Ram Dass said,

And you 'are' a statement of that love. And your every action is not consciously designed to assert that you love everyone, and everyone loves you, because you 'are' love. Then, there is no more need for anyone to love you. All you experience is a feeling of present flow with everyone in the universe. You are in love with the universe. You are not actively loving, but you are 'in' love; you exist in the space of conscious love, which is Christ love. That's what this whole game is about. (Dass 2016)

Self-Love, Actually

Self-love is very popular in contemporary wellness circles. And for good reason. So many of us, myself included, have had to learn how to truly love ourselves. That teaching and lesson is invaluable and life-changing. But there is a shadow side of unbalanced self-love. When attached to the world self, love can sometimes be stripped of its depth and meaning. When self is not the higher self of awakened consciousness but the self of the ego, then love gets linked to the unawakened realms and can be misunderstood. In the name of self-love, there is a trap that leads to self-aggrandizement and bears little relation to the potential of love expressed in alignment with one's true nature. Instead of being a deep healing power, when tied to the ego self-love can be delusional and take the spiritual seeker off track. I've fallen for this ruse, and it took me a good deal of effort to back up and rework my mistakes.

On the spiritual path, a common obstacle is called, in Sanskrit, *branti darshan*, which means false perception. Many would-be aspirants fall for what is considered an untrue teaching, masquerading as a true teaching. Without a distinction between the ego and the higher self, self-love can be a trap of false perception that further binds the mind in chains of delusion. Love of self is a delicate line to walk between truly honoring oneself as a spiritual being of great value and falling for the ego's game of clinging to the image of the false self. It requires a great feat of perception to delineate between truly liberating self-love and painfully limiting ego-building. What makes the terrain even harder to navigate is that there are no absolute rules. Sometimes, a person may need to build up his or her ego in order to heal and grow, only to find the ego is overgrown and in need of pruning. It's a balancing act that never seems to stop; at least, it hasn't yet stopped for me.

The teachings on self-love are quite confusing. After being told that we should love ourselves, treat ourselves well, value ourselves a lot, trust what comes up for us, honor our truth, and the like, it can be easy to center every circumstance around, well, one's own self. Centering one's own viewpoint as the be-all and end-all of every situation is not necessarily an act of love. It could even be seen as the opposite of love when an individual places his or her own desire and feelings above all else, even at the expense of harm committed toward others. For example, imagine this scenario: I am spending time with a friend, and my friend continually steps on my foot. When I tell my friend that her actions are harming me (to use a silly example, it hurts when she steps on my foot), my friend then says that it is her truth to occupy the space in the way that she is and that I should honor her pursuit of self-love. Of course, this is just an example and perhaps even an unrealistic one. But the danger of allowing self-love to be a spiritual bypass that avoids the egregious harm done by our actions, albeit often unintentional, is real. We are responsible for ourselves and our own happiness, but we are also responsible for the impact that our actions have on others. Without a social and spiritual check, the language around honoring ourselves could potentially lead to an endless circle of self-centeredness.

Similarly, if every desire is honored as arising from a deep truth, the pursuit of material, emotional, and even spiritual "nexts" might be endless. Sometimes we seek what is next just to fill a void of emptiness within. For me, when I have run the hardest from facing reality, I've engaged in grand acts of escapism that sought only to stuff things and experiences into a gaping hole in my heart. Self-love is something else—expressed with a calm and balanced mind that operates from the perspective of wholeness.

Humble Wholeness

Most people are not able to see this from the outside looking in, but I am someone with a kind of perpetual sense of low self-esteem. I work hard every day to value myself, and there have been many moments when my low self-esteem appeared to be humility. But there is a difference between humility and low self-esteem. Sometimes, it can be hard to tell the difference, yet that distinction is an important one to flush out a bit. The same conditions for love to flourish between two separate individuals must be present within oneself in order for self-love to flourish. That is, one must feel both safety and connection at the core of one's being if self-love is to be realized.

Whenever I feel the worst about myself, I want to wall myself off from any and all negative feedback. It can feel like there is no place to put any more negativity. But a bubble of artificially constructed positivity is not equivalent to self-love. Like any bubble, it is in danger of popping. When low self-esteem is present, the next step in any spiritual development has to be the cultivation of some sense of self-esteem. Without a basic value of oneself, the work of spiritual growth is very challenging. Low self-esteem takes constructive criticism and turns it into self-diminishment, or it gets defensive and denies everything.

Low self-esteem is an impediment both to self-love and to feeling real love for others. Being open and receptive to negative feedback, which could be called doing the shadow work of spiritual awakening, requires a stable sense of self. Without that, it is just too easy to internalize negative thinking and spin down a cycle of self-depreciation. Learning true self-love is not silencing all voices of conflict. Instead, it's about generating a feeling of safety and connection within one's own wholeness. When my sense of worthiness was at its lowest, I was not able to receive the love of others. No matter what signals of support I received, I disregarded them as transitory and unreal. Similarly, from a place of low self-esteem, I was not able to properly identify what was a safe space and what was an unsafe space.

The unfortunate downward spiral that happened for me has probably happened for many people. The misidentification of an unsafe space as safe creates the framework for harm and mistrust and gives one's power away. When I could not recognize whom to trust, I made the mistake of thinking that the way to express love was to be open to everyone all the time. Instead of truly listening to myself, I listened to people in positions of power and set up the scene for a lot of hurt. My boundaries were slippery and unclear, and I was unable to assess a situation for potential harm. When the harm did arrive, rather than seeing the signs and correcting course, I vacillated between blaming the world and imploding with guilt and shame. The voices in my heart said, "See? People are just awful," and "There you go; you did it again. What's wrong with you?" As I slowly reclaimed a solid sense of self, I realized the harm done to me and also integrated the learning that was available for me in my past. Blaming a person with low self-esteem for falling for the tropes of would-be perpetrators of harm only fuels the cycle of low self-esteem. There is another way toward healing, which we will explore in a later chapter. For now, let us continue to explore the polarity between self-diminishment and self-aggrandizement.

Hearing the dangers of low self-esteem and being steeped in self-help lingo, some students of spiritual development may attempt to flip to the other end of the spectrum entirely. Inflating one's self-worth can feel like quenching a thirst. But there is a danger in the unchecked focus of the self; that is, sometimes an inflation of ego masquerades as self-love. Internal low self-esteem can appear, then, as external self-aggrandizement. Focusing too exclusively on the positive is one-sided and sometimes divorced from reality. We all can think of a bully who wears a mask of protective armor to shield a negative view of self. Sometimes, what appears to be a grotesque display of narcissism can actually be a supreme act of self-diminishment.

Humility grounded on a stable sense of self acknowledges both one's value and one's worthiness, while accepting the truth of imperfection. A humble heart is strong enough to admit responsibility for mistakes, correct course, and offer apologies where necessary. Many people, like me, find it difficult to call up some of their good qualities and have quite low self-esteem. If that is the case, then there is work to do on the inner planes of self-love. It is possible to establish a kind of inner resonance of love that vibrates in every cell of the body. A kind of harmony can play as a tune in one's life. I don't always hit those notes, but when I do, it *feels* good.

We are often far away from a state of feeling good. Just think about how many times in each day you rehash negative thoughts, whether about yourself, another person, or a situation. Negative self-talk is like adding compound interest to debt—it only makes things worse. Sure, we may make mistakes; no one is perfect. I have certainly made my fair share of mistakes, both big and small. I know all too well the tendency to ruminate on everything I did wrong. That is a habit of the mind, just like anything else. It's not independently true. If the pattern of the mind keeps getting fuel, it will only accelerate, possibly leading to even more negative thinking. Self-love is not about removing all negativity. Rather, feelings of safety and security, irrespective of external circumstances, tie a sense of self-worth to an inner state of wholeness. If we are whole beings as we are, then anything achieved only adds to our already whole state. Thinking that someday, when we finally are thin enough, rich enough, strong enough, educated enough, or beautiful enough, we will be lovable is a trap of delusion. There is no day out there when everything will work out. The goalposts keep shifting in the paradigm of "someday, when." Instead, there is the here and now, where wholeness and happiness are available.

Love is not a prize for an elite few. Life is not a zero-sum equation with winners and losers. Love is not a finite source of scarcity. Certainly, love is in high demand and is the most valuable resource in the universe. But love is infinite. Every living being is a generator of love. In fact, love is the foundational nature of reality, including you and me. We are not only composed of the most valuable stuff in the world, but each being has the power to manufacture, or perhaps tap into, a wellspring of eternal love. We do not need a university degree to love. We do not need to be any size, shape, age, or religion to love. We certainly do not need a billion dollars in our bank accounts to love. We just need to be ourselves because love is who we are.

It's Not Always Sunshine

Love is not always positivity. When love gets equated with a persistent and ceaseless veneer of happiness, the depth of what love really is can get lost. The times when I felt most loved and supported in my life were often when a friend or family member sat with me amid my pain and sorrow. More than just being there for the laughter, joy, and good times, those beings who share both the highs and the lows offer a genuine depth and connection that expresses a fullness of true love. When love is embodied fully, it includes the full spectrum of beingness—the good, the bad, the happy, the sad, and everything in between. Love is total in its expression through us and demands a totality of our being, lest we betray the true nature of love's potential.

There is a state that is truly positive and life-affirming, while not always being positive in emotional affect or physical expression. Instead, love can be expressed as a kind of spiritual openness that sees that all is not swayed to look away from the darkness or to be too attached to the beauty. Love is both innate to our true natures and a skill that we can cultivate. Just like a talent may remain buried within your potential, latent until it is activated, love needs a bit of your awareness to sprout. It is my hope that this book will be a kind of activation or initiation to the path of love.

We all have the potential to fully actualize love's potential. But the state of love's realization requires a grand act of courage to dive below the surface level of the mind and tap into something deeper. Moving beyond the initial moments of positivity is like moving beyond the honeymoon period of any relationship. As our relationship with love evolves, we also evolve as human beings. Love is personal, not performative. It is the voice that speaks to us in the silence of solitude. Love shuns elaborately staged games. Love is simple yet holds all the complexity of the world. We are all yearning for love in one form or another. And we all sometimes fall for the counterfeits of love. We are here not to judge what love is but to remove the restrictions from the free flow of love within. There is no pretense, no shortcut, no way to wiggle out of the world. Only when love, as a state, takes root in the body will the flower really bloom.

At the core of the mind, there are many knots of repetitive thinking that color our outlook on the world. Very often, these thoughts do not come from a place of safety and well-being but are instead rooted in past experiences of hurt. Unless the core pattern of the mind is healed and updated, no amount of positive thinking can cover up core programming. If a deep program running at the operational level of the mind identifies the world as a harmful place that one must protect against, then no matter what positive affirmations float on the surface level of the mind, the core emotional basis will not change. It can feel frustrating beyond belief to appear to be checking off all the boxes of positive thinking while experiencing little result. I've been there so many times, wondering why my visualizations of the future just never managed to manifest. I felt blocked and confused. It just didn't make sense that the more happy thoughts I tried to think, the worse everything seemed to go for me. From the outside looking in, someone might have described me as a "shiny, happy person," but on the inside, my thoughts were dark and twisted. I was blind to my own inner reality. The more I force-fed a rigid view of the veneer of happiness over my life, the less work I was able to actually do on the much-needed plane of the subconscious mind. The state of eyes-wide-shut happiness is a hard edge that denies failure and rebels at the slightest hint of disapproval. Think of it as positive self-talk gone awry or as a classic case of narcissism.

Narcissism is a near enemy of self-love, and it is, unfortunately, quite easy to fall for it. I've been there, in the ungraceful space where I smugly believed that "they" just didn't get it. Instead of cultivating compassion and connection, I nurtured the seeds of judgment and separation. Far from seeing clearly and far from love, I had a long way to walk to get back on the path. I found myself in a delusional dead-end suffering from spiritual atrophy and had to dig myself out of that hole. I am not writing this book because I am done with the work of awakening. Think of each message that resonates with you as a real-time message from a fellow traveler, alerting you to possible traffic jams, congestion, and other obstacles along the road.

Many of us, perhaps, have been or will be in a space where talk about love and light is just a defensive move of self-protection, rather than true love for ourselves and others. At that moment, maybe we can remember this teaching like directions on a map of the soul.

It appears to me that we are all on a path toward love. Sometimes, the path is winding, sometimes it's blocked, and sometimes it's a dead end. Walking back to the path from the high cliffs of narcissism toward a healthy sense of self-worth is humbling. But once the vantage point shifts and the fog lifts, the view of love and of life is so much clearer. If these words that I write bring even a little more clarity to this day, the purpose is served sufficiently.

Love as Action

Love is not a concept divorced from the body. Instead, love is something we can all tap into through a felt sense of embodiment. Acting out of alignment with love hurts, just as it hurts when any being acts out of alignment with gravity. More than a performative act, love is revealed both in the physical body and in actions taken. John 13:35 (ESV) states, "By this everyone will know that you are my disciples, if you have love for one another."

By this standard, love and love alone accounts for proximity to God. Love is known and expressed through acts and deeds; that is, embodiment, incarnation, and manifestation. Words may profess love or hate, but action is definite and reveals the truth of the inner workings of a person. While the mind may deny the inner reality, emotions and bodily sensations cannot lie or hide their truth.

Christian spiritual thinker Benjamin Riggs says that "love is received, not created. It is a gift. When we get out of the way, love rises to the surface. Love is the natural expression of our True Life, unencumbered by the false-self. In other words, love is born out of freedom" (Riggs 2016, 172).

Embodied love is perhaps easier said than done. It is all too easy to skip over the groundwork of building a stable base of love within and to allow the flame of love to burn out. When the ground is too shallow or improperly tilled, the seeds will not take root. Instead, love flourishes when its seeds are deeply rooted in both freedom and truth. Love flounders when the ego gets in the way and acts with a motivation of self-preservation. If there are no friends in the world, and all are competitors and adversaries, then the world is a brutal place with little room for love. Instead of a confederation of equals, human interaction can easily devolve into the savagery of tribalism. Love is a calling to ascend and love others equally, as one loves oneself. But, of course, the ability to truly tap into love stems from the realization of one's own self as valuable and worthy of love in the first place.

Actions taken without a solid root in true self-love are often transactional. One being wants something from another and then acts with the expectation of receiving something specific in return. Love is unconditional in its true nature. Love is action freed from the attachment to results. Love is a happening, not a possession. It cannot be controlled or forced. Instead, love flows in when there is openness and receptivity. Love is holy and sacred, so much so that love is the sacrificial offering needed to even approach the altar of God. It is not through words or thoughts but actions that love is most wholly expressed. The Bhagavad Gita says, "Ordinary action (performed with desire) is greatly inferior to action united to the guidance of wisdom; therefore seek shelter in the ever-directing wisdom. Miserable are those who perform actions only for their fruits" (Bhagavad-Gita 2:49).

When every action taken is imbued with a sense of the holy, then that action is in total alignment with love or, as some may prefer to call it, God's grace. Action taken without desire for a goal brings the actor closer to the presence of divine love. Strings attached to love stifle the flow and sully the waters of love. The sweet fruit of every act is love. When eating, talking, cleaning, listening, working, walking, moving, and breathing all are done as a natural, spontaneous act of love, then your whole life is a prayer, a benediction, and you live within God's grace.

Love is oneness, a total immersion in the allness of being. But love is also an equitable honoring of every part of the world. A clear, holographic view of love validates both the grandness of oneness and the individual being. Love is a renunciation, a kind of willingness to die, to be submerged, to kill the ego of separation. Feel, cry, love, dance, but do it all from the heart as an act of love. Then every act of love will feel like a joyous transformation.

Moment by moment, we are all acting, consciously or unconsciously. Perhaps the first step in learning how to act in love is to realize what the root motivation truly is for every action. It is through deep introspection and contemplation that self-knowledge comes. Too much thinking and overanalyzing can sometimes be a hindrance. The mind is able to engage in great acts of self-deception that sometimes conflate love with hate, generosity with jealousy, rejection with acceptance. Yet the rational mind is a vital component of our ability to see clearly. If love is truly a field and a presence in which liberation occurs, then every aspect of one's being must be fully invested. Along those lines, let us now turn to the scientific and measurable in regard to love.

The Science of Love

Love researcher Barbara Fredrickson defines love based on metrics that can be seen in the body. She says,

> To put it in a nutshell, love is the momentary upwelling of three tightly interwoven events: first, a sharing of one or more positive emotions between you and another; second, a synchrony between you and the other person's biochemistry and behaviors; and third, a reflective motive to invest in each other's well-being that brings mutual care. My shorthand for this trio is *positivity resonance*. (Fredrickson 2013, 17)

According to her view, love does not belong to the person who feels it. It is any moment of warmth and connection shared with another living being, where a tangible sense of oneness and self-transcendence can be felt. It is an action that bears the feeling of connection and can be found between any beings that share positive emotion. Positivity resonance is the signature of love, and it can be felt in so many more places and instances than one might at first think. While love is usually understood to be a happening between beings who are in your intimate circle, it has the potential to be more than that.

There is a biological component of love that occurs when the felt presence of connection resides and flourishes. The presence of love influences not just the lover and beloved; love has the power to enervate communities, spread through social networks, and knit beings together, even if just for a brief spark. The power of love as the true nature of every being is so powerful that even a momentary uprising of love can alter the course of a series of events or even one's life. Whether positivity resonance arises between two people or two thousand people, there are certain conditions that create the ideal conditions for its occurrence. Fredrickson says that positivity resonance needs two things in particular—the perception of safety and real, true, sensory temporal connection with another living being that establishes rapport, intersubjectivity, eye contact, and shared experience. This state is felt in the body and feels good in the body.

Love, it seems, isn't random. Love is something we can consciously cultivate with the right conditions for its thriving. Perpetual states of busyness, rushing, and general distraction erode the foundation needed to experience the love that every being contains within. It takes time to be present and notice the signs that love is potentially in the air. Whether that means pausing for an extra few seconds to make eye contact with another human being, tuning in to the breath and body, or stopping to feel a gentle breeze wash over the skin, love happens in slowed-down moments when the mind drops below the tune of repetitive thinking.

Princeton social psychologists John Darley and Daniel Batson tested the effects of time pressure in what is now a classic study in human behavior. The single most determining factor in regard to establishing true connection is hurrying. Participants in the study who were late were much less likely to connect and offer help to a stranger in need than those who were given excess time to complete their task. Regardless of the moral, ethical, religious, or ethnic background of the participants, very few of those who were rushing to complete their assignment took the time to reach out and help. Positivity resonance only would be possible between those humans who took the time to stop. While stopping to help a stranger isn't necessarily a litmus test of true love, this study shows the impact that a culture of perpetual rushing has on the potential for any human being to dive into the depth of love. After all, who knows? Maybe the priest and the Levite were late for an appointment, and only the Samaritan felt like he had time to stop and be a good neighbor. So when Jesus says, "Go and do likewise" (Luke 10:37 NKJV), perhaps it is not only about being a good neighbor. Perhaps there is a deeper teaching about the need for a spiritual seeker to make time and space for love and connection.

It's about Connection

Human beings bond over strong emotions, positivity resonance, and what we experience as love and goodwill. But human beings also bond over hate. Any emotionally intense experience, whether high or low, often will bond people together and form a kind of affinity group.

Emotional synchronicity is powerful. When we smile, laugh, cry, or share any other emotion with another being, our brains sync up, and we become, at least for a moment, one. Openness from one being allows others to be open as well. The same is true for harmful acts. One act of aggression normalizes and activates other people's aggression. The brain is connected to the brains of other people around, whether we realize it or not. Identifying with another being increases the amount that the brain synchronizes with the other person's brain, for better or worse. This process is called neural coupling, the process by which at least two brains establish coherence by the firing of *mirror neurons* in the part of the brain responsible for listening. This usually happens between a storyteller and a listener, but it can also happen whenever a human being experiences a connection with another human being.

Neutral coupling happens and creates a sense of belonging, whether the emotions are positive or negative. Princeton neuroscientist Uri Hasson says, "The people who we are coupled to define who we are." There is often a shift in orientation from *me* to *we* while neutral coupling occurs. Both good and bad moods can be contagious. The emotional state that one person is in has the potential to impact others, for better or worse. We are all impacted by the other humans in our lives, and we all impact the other humans in our lives, perhaps more than we know. Resonance will happen; the choice is whether it will be positivity or negativity resonance with others. In negativity resonance, a bond is established with others who share the same anger or fear response. This creates a close-knit bond and a momentary hit of intimacy and connection. When the brain goes looking for a second hit to keep the feeling of closeness going, the brain will look for anger and fear, as that is the root of the connection. This type of identity-driven action is the root of identity politics, tribalism, racism, and other forms of oppression.

Positivity resonance is different from the false positivity that is projected but lived and different from negativity resonance. Since the human brain is responding to the actual embodied emotional state expressed primarily through nonverbal cues, the connection facilitated from a space of love felt in the body bonds humans together and helps elevate all involved. Furthermore, the state of an open heart encourages connection, not just to the people in one's immediate social group but to all beings. Teachers, speakers, influencers, and other leaders with a powerful platform may feel the temptation of power that comes from egging people on through shared anger or fear. This fuels a seductive cycle of craving the next outrage and leads to burnout. Using anger or fear as the driving motivation will not only fizzle out but eventually will turn back on you and those you seek to lead. Eventually, there will be more disconnection and disillusionment. Anger and fear cannot heal the world.

It's not to say that you cannot feel anger or fear. We all, myself included, certainly will. There is no escaping that. But the question at the heart of this journey is a choice about whether to act in love or to act in anger or fear. This one small shift changes everything. Once the world is no longer seen as an enemy, against which to throw hate and rage, but a mirror for one's own process, a change that could be called *awakening* happens. Then, all actions can be rooted in the depths of spiritual development. The inner and the outer, together, grow and evolve. Feel the pain of the world, and then—not in anger or hatred but in love—work every day to heal the wounds of the past and build a better world. There is simply no way that an open heart can turn a blind eye to injustice. It is not enough to preach love and light; actions matter as much if not more than words. Connecting honestly and openly with the heart creates the possibility to embrace the sorrow and suffering of others. Coming into emotional resonance with another being means opening fully, not closing down or defending when things get difficult. Action taken from an open heart is action taken in love.

The brain is constantly changing and will adapt to new circumstances. The body transmits the frequency of one's mental and emotional state, opening the door for connection or division. Emotions are like a self-fulfilling prophecy that sets the stage for future life interactions. Barbara Fredrickson says, "When you feel good, you see beyond your cocoon of self-interest to become more aware of others, more likely to focus on their needs, wants and concerns, and to see things from their perspective" (Fredrickson 2013, 67). Feeling an affinity with another being opens the heart and mind. When others are seen as part of a "unified whole" that feels like an "us," rather than two separate selves, or "me's," the world changes. Naturally, more care and concern for the other person arises.

Love is big and encompasses all, both the positive and the negative. Each shared moment primes the body and brain for more such moments in the future. Love is what allows the brain to grow big enough to embrace pain and even anger without acting in hate. Learning to live in love builds emotional resilience. As someone who has struggled with long-term depression, I know how hard it can be to feel truly connected.

The negative-skewing nature of the mind is nothing more than a learned behavioral pattern, embedded deeply in the neural pathways and programming. It takes sincere, dedicated effort to reprogram the mind. It takes a combination of intent and action. Changing the operating system of the mind requires systematic unlearning, something like washing out the old thoughts in your brain.

Love is like a ripple that expands outward from the heart and touches every single interaction in life. Not only are we more relaxed and happier when we are able to feel love, but we are also more able to consider the needs of others and be more empathetic. A happy, relaxed mind, acting in love, is expansive and open, not closed and rigid. It has to start somewhere, but once we begin to experience and focus on the moments of love that are already present in our lives, those moments can change who we know ourselves to be. The ripples of love don't just affect us as individuals. As we upgrade our concept of love, we will not only get more love, but we will give more love too. This give-and-take cycle reinforces the patterns of love. Resonance and vibration till the soils of our lives. Every email sent, word spoken, post shared, casual glance—each of these actions carries a charge that expresses the underlying tone of our connectivity potential. While we have certainly already stumbled upon numerous instances of love by happenstance, now is the time to cultivate the fertile ground to nurture the growth of love. Rather than just luck or fate, we can deliberately plant the seeds of love in the garden of life.

Meditation and Reflection

1. Let the Good In

Sit for a few moments with your eyes closed. Bring your attention to your heart center. After you feel connected to your heart, think of a few of your good qualities. Be specific. Don't just generally say, "I'm good." Find a specific thing that you can say is good about you. You might say, "I'm a good driver," or "I'm a good cook." Or you might focus on a quality about you, such as, "I'm generous and kind." If you feel deflated, thinking that there is nothing good about you, pause, name the pattern of self-diminishment, and then return your awareness to yourself. No matter how hopeless you may seem to yourself, I promise you there is so much good in you. You don't have to wipe away all the bad; you just have to be open to finding at least one good thing about you right now. Start with a few deep breaths, and bring to mind at least one quality about you that you can label as good. You might find that when you begin, a floodgate will open and a wellspring of goodness will wash over your whole body. If that happens, go with the flow, and steep in your goodness. Recognize the inherent truth about this state, and let the good in.

2. Love Memory

Call up a time in your life when you felt the presence of love. Where were you giving love? Receiving love? Did you feel the love of the universe, of God? Can you identify the signs of emotional resonance?

Chapter 2

Love in Action

> The more you understand the more you love. The more you love the more you understand. They are two sides of one reality. The mind of love and the mind of understanding are the same.
>
> —Thich Nhat Hanh

> You have a right to perform your prescribed duties, but you are not entitled to the fruit of your actions. Never consider yourself to be the cause of the results of your activities, nor be attached to inaction.
>
> —Bhagavad Gita 2.47

The difference between an action and a reaction is consciousness. To act is to engage with awareness. To react is to engage without awareness. To act in love is to act with fully alert consciousness in each and every moment. This is the path we are on together, as spiritual seekers.

The majority of human actions, mine included, are not conscious creations. Instead, we most often act based on patterned unconscious reactions. Liberation means freeing the mind from these old patterns and consciously choosing how to respond spontaneously, moment by moment. Even one act done in full awareness has the power to change the course of everything that follows.

Once a thought, feeling, or mental picture manifests itself as concretely as an action, the pattern has been working internally for a very long time. The benefit of having choices, deeds, and words on display in the realm of the physical body is that the root cause of the direction is shown more clearly. Think of every action or reaction as a tree branching from a root. It may not at first be evident that the roots of a vast tree are planted within the field of one's own psyche, but with time and awareness, those patterns are revealed. Various patterns may grow and receive nourishment from life situations and repetitive thoughts without any awareness. At some moment, the sprouting tree may perk up to the surface, but most people usually assume that it is harmless and ignore it. Sometimes, patterns are so familiar and known that we may even rest under the shade of the canopy of the tree. But when the tree bears its fruits, then the quality of the tree will be manifest and unavoidably clear.

Actions rooted in anything other than love bear the fruits of suffering. Actions rooted in love, true divine universal love, bear the fruits of liberation. Some people may even refer to actions done in love as miracles. Working with the mind means weeding out centuries of overgrown trees. The fruits of these trees are ripening all around us. Once the tree fructifies, it can sometimes feel overwhelming to sit in a rotting stench of the poisonous grove of old patterns. But it is actually exactly at this point that there is the highest motivation and chance to alter course.

The key to spiritual awakening is developing enough insight, clarity, and wisdom to know whether an act is done in love or whether the root of the tree is something else. Sometimes, I feel so tired of the old stories of the past and am desperate to change them. My quest has led me to the discovery of an inner GPS that helps me navigate through the exhaustion and confusion of repeating the same thing over and over again, while hoping for a different result. There is a navigation system hardwired into the structure of the body and mind. With practice, I have learned how to traverse the inner circuitry of my own being and enjoy the ride. If I found a way through—toward more wisdom, peace, and joy—by acting in love, then I know we all can too. I'll discuss in greater detail later the gift of the body, but for now, let us dive a little bit deeper into what action really is.

Unconscious Action

Feeling stuck in a repetitive pattern is never fun, but it can be the right type of pressure needed to break out of unconscious action. I can't count the many times that I've been there myself, caught in a web of my own thoughts, emotions, reactions, and habits. Feelings of depression, overwhelming anger, or debilitating anxiety can drown out any moments of happiness. Sometimes, struggling against these states only makes it worse. There is a paradoxical desperation to find the answers, paired with a kind of veil that occludes all sense of hope. For me, it helps to realize that the only locus of control that I have remains always and eternally within me. I had to find a way to shift my own state; otherwise, any action taken only perpetuated the cycle I was already in.

Unconscious actions and reactions are a complex riddle to solve. The tools of reason and logic often lead to dead ends. Fighting these patterns directly frequently has a counterproductive effect of making the patterns even more entrenched. Instead, shifting the paradigm and updating the subconscious operating system is a way to work on the patterns in a nonconfrontational way that addresses the true source. As long as the energy of the problem is most salient, the solution will remain hidden. Fighting with problems head-on often locks the problem in place. Instead, try finding an indirect approach by changing the framework of thinking that grounds the problem.

The small *I* that is associated with the ego likes to think that it is the responsible force behind all the success in life. The ego envisions itself as a demigod whose power moves mind and matter and solves the hardest problems. But the truth is that the ego does not *do* anything of substance in the world. In fact, the very notion that there is a master doer within the mind who solves all the problems is based on a limited concept of self, rooted in the illusion of ego. Fixing, solving, working, pounding, forcing, and fighting to bend reality to the wishes of personal likes and dislikes is far from an enlightened course of action. On a certain level and for a certain time, the appearance works, and then, at another level and in due time, the facade crumbles. No matter how strong the ego is, there will be a situation that simply cannot be controlled by sheer willpower. Rather than a moment of failure, these often upsetting and frustrating situations, where the ego's limit has been reached, are opportunities for true spiritual growth.

Patterns are sometimes best revealed and seen in the pieces of destruction left in the wake of a big crash. In retrospect, the core pattern at the heart of each action is evident, much like the logic of architects can be read in the structure of their building. What can be done when the end of human effort is reached and no result is in place? Well, the only thing to do at that point is to let it go.

Learning to Let Go

Letting go is not doing nothing. Instead, the act of surrender is perhaps the only effective course of action that follows the cataclysm of ego and "stuckness." It is so easy to nurture the seeds of bitterness when things don't work out, but the practice of nonattachment promises peace amid releasing the fruits of one's labor to a higher power. The moment of surrender is also a moment of humility and honesty, a recognition that there is no "I" that does anything anyway. The heart opens to an eternal source of love and strength, once the need to attain one's goals is released.

I have been on my knees, humbled and aware that I could do no more. While I hated the idea that I would "lose" the fight, I knew that the only viable path for me was to surrender. Giving up the struggle, in this instance, was a careful articulation of the surrender needed to walk the spiritual path as a kind of softening of the heart. But it isn't easy. It hurts to let go. There is a feeling akin to grief and loss that comes from throwing out old attachments and habits, but there are big and small gifts that grace can deliver.

In the physical practice of yoga, many students have a strong desire to be more flexible and embark on an ambitious journey to open an inflexible body part. I can be like this myself, and so can many students. Keisha is a committed yoga student who practices with me regularly. While she is naturally strong, her hips are not naturally flexible. Seeing other yoga students easily fold their legs into Lotus Pose made her feel frustrated. One hip was tighter than the other, which made her concerned about a lack of symmetry in the body. Keisha attacked the "problem" head-on; she stretched her hip in as many postures as she could bear, analyzed the anatomy of the pelvis and hip joint, and pushed and pulled on her left hip every day during practice.

After an intense period of practice, she felt defeated because her hips just wouldn't open. I suggested that she take a few days off the intense program of hip opening and just relax her body and mind. Perhaps, I offered, she could go for a walk in nature, sleep in, and catch up on reading. Keisha didn't like my suggestion, but after a bit of prodding, she agreed to take the weekend off from practice. When I saw her again on Monday, she looked like a different person, as though a burden had lifted. She told me that over the weekend, her left hip cracked nearly every time she moved. It started Friday after our conversation and her decision to take the weekend off. The cracking continued all day Saturday and Sunday, while she went for a gentle walk, as she shifted position reading, and as she got out of bed (later than usual). Neither of us knew what would happen on the mat that day, but we were both curious. I advised her to explore the practice without any expectation. To our great surprise, she discovered a totally different left hip. It was open, and it had stopped cracking. It felt like magic—there was no pain, no struggle. Something had shifted.

As a metaphor, there is something to be learned from this experience. Whenever the logical mind tries to figure it out, and the ego forces the will into being, the competing attachments tighten what can be endless knots in the body and mind—and perhaps also in life. When all appropriate effort has been done, there is only one solution left, whether the problem has been fixed or not, and that is to let it go. As long as the problem is front and center, the problem has priority. But in the act of diversion, release, and surrender, a change happens. Perhaps the body finally gets a chance to integrate all the work done. Or perhaps the grace of the universe pours in and works a miracle. Either way, the shift in energy and vibration is itself worth the act of letting go. Instead of pounding away at the same repetitive cycle, there is a bit more space to see what else might want to happen. I believe that every gift we receive, whether an opening of the hips or an inspired idea, is something we receive from a source that is beyond the world of our problems. When that contact is blocked, it is usually blocked for a reason. Instead of generating tension around the problem, focus on releasing your resistance to the answer.

Not every situation is as clear as a muscle or joint that is not open. Sometimes, choices in life are big and heavy with big consequences. Yet here too, there is a limit to what can be done by the force of ego alone. Admitting that a problem is unsolvable hurts. Sitting with irreconcilable differences can feel like heartbreak. That moment, however, is not the end but a beginning of a different type. If, instead of quitting, the path of surrender is chosen, the urgency that surrounds moments of exhaustion and defeat can be truly transformational moments of liberation. There is at least one moment, if not many moments, in every spiritual practitioner's journey, where the lesson of surrender presents itself. Each person's journey is unique, and the situation that presents itself may be totally different. Yet the lesson of surrender is universal—release the struggle to receive the power of grace.

Wanting Is Not Action

"I want ..." When these words begin a conversation or thought, it is highly likely that the ego is involved, and old patterns are activated. The paradigm of *want* is the root of much suffering. Desire, the state of wanting, is something that colors one's worldview. Craving. Clinging. Wanting. These are all states that many spiritual paths say lead to suffering.

Desire colors human relations. When the root of an interaction stems from the sole purpose of wanting something, it feels off. There is a subtle form of manipulation that occurs when another person operates from the paradigm of wanting, even if what the person wants is not too unreasonable. If it is decided before a meeting that the foundation of the meeting is to get something, then that is the lens through which the entire meeting will be viewed. Once the seed of wanting starts growing, that very seed defines so many other actions, which almost act like a nearly entirely predetermined route. The state of craving is bottomless, like an unquenchable thirst. In fact, the word for *craving* used by the Buddha, *tanha*, is translated into English from the ancient Pali as thirst. Once a small sip is given, there is yet only the desire for more. Wanting, as a state, breeds more wanting and is not satisfied by any attainment.

The root of wanting is not actually about the object of our desire. We want because we think that act of possession will fill some vacuum within ourselves. But the sad truth of material objects is that the acquisition is a temporary high that, like any drug, leads to addiction. Craving begets more craving. Momentary relief of the pain of an inner emptiness will only compel an individual to strive even harder for the next hit of relief. That is true whether what desire is focused on a steady stream of objects, unique or extreme experiences, or favor, influence, time, information, or power over other people. Nothing, no thing, can fill the spiritual void within. Many spiritual paths discuss the dangers of chasing the material pleasure of the world. For some long-term seekers, it is all too easy to look at the fleeting happiness, promised by consumer culture, with skepticism. Yet the state of wanting can infiltrate more subtle layers of being. For example, it can be so much harder to penetrate beyond the veil of emotional materialism. Rather than consuming objects or wanting things to fill a void, emotions consume other people in the same way that products are purchased, used, and discarded. Even though a physical product is not exchanged, bartering with emotions can be just as scintillating, if not more, to the state of craving. By clinging to attention, the object of desire becomes a kind of idol to worship, possess, and control. But just like any possession, the driver of the pursuit of wanting will always be left alone to face his or her own void.

When the foundation of human interaction is a desire, the action is rooted in ego, like a spiritual quid pro quo that taints the authenticity of both parties. I get many requests for collaboration each day. Recently, the owner of a yoga-related business asked me if I could give them any tips to grow their social media audience. Now, I understand how prevalent and necessary social media is for a successful business venture and also how perplexing of a beast it can be. I also usually like to chat about business strategy and help others who are just getting started in the pursuit of their dreams. But not this time. So I had to ask myself what was different.

The person wanted something from me—information, time, favor, influence, promotion. While these are common things to ask for, the quality of wanting was more heightened than usual. I'm not entirely sure how to describe the sense I got of this. It was a look of longing, exacerbated by prolonged eye contact, filled with a kind of hunger that seemed both insatiable and impossibly full. The gaze felt like it was searching for something to hook into, rather than meet honestly. The body posture was leaning in, invading, lingering, and uncomfortably close. There were pointed questions, a dragging tone of voice, and a kind of disregard for time—it just so happened that I was on the way to catch a car to the airport, and I indicated that I was short on time.

The wanting personified a character trait that reminded me of the Tibetan Buddhist archetype of the hungry ghost. I was repelled by the urgency of the desire and the intensity. To be "wanted" like this felt like I was in the presence of an energetic vampire, searching for a place to latch on. It wasn't so much the actual desire as the craving attached to the desire that spawned a kind of visceral rejection of the request. Of course, I myself am not beyond that type of insidious desire. None of us is. It is a fact of being human. But the purpose of the spiritual path is to be aware of the hooks when they arise within us. I have wanted, desired, yearned, and pined for so many things in my life. I see people through the lens of my desire.

I'm not suggesting that the path to happiness is to renounce all worldly possessions and make a hard claim to reject all materialism, whatever forms it takes. Many students do this when they embark on a spiritual path. For a time, many new students do things like shave their heads (I did that!), give away their possessions (did that too), or eat only organic food (I'm still doing this as much as possible). It is a wonderful process to let go of attachments, and maybe we all do need to go through it ourselves.

Unpacking the root of action is at the heart of the spiritual journey of awakening. Without conscious, inward seeking, it is just too easy to trade one type of materialism for another. Attachment to material objects can even be replaced by attachment to antimaterialism. It is the attachment itself, the quality of mind that uses wanting as the basis of action, that defines spiritual liberation. Attachment, even being attached to *not* having things, is still, after all, an attachment.

Trading one form of attachment for another is a sometimes-necessary step along the path. Materialism and greed, as a state of mind, are closely related; this state may or may not be expressed in the accumulation of material possessions. Greed and desire can be directed to more than material objects. Hunger for attention and approval causes much suffering. Insatiable desire for adventure, mystical experience, or exciting highs is a kind of addiction in and of itself. In other words, every human being has some element of desire and attachment, whether that points toward material objects, emotional states, or other experiences of one type or another. The teaching presented here is not to present a purity litmus test for spiritual practitioners. Instead, we are on a very human path together to know desire, address its root, and—hopefully, in the process of knowing—gain a bit more freedom from it.

Action rooted in desire leads to suffering. Action rooted outside of the realm of desire has the potential to lead you out of suffering. This axiom is one of the foundations of the spiritual path. To be *in* the world but not *of* it is a riddle every spiritual practitioner is encouraged to solve. There is a pure heart within that can never be defiled or harmed. Walking the line between desire and attachment, between craving and clinging, without being ensnared by the hooks is freedom. Boxes of absolutes often perpetuate attitudes of desire and craving. But even if all the "right" actions are taken, there is no guarantee that the attainment of the checklist will lead to happiness. There is no substitute for the inner work of changing the paradigm and waking up to our true thoughts.

Behavior is nothing but the patterns of the mind made manifest. The impact of behavior is the fruit that tells the story of the root of that action.

Whether we are casually scrolling through social media, reading the news, cleaning the house, listening to music, practicing yoga, or doing anything else, there is a root to every action. Actions rooted in the paradigm of desire are founded in the ground of self-rejection. In order to be free from the fruits of suffering, the ground upon which the seeds of those actions are grown must be tilled to make room for new seeds and thoughts, the fruits of which will be the sweet fruit of love.

Question Impulses to Change the Paradigm

Cindy is a private student of mine who has a troubled relationship with her sister. She spent years feeling mistreated by her sibling. During practice, Cindy would often be filled with angry thoughts about the way her sister treated her in the past. While I advised her to speak with a trained therapist, I also advised her to avoid acting while her anger and aggression were stoked. But she felt justified. She told me that her anger made her feel powerful and that it was healing the weakness she felt when she was around her sister. There is something that feels kind of intoxicating about anger—anger makes us feel powerful, at least for a moment. If we have felt victimized by a powerful person and tend to drop into depression, then getting angry and lashing out may give a temporary high. It can feel like a rush of energy and may even make us think that our anger is a way of reclaiming power.

So Cindy gave herself permission to act in anger. She lashed out at her sister and spoke harshly about how she felt bullied, victimized, manipulated, and used. Expecting to evoke a behavior change in her sister, Cindy was shocked when her sister dug into her past patterns and lashed out even more. They haven't spoken since, and it's been years. Maybe one day, they'll heal the wound.

Now, I'm not saying that expressing anger is wrong, nor am I saying that Cindy's sister did nothing wrong. I am saying that actions bear consequences far beyond what we can see from our limited perspective.

The only power we actually have is over the actions and reactions that are done directly by us. No one has power over the actions and reactions of others. The quality of any course of action is eventually shown by the fruits of that action; allowing attachment and desire to be the cause of action are certain to bear bitter fruits. Feelings of despair, disillusionment, separation, hopelessness, and more anger only grow under the paradigm of desire. Worse still, once the taste of bitter fruits grows, it sometimes precipitates a downward spiral, where loss of self-esteem generates even more suffering. Sometimes it takes years to process all that happens when an act is done from a place of wanting.

Yet for the spiritual journey, that too can be ultimately useful. It is only after patterns bear their fruits that the most deeply rooted ones come to the surface. Once revealed in clarity, there is a chance to heal and be free of those old patterns. While it may seem overly optimistic, there is a time when it may even be possible to be grateful for the learning that came from suffering, at least on a spiritual level. The process of spiritual evolution and growth is rarely a straight line of upward growth. In fact, even some small shifts can make a qualitative difference in life. While few people may truly get beyond anger or desire, everyone can begin the work of operating from a different paradigm, one that is much better equipped to lead to peace and happiness. The journey would not be the journey unless both the malady and the antidote were part of the process.

The paradigm changes when the ego drops away. Questioning the exceptionalism, toward which so many people have a tendency, is a big step toward chipping away at the ego. In the acceptance of the average, ordinary struggles (anxiety, depression, anger, desire, low self-esteem) and average, ordinary highs (love, joy, and bliss—although you could argue that there is nothing ordinary about love, joy, and bliss), there is a kind of simple truth. I'm not on some higher plane. I'm a person who has been practicing yoga and meditation for over twenty years. I'm not an enlightened master. I may not even be a few steps farther along the path on some things. But I'm still on the path, and I've put in a lot of work to shift the paradigm in which I operate. I am now living in a state of self-awareness and self-acceptance to a degree that I previously thought impossible. As a result, I no longer want things from other people like I used to do. I no longer spend my days wanting and doing and worrying about what the next things to want and do will be. I spend hours of my day, if not my entire day, just being.

While I still have goals, and I work hard, the root cause of the action has shifted. Instead of running fast and hard to fill a void within myself, the foundation of my being is wholeness, and what I do is now about purpose, depth, meaning, and service. The question I ask myself today is, what can I give? How can I serve?

Desire. Wanting. Craving. Clinging. Control.

This was the old paradigm.

Purpose. Service. Surrender. Respect. Humility.

This is the new paradigm.

At least, this is how I see it. I am not here to give all the answers. Instead, I hope to present a teaching about how to ask questions that will lead deeper down the journey of discovery and awakening.

The Root and the Fruit

Every action has a root. The root determines which fruit will be born. Fruits do not lie about their roots. Yet not everything that happens is our fault or the result of our vibration, our negative thoughts, or our karma. Instead, sometimes things just happen due to forces that are beyond our control. How we respond to the various situations of life, which are sometimes painful, sometimes pleasurable, and sometimes neutral, determines which seeds are nurtured within the garden of our own minds.

Many people claim to act with kindness and generosity, but the fruits of their actions tell a different story. Conscious intention is often at odds with unconscious patterning. We are responsible not only for our intent but also for our impact. Even more, we are responsible for the subconscious thinking that our actions carry, even when we may not be aware of the patterns at play.

The cognitive dissonance that many people face when presented with evidence that either proves or refutes consciously held notions about themselves is hard to handle. When the impact of one's action is contrary to one's intent, the paradox can feel like a trap with no clear path out. In order to untie this knot, look to the deeper root of action.

Love is expressed not only in conscious behavior but in the deep programming of the subconscious mind. Love is shown by that to which we are most devoted. Whatever is front and center when talking, thinking, reading, and reflecting is an expression of where the energy of love is directed. Most people are not conscious creators of their daily life experiences. Most people are unconsciously pulled by cycles of distraction, an endless sea of news headlines, and the problems that need attention.

It may be hard to accept, but what garners the most attention is whatever carries the most energy. Love is a function of attention, first expressed in thoughts and then manifested in action. If family is a stated top priority, but the majority of time is spent at work, actions might appear to tell a different story about what is loved. People express love in all sorts of ways, and those ways are often colored by the root patterns carried in the subconscious mind. The twisted knots that the old paradigm carries sometimes betray the consciously stated intention of actions. If love, peace, and kindness are a priority, but each day is consumed by arguments and judgments, then actions reveal a deeper truth. Actions are physical manifestations of thought. While thoughts are hidden from view, actions reveal their supporting paradigm clearly. Actions will only change once the root of the action is changed. Simply piling on a bunch of "loving" behaviors while failing to dig deeply within dooms those mighty proclamations to failure.

When I suggest that everything should be an act of love, I am not suggesting sugarcoating everyday life. The journey that I am offering begins with the brave excavation of the true root of all current actions in life. All the places founded without love—or worse, with hate—must be dealt with in the clear light of day in order to truly learn how to love.

Action without Attachment

In the Bhagavad Gita, the warrior prince Arjuna enters the epic battle armed with the teaching of yoga. Arjuna is an archer who has taken Krishna as his guide and charioteer. Krishna is one of the most revered of all Hindu divinities, worshipped as an avatar of Vishnu and also as a supreme god in his own right; in aligning his interests with Krishna, Arjuna takes refuge in God himself. The night that precedes this cataclysmic battle is spent with the young prince Arjuna in communion with his teacher, the manifest God, Krishna. Among the many questions that the young prince has for his guru, his most pressing one is about how it is possible to commit the terrible act of war without violating the precepts of yoga. To which, Krishna replies, in chapter 3, verse 19:

> Therefore, always perform prescribed actions diligently without attachment; for, by performing action without attachment, an individual attains the supreme.

Selfless action, rather than selfish action, is the path for how to act without attachment. But the question of action is presented through the lens of effort and surrender. The actor is entitled to his or her own effort but not the fruits of his or her labor. There are two parts to every activity— the active and passive, the yin and the yang. By balancing these two points together, the spiritual aspirant attains true and lasting peace. An action done in balance between these polarities can be considered an act of love, one that engenders no negative karma.

Krishna instructs Arjuna to surrender the fruits of his labor to God, or, more specifically, Krishna says "to me." In releasing the arrow from his bow, the young warrior prince is to let go of the idea that he is the doer and turn the results over to God. If this act is done sincerely, then Krishna says that the arrow and its karma will no longer belong to Arjuna; instead, the karma will belong to God himself. Arjuna's great act of love has many layers. First, in turning over the ownership of his efforts to Krishna, Arjuna releases his ego and attachment. The selfless act of surrender is an act of love. Second, flowing forth from that pivotal change of heart, every arrow fired in battle now falls in line with love's path. Third, it is only through a great devotion to Krishna as God that Arjuna finds the path of love and frees himself of the accumulation of negative karmas otherwise incurred by the act of warfare.

Exploring the notion of karma and the fruits of karma are integral to the idea of what action means and what acting in love truly means. To act in love means to act without any strings attached, to give freely without any expectation. Karma is translated into English from Sanskrit as action, work, or deed and is often used to refer to the law of cause and effect. Take, for example, karma yoga, the yoga of action that often takes the form of acts of service. Karma is often used to refer to the universal law of causality, most commonly understood to be that every action causes ripples in the lake of our lives, spiraling outward. There are said to be direct, indirect, immediate, and distant consequences to every action. Sometimes, on a very basic level, people think of karma as the police department of the universe. Even then, it is important to note that karma, in its most traditional sense, has no emotion associated with it. It is not out to get anyone or make anyone "pay."

A popular, if somewhat vulgar and culturally appropriated phrase, is to say that "karma is a bitch." Ironically, another quite popular phrase that seems antithetical to this statement is to say that "God is love." These two statements seem, at first, irreconcilable. Unpacking them both might make sense of what appears to be a logical inconsistency and help understand a central principle gleaned from Arjuna's great act of surrender.

When I've heard the phrase, "karma is a bitch," it seems that people are often referring to their own hurt feelings and the desire to see the person whom they have identified as the source of their suffering pay a price for his or her actions. Instead of referring to universal yogic principles, in that case, karma becomes a messenger of personal justice, vengeance, and retribution. I know all too well how hurt feelings, especially powerful emotions, betrayal, abandonment, and anger, can fuel a desire to extract a type of payment for the debt created. This could be called an eye-for-an-eye, tooth-for-a-tooth sense of justice and is perhaps the most basic and elementary form of righting the wrongs of the past. Yet while it is totally human to yearn to see the perpetrators of wrongful actions pay for their crimes, this desire is, at least, only a rudimentary understanding of how people truly atone for their actions in life.

Karma is not really a bitch, nor is it at anyone's beck and call. Karma is a divinely created law of order. It is impersonal and formed in love. Formed as a guiding principle in this life and beyond, karma is of the highest order of life and a key philosophical principle, borrowed from the spiritual traditions of the East, including Hinduism and Buddhism. Personal feelings of pain and hurt may close in so tightly on us and spark a desire to seek an avenger of some type to set things right again in the logic of our own moral universe. When we feel victimized, we often search for a hero to step in and make things right again. Following this logic, it feels safe to claim karma as our champion and send off this force to perform the punishment that we see fit. Thinking of karma in this sense is short-sighted and ignorant of the vast cultural context in which the concept is presented. Karma is translated from Sanskrit to English as action, work, or deed. The principle of karma is a spiritual notion of cause and effect, as impersonal as the law of gravity. The consequences of one's actions are typically described in two forms: the fruits (*phala*) and the residual patterns (*samskara*) generated from any given action. Like this, all karma is revealed in due time. Traditionally, it is also understood that the implications of karma follow an individual from one life to the next in the cycle of reincarnation, until all karmas have been burned up, and no more fruits or residual patterns remain. Regardless of one's personal belief regarding rebirth, the implications of karma on action are immediately apparent.

Wishing harm upon others, even through the invocation of external forces, perpetuates suffering. Genuinely wishing others well has an immediate impact on one's entire being. Of course, karma is much more complex than that, as can be illustrated in the relationship between Arjuna and Krishna. Or maybe it is also that simple. Arjuna never truly wishes harm upon his enemy, and it is his desire not to commit a hurtful act that opens the door to Krishna's great teaching.

I know all too well the harm that one inflicts on oneself from hating someone or something that is seen as a perpetrator of wrongs in the world and then acting on that hate. Whether through thoughts, words, or deeds, the desire to see someone (or even an organization) suffer contains a kind of darkness, or at least, it did for me. I am not proud to say that I have sat on the sidelines while people were ridiculed, and I remained silent, simply because I thought they were getting what they deserved. This is evil at its root. To cheer on the demise of a fellow human being is, quite simply, cruel. Remember that devotion to God is at the heart of Arjuna's ability to turn over the fruits of his actions. Proximity to the divine is illustrated least of all by acts of hate and cruelty, even those that appear to be justified by circumstances.

How can we become like Arjuna and enter into the battlefield of life with the same devotion and surrender? We all have desires, whether for clean water, a good job, a romantic partner, a vacation, a good cup of coffee, or something else. If the state of wanting merely attempts to fill a hole inside, then it is highly likely that the action will generate more suffering. Running away from the void within, consciously or subconsciously, means running away from the path of awakening. To the degree that we have each surrendered our desires, we will be free from the chains of desire. Whatever unresolved hooks remain within will ensnare not only ourselves but those around us, creating sometimes messy, dramatic interactions. Arjuna is a model for every spiritual practitioner to strive toward, a true yogi, whose ability to be in the world but not of it sets him free. I can only say that I feel like I have a long way yet to go.

Overwriting the Fear Program

Being kind to others increases the likelihood that kindness will flow in both directions. It's not a guarantee, but even a small act of kindness has the potential to make a positive difference in the world. Lending a helping hand by opening a door for a stranger or simply sharing a warm-hearted smile might just be enough to change someone's day. If nothing else, it feels good to do good. Perhaps the universe is a much more benevolent place that we tend to think it is. Perhaps in realizing that we are all here to live, learn, and, ultimately, to love, we can find a way out of cycles of fear into a path of love. Understanding our brains and biology is a key access point to the work of reprogramming old patterns of reactivity, fueled by unchecked desire.

Two biological systems in mammals play an important role in how human beings operate. The fear response is called the fight-flight-freeze response, and this state of fear, anger, and shock is the source of much suffering. Associated with stress, racing heartbeats, digestive dysfunction, anger outbursts, aggression, rage, and PTSD, this neurological state can feel, quite simply, like hell.

The second, less-well-known state, is called the calm-and-connect state. Associated with the release of the neuropeptide oxytocin, this state within mammals calms fear and opens the heart for deeper connection. The vagus nerve, which has its roots in the perineum, runs the entire length of the spinal cord up and has its origination point all the way up in the brain; it speaks the language of safety to the body and mind.

Love and health are intimately intertwined. Prolonged periods of the fight-flight-freeze response place burdens on the body and mind that predispose disease. The vagus nerve plays a crucial role in the lived experience of love. More than any other nerve in the body, the vagus nerve interfaces with the parasympathetic nervous system and influences the functioning of the heart, lungs, and digestive tract. It is also the longest running nerve of the autonomic nervous system, and its regulation directly impacts the muscles of facial expression. A well-balanced vagus nerve increases the likelihood that two individuals will be able to maintain sympathetic expressions, like maintaining eye contact, and be in sync with one another. When the vagus nerve is balanced, it is sometimes called having a good vagal tone. The middle ear benefits from vagal tone by heightening the ability to tune out background noise and focus more intently on the intimate sounds of another person's voice. This all normally happens entirely outside of the field of conscious awareness. In *Love 2.0—Creating Happiness and Health in Moments of Connection*, Barbara Fredrickson says, "Keeping in mind that love *is* connection, you should know that your vagus nerve is a biological asset that supports and coordinates your experiences of love" (Fredrickson 2013, 57).

Studies show that practicing meditation increases vagal tone. In 2010, scientists discovered a connection between high vagal tone, physical health, and positive mental states. Mladen Golubic, MD, the medical director of the Cleveland Clinic, states, "The vagal response reduces stress. It reduces our heart rate and blood pressure. It changes the function of certain parts of the brain, stimulates digestion, all those things that happen when we are relaxed" (Fallis 2021). Meditation reduces the sympathetic nervous system's warning bells and disarms the fight-flight-freeze response. But it's not only meditation that increases vagal tone. Lifestyle, diet, exercise, massage, breathing exercises, yoga, singing, chanting, humming, and, perhaps most importantly, socializing and laughing all stimulate the vagus nerve.

Actions that establish a balanced vagus nerve literally make the body and mind healthier. Instead of those actions only being done at certain times during meditation or in the therapist's office, imagine if our whole lives could be structured in such a way as to have a root in vagal tone every day. Perhaps then, loving-kindness would be the root of every action and every thought, every moment of the day. Quite simply, imagine if everything done was an act of love. I'm not sure life would suddenly feel like heaven on earth, but I am pretty certain that life would feel a few degrees better than it does right now. What's so wonderful about learning the tools of self-regulating the nervous system is that there is no need to wait for any external circumstance to change before experiencing deeper states of relaxation. All that needs to happen is a shift in inner perception, a kind of update to the operating system.

Love in the Real World

I understand that this may seem impossible or incredulous that the whole experience of life will change, just by shifting one locus of control. It might sound like unrealistic, spiritual woo-woo talk from a privileged person. And to be honest, I have been blessed with certain privileges. As a cisgender person from a two-parent middle-class family, there is much I have received as advantage, simply from birth. As a multiethnic person with Japanese ancestry who grew up in Florida, where the Asian population was nominal during my childhood, I never identified with being of the dominant culture, even though I am white-passing. I am also an early childhood sexual trauma survivor, as well as an adult rape survivor. While I cannot know directly the pain, fear, and anger associated with certain types of systemic oppression, I have certainly felt the pain of trauma and an imbalanced nervous system. On the other side of that, I have also felt the peace and tranquility from a down-regulated nervous system. Part of my work in the world is to make the tools I have learned through my over twenty years of yoga and meditation practice available to all.

The reality is that many of us face staggering odds that seem to make it impossible to simply relax, take a few breaths, and stimulate the vagus nerve. There are many people, myself included, whose life circumstances may not immediately make it feel safe to trust what lies on the other side of the calm-and-connect response. For survivors of trauma and members of marginalized communities, the world, quite frankly, has not been a safe space. To create a world where love is the dominant force requires a massive shift in consciousness. The burden cannot be placed only on those who are victims of oppression and acts of harm.

Perhaps acting in love looks different for us all. Perhaps acting in love from a place of privilege looks different than it does from a place of disadvantage or hurt. The purpose of this book is not to weaponize the language of self-development to pass judgment on others, giving free license to label people as "negative" when it appears their actions do not look like love from the outside. While I have sought to explore the definition of love and action, my writing here is by no means the final and ultimate truth about these principles. I encourage everyone to keep striving and searching, as I will continue to keep striving and searching along my own path of awakening. The fruits of love may take many years to bear their fruits. Meanwhile, the seed of every action is held internally, in the secret chambers of the heart. The seeker's path is about uncovering these inner realms to know oneself deeply. None of us can truly know the root of another's action. Our ability to feel is so deeply impacted by our social conditioning that it may not be possible for each of us to see clearly. In fact, it is, quite frankly, not possible for any human being to always see the whole picture.

From a place of privilege, an act of love might look like empowering those who do not share your privilege. An act of fear or hate might look like entrenching and protecting privilege at the harm, intended or not, of others.

From a place of disadvantage, an act of love might look like self-preservation or self-love, even and especially when those in positions of power resist the efforts to lift up or call actions hateful. An act of fear might look like going with the flow or preserving the status quo, seeking approval, or not rocking the boat or upsetting your superior.

For all parties, an act of hate can often stem from self-directed hatred that implodes through substance abuse or physical or verbal aggression directed toward oneself or others. Low self-esteem, cultivated and confirmed by actions that betray one's true heart and highest potential, further the cycle of suffering.

The burden of love cannot simply fall entirely on the disadvantaged and hurt. If the basis of societal structures relies on a violence committed to a member of that society, the dominant culture simply has to participate in an update to the cultural ethos if real change is to happen. The very North American premise of individualism gives false equivalence to two human beings whose lives start off on entirely different playing fields. There is only so much those born into disadvantage can do by changing their own minds. The daily constant onslaught of aggression would require those facing intersectional prejudice to evolve to the level of Jesus Christ manifest, just to go about their day without being triggered. Privilege of any type—class, race, gender, age, ableism—comes with the responsibility to use it wisely. The operating system of the individual mind and of the social mind contains generations of deeply entrenched beliefs. To be the force of change requires enough courage to change course and question the status quo.

Even these parameters are flawed, imperfect, and inadequate to express the complex network involved in changing an entire paradigm. To act in love is a personal choice to break an outdated model for human interaction. It is a private affair that cannot be judged, except, perhaps, by the long-term fruits made manifest in body, mind, and life. Committing to the work of spiritual awakening has the power to change everything. But like any change, the impact happens first internally and then spreads outward, like a plant that first takes root and only flowers over a course of time. It cannot be rushed, and most of the process will be internal and unseen. Just as the tree works hard to sprout, grow, blossom, and fruit, and most of the work is done deep within its trunk and root system, so too must the work of personal development be done on the inner terrain. To change the root is to change the very nature of the plant. Perhaps that is where we all are right now—in the darkness of the soil, feeling the pain of change, while the dormant seeds of love begin to activate.

1. Unpacking Desire

Come to a comfortable position. Close your eyes. Allow yourself to focus on your breath for a few moments. Settle the mind until you feel centered within yourself. Open your eyes, and pick up your journey. Draw a line down the center of a blank page. Write the word *desire* at the top of the left-hand side of the page. Then, write out everything you most desire in the left column. Then, after you complete your list, write the word *feeling* at the top of the column to the right. Ask yourself what feeling each of these desires is connected to. Begin to understand why you want each of these things or experiences by reflecting on how you would feel if you were to have what you desire. It could be a feeling of wholeness, success, relief, peace, acceptance, love, happiness, freedom, or anything that comes up for you. Take the time to identify what the root of your desire really is about. Once you've completed your list of desires and the corresponding feeling that each desire represents, reflect on the feelings. Is there a theme? Or are the feelings quite diverse? Finally, open a new blank page in your journal. Write at the top of the page *fulfillment.* Ask yourself if there is any way that you could give yourself the feeling of what you desire right now. Is there anything you could do in order to unify with the deeper object of your desire—that is, the emotional state—with or without the physical object of desire? Write your answer down on this new page, and take it outward as a practice to embody the fruits of desire in fullness and wholeness as you are.

✳

Chapter 3

Update the Operating System

The process of change requires unlearning. It requires breaking the habit of the old self and reinventing a new self.
—Joe Dispenza

What we consciously think about is only a small portion of what we actually think about. The foundation of our thinking is rooted in the subconscious mind. Every human being (you and me too!) is primarily unaware of the recurrent thoughts that play in the background of the mind. Past experiences accumulate, first as memories and then solidify into preferences, judgments, and deeply held beliefs about the way things are. The aggregate impact of these old assumptions rooted in the past is a powerful inertia that casts a shadow over the present that looms over the future. What seems fresh and new is often just a recycling of the familiar with a fresh coat of paint. This largely subconscious pattern is the source of much suffering; freedom begins with unpacking the systemic thoughts that form the basis of this largely hidden programming.

The mind is like a computer and contains elements of software and hardware, but unlike an inanimate object, the brain is constantly changing. Experience-dependent neuroplasticity shows that behavior has the power to influence biology, but it's not so easy to change. When we try to think new thoughts, it's hard to actually make the new thoughts stick. When we want to break an old habit, the sheer inertia behind past actions is daunting. Yet that is what we are here to do—to update the operating system of the mind and consciously create the foundational principles that guide and govern each of our actions. It is nothing short of a revolution of consciousness that occurs with what may be a subtle yet impactful change in perspective.

The stories of our lives are told at the intersection of thought, emotion, and action. Not everything you think or feel results in action. And not every action is aligned with intention. The potential to truly awaken as a human being is a call to align thought, emotion, and action with the highest path; that is, the path of love. Each of us decides, moment to moment, consciously or unconsciously, which system we support and the value that system upholds. No one but us has the potential to truly reshape the fabric of our minds and thereby our world as well. By adopting a new view of reality, thinking new thoughts, embracing new actions, and feeling new feelings, we can be agents of real change. This is the work of spiritual awakening and the purpose of our journey together.

The promise of a life fulfilled or, as we say in the yoga tradition, fully realized is a unity of mind and body, matter and spirit. Western societies tend to be very good at intellectualizing things. We philosophize, we think, we believe. We formulate theories and moralities, but we are not truly embodied. Just look at one of the key philosophers of Western civilization, René Descartes, who proclaimed, "I think therefore I am." Our sense of I-ness in the West is tied to a sense of the thinking mind. While many in the West have recently worked on integrating feelings, there is a tendency to think and philosophize about feelings, rather than actually feel them. Through my spiritual practices, which are rooted primarily in the wisdom traditions of the East, I have learned how to be more fully alive in the body. The ancient practice traditions of Eastern spirituality have preserved a path to bring home the true promise of being human. But first, we need to update the operating system of the mind.

Updating Your Inner Software

In order to update the operating system, though, we first need to recognize the role of the subconscious mind. Most of what happens in the mind occurs at a subconscious level. Harvard professor Gerald Zaltman, along with many contemporary neuroscientists, says that 95 percent of all cognition occurs in the subconscious mind. That means that around 95 percent of the mind's power is directed to the subconscious level, which can be somewhat scary news for some of us. By definition, we do not consciously know what is happening on this level of thinking, even though our most powerful and systemic thinking takes place here.

In the realm of the subconscious mind, we have deeply held behavioral patterns that run without our being aware of them. These patterns are often ones that were set deeply within the subconscious mind at a young age—before the conscious mind was fully formed. It is reported that after age twelve, the door between the conscious and the subconscious mind usually closes (MContigo 2017). Until the pivotal shift through puberty happens, the mind is like a sponge and soaks up largely subconscious programming, communicated through nonverbal cues, thoughts, and feelings. But these thoughts, behaviors, and reactions actually define our lives and identities as much as, if not more than, any conscious memory, thought, or intention. Unlike the conscious level of the mind, of which we are aware even now, the subconscious mind does its work automatically, and we are often not aware of it.

That's the danger of the subconscious mind. If we do not directly work with these deep behavioral patterns, which have largely been imprinted in the mind because of what may have been painful, traumatic incidents early in life (or perhaps in a previous life), then these patterns will literally run our lives. This happened for me. I felt like I was repeating the same patterns of suffering, despite my best efforts. I was frustrated, and it felt like no one could help me find the way out. The names and situations may change a little, but an ever-present knot that I just could not untie sat at the core—that is, until I untied it and shifted my thoughts.

Thoughts exist in a realm of the mind and intellect. They seem to emanate from within a space of selfhood. We may think we are thinking, identifying with the thought, the action of thinking, and the thinker itself. It is easy to assume that if we are the thinker, then our thoughts must be linked to a permanent self. Again, in the West, we tend to elevate rational thinking and institutions of higher learning to the degree that many people operate as thinking heads, attached to a dismembered and forgotten body. But thoughts do not actually come from anywhere external. If the eyes close for a few moments, thoughts appear in the silence and seem to think themselves. And even more confusing, thoughts are not necessarily true or untrue. Thoughts are merely stories that we tell about ourselves, our world, and everything around us. We do it with our conscious minds, and we do it with our subconscious minds. At least, we are aware of the conscious stories. Only when a thought pattern becomes conscious can we work with it, deconstruct it, or decide to give it authority over our lives.

Psychologist Timothy Jennings has devoted his work to unpacking deeply held assumptions about self-worth, God, and identity, as they are held in the subconscious mind. He writes,

> The brain will actually rewire itself based on the things we think, do, see, and experience. Indeed, the brain is constantly branching and pruning its neural network. The choices we make—what we think, believe, admire, and worship, as well as the behavior in which we engage—all have profound effects on the ultimate behavior in which we engage development of our neural network and thus our characters. The software (what we think) can actually change the hardware (the neural network). (Jennings 2012, 33)

We all have knots of delusion that bind us. Think of these knots as blind spots that will define reality and be the foundation of personality. As long as they remain unconscious and shrouded in darkness, these patterns have power over us and our lives. These hidden premises of subconscious thinking will often be known to the subject as the feeling of "the way things work." Subconscious thoughts are assumptions and, as such, are often taken for granted and so sublimated that it takes great effort to reveal them in clarity. However, it is precisely by tuning into this realm that the real work of personal growth happens. Some refer to a deep dive into the subconscious as "shadow work." And it is true that all who enter will walk through what might be called a "dark night of the soul," where every single deeply held belief about oneself and the world is challenged and put through a trial-by-fire test.

The most common reaction to facing the shadows that lurk within is not a willingness to dive in; instead, it's a willingness to tune out. I felt it too. When I sat with the shattered pieces of my thoughts, I wanted to do anything but work on myself. I felt the pull toward distraction, diversion, and any activity that would allow me to tune out rather than tune in. I vacillated between extreme experiences, the sheer intensity of which blurred out the pain, and mind-numbing hours spent zoning out like a zombie, scrolling endlessly on social media. It works for a time, but sooner or later, the effect wears off, and reality is always waiting.

In order to break the cycle, the operating system of the mind needs to be updated. This book shows how to reset the mind in much the same way as a computer reboots after installing a software update. Let me be clear on where I am in the process: I do not assume that the updates I've made are the last to be made. The teaching I share here is but a small piece of the infinite learning of my own journey. I am not sitting on a perch of enlightenment, far away from everyone. I struggle and continue to awaken with new lessons each day. Yet there is a method I discovered that fixed some of the buggiest aspects of my mind, and I am sharing it here. If it works, great; apply it, and put it to work. If it doesn't, keep searching. I am sure there is a teacher or a teaching out there that will shed light on the path.

Understanding the Jungle of the Mind

The mind is sometimes described as a jungle of thoughts. Within the network of interweaving thoughts, there are the manicured thoughts of the conscious realm. These are lighter thoughts that we advertise to others and have no difficulty discussing. But there are also the wild, untamed thoughts of the jungle within. These intense thoughts, overgrown with instincts, obsessions, impulses, and other behaviors rooted in the unconscious, are often held tightly—so tightly that few people are even aware of them.

Consciousness is fragile. Exploring the jungle of the subconscious mind challenges the fragility of the conscious mind. Anger and other intense emotions seem to emerge from a great chasm within that appears to be an unruly, unconquered place, where instinct and animal nature rules. Before the conscious mind knows what's happening, the impulses of the subconscious can grow and overtake it, leaving a residue of confusion and befuddlement. The conscious mind, clouded by a thick fog, drunk with the intoxicating aroma of pleasure and pain, engages in actions that are often unacceptable when assessed from a clear mind. The cycle of unconscious action happens more often than we realize. In the freewheeling space of the subconscious mind, there is very little space between the stimulus of the world and one's own response. Spiritual awakening cuts a path through the thick jungle of the mind, revealing clearly what would otherwise be kept in the dark. Remember that the purpose of this discussion is not to create dichotomy and division but to heal and make the conscious and subconscious mind whole. Sort of like how cleaning out a computer's hard drive allows the machine to function optimally, the process of personal growth integrates all the disparate thoughts and desires into one being.

Many spiritually oriented people fear the jungle-like nature of the subconscious mind. There is, perhaps, something satisfyingly safe in rules and dogmas. Sometimes, the massive job of weeding out the garden of the mind gets relegated to strict rules and lists of dos and don'ts. Weeding out the mind is a useful endeavor when done with a heart full of love. But if it's a crusade, launched on the inner world against thoughts labeled as dark, then a war of self-rejection begins. Keeping thoughts and patterns labeled as "bad" under lock and key fuels a cycle of fear and creates a vicious cycle that is far from true liberation of the mind.

There is nothing to fear in the world of thoughts, especially the angry ones. All that is within the nature of being. Even the most apparently destructive thoughts that conjure up trepidation are nothing other than broken, wounded parts of the self, relegated to repression within the jungle of the mind. Once those sleeping demons are brought out into light, they are disarmed and befriended. In fact, there are no demons surreptitiously slinking in the background, waiting to pounce. There are simply patterns woven into the fabric of the subconscious mind. Patterning itself is neutral; it simply is a quality of being. But which type of pattern is programmed has the power to create quality of life. Liberation of the mind is not a rejection of the power of the mind but a repatterning of the most foundational program. Instead of rejecting the wounded parts of ourselves, wholeness is about growing big enough to include both the light and shadow.

Healing Crises and the Power of Yoga

Some people are forced, through a pivotal crisis, to make changes to the inner workings of the mind. Others choose voluntarily to participate in the work of awakening. While life often seems like a perpetual-motion machine, driven by forward motion through goals, such as a career, family, travel and other similar achievements, life is not just about checking off boxes of accomplishments. Instead, we are here for an entirely different purpose. But we will only be able to discover what that purpose is if we are willing to unlearn the old patterning of the mind and update our inner software.

Nicolette was a student of mine who showed up one day and practiced yoga with all her heart. She sometimes took two classes a day. Our yoga center became her second home. I later learned that she started practicing yoga after her world shattered. Raised in a traditional Christian family, she assumed she had realized her life's purpose of being a wife. Planning ahead, she hoped to be on her way to building a family with the man she thought was her life partner. But one day, her world came crashing down; she found out that he had a secret life. Not only was he seeing another woman, but he had bought that woman an apartment and was living with her when he said he was away on business trips. The nest egg that she thought they had been saving for their child was depleted; he locked her out of their bank accounts and apparently vanished, ghosting her and leaving her with their bills and joint responsibilities. Although Nicolette had a law degree, she had never worked a day in her life. To make matters worse, she had no friends of her own because her entire social circle was defined by her marriage. It was out of this desperation that she found a yoga video online and, after practice, felt a tingling of life return. It was my video with which she practiced, and it was in my class that she would begin the long road back to herself. Now, years later, she is a successful lawyer in a happy relationship and a dedicated yoga practitioner.

Over the more than twenty years I have spent in the yoga world, I've learned of countless stories of students who turned to the methodology of yoga in times of great need. Yoga is not the only balm for a searching soul, but it is one of many ancient techniques that seek to liberate the mind. Maintaining or developing a yoga practice isn't a prerequisite to benefit from this book, but some sort of mind/body practice can be immensely beneficial to the work of rewriting the mind's code. The mind and body are intimately connected, and the work of liberation happens in tandem in the spheres of the physical and the mental or emotional. We cannot work one without the other, for the physical and the mental/emotional are the yin and yang that create the balance of our being. In his book *Could It Be This Simple?* Timothy Jennings suggests,

> All of us reach adulthood with beliefs, values, and morals that need modification. As adults we have a responsibility to evaluate them for ourselves and keep all those that are healthy, all those that are supported by the facts and truth, but discard or change all those that are remnants of a child's way of thinking. (Jennings 2012, 25)

People practice yoga for their entire lives, not because they get a better handstand but because yoga works in powerful ways to provoke substantive changes in both body and mind. Every yoga practitioner has a story about starting practice when feeling angry, sad, anxious, or in some other way unsettled, only to finish practice feeling happier and more peaceful. I consider it an act of kindness each time I choose to practice. I'm a nicer person when I practice, both to myself and others. I think kinder thoughts, say kinder things, and engage in kinder acts. Somewhere in every practice is a door that leads to peace. It's magical, sacred, and holy. My practice is a space of listening and worship, and, even on the days it's difficult, there is an element of transcendence, a kind of movement beyond the physical into the realm of spirit. I leave every practice changed, just a little bit. To me, this isn't discipline but more like a ritual of love. Until we see that choosing the practice is an act of kindness, some part of us might rebel against the monotony of it. Unless we see how the art of yoga is an act of compassion, we might feel that it's just another dogma. The practice is where I go to drink from the source, a deep inexhaustible source of the purest energy. Of course, I want to return to that altar every chance I get. But it's up to each of us to find that sacred space for ourselves.

This isn't a yoga book. I have written four instructional books about yoga, so if reading this sparks an interest in yoga; there are many yoga resources available. This is a book about reprogramming the mind. If we truly want to do this, the changes we make will have to find a way to live in our bodies. The body, as the receptacle of the subconscious mind, is perpetually feeling, thinking, and creating reality. To make any lasting changes in our lives, the system update cannot be only in the level of conscious thought. We will have to learn how to live and be in the body in a radically new way. Without the disciplined methodology of some behavior change anchored in the body, we will feel overwhelmed with the old patterns of the past. The familiar stories of jealousy, victimhood, vengeance, blame, shame, saviorism, and anxiety are too deeply entrenched. Retraining the mind is not like flipping a switch. It requires dedication and determination. We will need real and effective tools that focus our intention back toward awakening. We will need reminders to come back, over and over again. What's more, we will all fail, fall, and stumble along the way.

Silence, contemplation, meditation, yoga, prayer, and all activities that focus intention toward awakening walk this inner path. These practices are ways to embody acting from love, but it needs to be a deliberate practice. It's not enough to just repeat the same things over and over again. Instead, we need to be intentional in how we apply the teaching contained with our daily devotional exercises. Throughout this book, I share the tools and techniques that have helped me and many of my students ground the often-esoteric work of spiritual development. It is up to each of us to choose which path helps us answer the call of the soul that yearns to go home.

Divine Humanity

Seeking, the spiritual quest, is built into human DNA. It is the thing that defines humanity's promise. From ancient times to our present day, the human being has been essentially a seeker. Buddhist teachings state that the human incarnation comes with the perfect mix of suffering and joy to stimulate the desire for awakening. Friedrich Nietzsche likens human beings to a rope stretched between the two externalities of nature and God. In this way, the human being is a promise of awakening, a middle path that leads from duality into wholeness. The question that underpins every human's existence is how to contain these seemingly contradictory halves—the human/the natural and the individual being/the divine. The world at large mirrors this inner dualism in polarizing political extremes, the pass-or-fail litmus test of cancel culture, and all-or-nothing thinking. We may feel this pull within ourselves as an apparent duality. To believe in the separation aspect of dualism is easy and tempting, but it would be a false promise. Instead, we expand our minds so we can start to see our incarnation not as bondage or punishment but as a path of liberation.

The promise fulfilled in being human is to bring divinity onto this earth. We each are the promise. We each are the miracle. But we remain unfulfilled as long as we separate ourselves from the truth about who we are and believe the lie of separation. The more time that we spend focusing on what divides and defines us in this particular incarnation, the less time we spend in the realm of the eternal. There is a new code language built on an entirely new logic. If the concept of oneness appears delusional, triggering, or false, it is most likely because we are using the old database to query the new paradigm. This teaching is here, not only to help us understand who we are but also to help us realize who we are not. In that recognition, we can then transcend the plague of duality and realize true wholeness.

Some people believe that there is a seed of divinity within DNA and that by changing our thinking, we can activate this true and higher human potential. Neuroscientists Elizabeth Blackburn and Elissa Epel write in *The Telomere Effect* that it is possible to up regulate and down regulate strands of DNA and RNA with emotions, thoughts, and behaviors. When we change the way we think and feel, we literally have the power to change our genetic code. This concept is called *epigenetics.* The emergent science of epigenetics documents the relationship between the body and mind and helps verify the impact that we have on rewriting the logic of deeply programmed subconscious thoughts.

Only by liberating the mind from limiting beliefs, such as persistent feelings of low self-worth, will the inhibiting factors that prevent us from fully awakening be removed. Repetitive thoughts that run on the implicit framework of the body and brain need a massive update to unleash the power of consciousness contained within us. Change must be rewritten on a systemic level into the structure of our biology. We are here to awaken, and the first step on the journey is unlearning all the ways in which we are still asleep.

The Path We Seek

We are not subject to external forces beyond your control. We have the potential to be the creators of our world. There is both freedom and responsibility that comes with that. We can be free, or we can create our own chains, but *we* ultimately hold the power to liberate ourselves. It's our choice, moment to moment, what to worship or where to place attention. Remember that conscious choice is often obscured by subconscious programming so that many of us feel trapped, frustrated, and confused.

This is where the seeker's work comes in—the body and the breath are avenues that lead toward the subconscious mind. When we feel sensations, our thoughts are made manifest. When emotions disturb the breath, we stand on the bridge between the conscious and subconscious minds. It's only when our choice originates from and adheres to the subconscious mind that we start to break free of the past and tap into the creative power vested within.

Remember that every living being is, in some ways, a seeker. Whether we realize it or not, the seed of awakening is within us all, waiting for the right conditions to germinate. Once the process of awakening begins, life changes, perhaps dramatically. We are not alone on this journey. We are taking it together. There will be a time when we will look back on every moment of our lives and see how each instance fits together, like pieces of a puzzle. The soul is on a quest for the truth about life, for inner peace, and to answer life's deepest questions directly. The quest of soul-awakening is not easy. Based on the past, we are invested in our ignorance by the sheer fact of how long we have been living in a delusion of separation. The task of liberation is arduous, and the battles are fought on the most sensitive territory. Yet there is a calling in each and every human being's heart that beckons them to the spiritual path. It could even be said that all are called, but few choose to heed the call. Even those few who answer the call end up inadvertently perpetuating the very system they seek to challenge. Many more end up at a spiritual dead end, more disillusioned and deluded than when they started. A few rare souls have truly awakened, and they are a clarion call for us all.

I am on the path too. We are friends. I am not on the other side, looking in. I realize that not many people think they need to bother with this spiritual awakening stuff. In fact, you may think that this book is not for you, but before you close the book, let me pose a question: were negative thoughts, like worry, stress, and anxiety, present this morning more than blessings? I would imagine that within the first few moments of the day, the old patterns of complaint, annoyance, or general malaise took over. If so, this teaching will be immensely helpful.

The past is just that—familiar. The future will look just like the past unless we break the cycle of all that we have known. Rehashing the past brings about the predictable future and deprives us of the miraculous present, the only power point from which all things are possible. There is a way that we can step out of the familiar past into the pure joy of the present. It doesn't come from mere desire. It requires effort and a willingness to step into the unknown. Why the unknown? Well, because all that we have known has led us to this very point, and if we want to change, we will have to try something new. Once the catalyst for this process has begun, it cannot be stopped. There will be a day, perhaps in the not-so-distant future, when the system upgrade will be complete. That which is unknown now will be familiar. If the new program is effective, there will be more peace, happiness, and love all around.

In the time between then and now, the work will center around being receptive to the unknown, spontaneous to the present, and willing to let go of the past. The promise that I make today is a promise I made myself— that is, that there is a way to live a life of real peace, happiness, and love. This is not a hollow promise; I am not selling snake oil. I am walking down a path that I and many others have walked. I know we can find our way out of suffering to lasting happiness because I did. We don't need to know how all the pieces of the puzzle will fit before we start the journey. All we need is enough faith to take one step at a time.

It may be surprising to realize that happiness and love are available at every moment, even in our traumatic and painful moments. Happiness and love are always within us. In fact, happiness and love are our natural states. If we can break free from the repetitive cycles of the past and walk in the realm of the present, we can find true freedom and love. It may be difficult to understand that love truly is limitless, but it is. Even more, love is more than something we do; love is who we are at a vibrational level. Truth is liberating, and the deeper the truth, the more profound the liberation. Once we experience our true natures as energetic beings, as spirits, that transcendent state heals the wounds of the past and sets us on our highest path.

Choosing Our Thoughts

We think we are free, yet everywhere, we are in chains—chains that bind us to the past and call into being a future we fear. Thoughts anchored in pain suck us into an inner tornado, and we get thrown for a loop in its supercell spin. Emotions of suffering drain us of vital life energy and program us to repeat the very mistakes that we swear we will grow from. No one can set us free but ourselves. External circumstances, no matter how dire or how privileged, do not define us. We are not this body, not this name, not the things we own, not our accomplishments or accolades, not our history. Each of us is a pulsating, vibrating being of light, and we have the power to create worlds. A part of us knows this already. Acknowledging our vantage point of power is crucial to our success on the spiritual path. If we do not accept that we have created the world we live in, then we will not believe that we have the power to change it.

We have a collective consciousness that has created our collective world; we have a personal reality for which we are directly responsible. When we resist the collective story, we will not often be met with acceptance. When we seek to change our personal narrative, we will meet the great power of the ego. Neither are stronger than we are, but it often seems that way. Nothing is insurmountable; no odds stacked against us are greater than the power vested within.

The illusion of the permanence of the material world is easy to believe. It all feels so solid, but, in fact, it's nothing but emptiness. At the apparent level, the world of matter is manifest, yet physics tells us that at the center of every molecule is mostly space. The world is 99 percent emptiness and 1 percent subatomic particles, arising and passing away. We live in a world of illusion and our suffering stems from our belief in the permanence of our dreams.

Perhaps we can accept that the world of matter is impermanent. If we are not convinced by particle physics, perhaps we can be convinced by the inevitable process of aging and decay. All things that are born eventually must die. The cycle of life is built on the fact of death. The physical cannot last forever. With just a small stretch of the mind, this basic truth is easy to accept. But what about our thoughts?

Understanding the brain from this perspective means that our actions and choices are hardwired directly into the brain. Subconscious thoughts are harder to work with. Often programmed at a young age, prior to the activation of the prefrontal cortex, or taken on through cultural osmosis, these are the sneaky thoughts that can often create so much suffering. Stories told by the subconscious mind are often held in emotions and imagery, preformed and latent, yet powerful in their ability to create repetitive cycles of suffering. Thoughts that are programmed in the subconscious mind think themselves without any conscious activation or awareness. They carry on, fueled with the raw power of emotions, proliferate, and attract similar experiences. Eventually, these manifest as "truths."

But no thought is eternally real. Just try to follow any train of thought for one full day. Write thoughts down. Revisit those same thoughts in a year. Thoughts that we once held will often shift and change, while others may harden into beliefs or dogmas.

There is much work to be done in the realm of bringing subconscious patterning to light, both in the personal and social. It can sometimes be difficult work, whether we have to face the stories we hold in our hearts about grief, casualty, shame, blame, anxiety, or self-worth—or, even harder, if we are charged with outing a largely held subconscious cultural belief that is systemic. Remember that no thought is true. What we think is who we are. Yet thoughts can deeply influence the world. One of the most impactful lessons of the spiritual path is this—we each have the power to choose what type of thoughts we think. If we hold fast to a belief system that perpetuates injustice, we become part of the instrument of oppression. If our subconscious minds tell a story about failure, chances are, despite our best efforts, we will fail.

No thought is always absolutely true, and every thought can appear to be true. Choosing our thoughts wisely is the work of awakening. Buddhist teacher Jack Kornfield says,

> Unhealthy thoughts can chain us to the past. They arise as vipaka, the result of past karma that we cannot change. We can, however, change our destructive thoughts in the present. Through mindfulness training we can recognize them as bad habits learned long ago. Then we can take the critical next step. We can discover how these obsessive thoughts cover up grief, insecurity, and loneliness. This underlying suffering needs to be held with compassion. As we gradually learn to tolerate these underlying energies, we can reduce their pull. (Kornfield 2009, 304)

It is up to each of us to make a credible assessment as to whether our thoughts are valid and worth keeping.

Let me share a story from my experience as a teacher to make this discussion more relatable. Richard was a long-term yoga practitioner who suffered from many bouts of depression, sometimes facing suicidal ideation. After years of consistent practice, he thought that he finally had defeated the old destructive pattern. But one day, in the midst of a relatively happy period in his life, a casual comment from his sister threw him into a negative tailspin. All the years of training could not stop him from experiencing an anxiety attack, but all that training did seriously change his response. Instead of lashing out at his sister in their old pattern of blame and shame, he left his sister and withdrew to process. Unable to see his thoughts as words, he simply felt the physical constriction and shortness of breath. The world seemed to close in on him, and he struggled to speak. While he tried to meditate, it was overwhelming. He would sit and feel harassed by dark thoughts that he could not name.

Then Richard came to my yoga class. Normally a home practitioner with good discipline, he sought guidance amid a particularly challenging time. During the movements of the yoga practice, the previously preverbal thoughts started to take a form that he could name. As he moved his body, he could feel his thoughts as though they had taken up residence on various body parts, as squatters and unwelcome settlers. I encouraged him to give these thoughts simple names—fear, shame, judgment, resistance, rage, loneliness.

While Richard didn't immediately feel peace, he left the session feeling more empowered to do the inner work of meeting his repetitive negative thoughts with a more skillful response. Instead of feeling caught by an emotional storm and not knowing what he was up against, he finally could see through the raging wind to a larger view of the storm as a whole. As a spiritual practitioner, Richard already knew he wasn't his thoughts, but the reactivation of his old trigger allowed him to see more deeply into his inner terrain. It also kept him humble. He thought he had conquered his demon, but he hadn't. Perhaps we never really conquer our demons.

When thoughts are preverbal, hidden in the shadowy realm of the subconscious prior to yoga practice, they have an inertia that is nearly impossible to resist. As Jack Kornfield says, "Painful thoughts can appear so quickly that I don't see them: they are the atmosphere through which we move" (Kornfield 2009, 298).

No matter how long we have been practicing, the old triggers can still remain dormant, waiting for the perfect conditions to become active again. It is a lifelong work of vigilance. Sometimes, despite our best efforts, we get trapped by the web of our own thoughts and find ourselves locked behind bars of fear.

It can come out of nowhere and be about nothing. But when the destructive pattern gets just enough stimulation to begin again, it can build momentum quite quickly. The thoughts run themselves down a familiar path that seems to lie in anticipation of the next hit. It is well-documented in neuroscience that the more we think a thought, the more we will think that thought. Repetitive thoughts create pathways in the brain that make it easier for the mind to travel down that road. And what's more, the more we think a thought, the more those neurons actually get programmed to want to fire again. The cells become interested in searching for the next hit, much like a drug.

Weathering the Storm

Sometimes thoughts grow so big that it feels like a storm. The best thing we can do, while caught in the middle of a thought storm, is to stand still and wait for it to pass. Choosing to watch instead of engage is an important pause between stimulus and response. Once we become aware of the implosion of thought, we can detach from the thought stream and choose a different response. Observing nonverbal cues is a great way to both break the cycle and become aware that we might be getting caught. Signs such as tightness in the chest, shortness of breath, accelerated heartbeat, slight trembling in the limbs of the body, time slipping away at a rapid pace, claustrophobia, or a feeling of no-way-out can lead to freedom or bondage—we get to choose.

Maybe the whole spiritual path is an elaborate system of cleaning house, except instead of doing the dishes and taking the rubbish out, our thoughts get scrubbed and cleaned and selected, until all that is left sparkles with the clear glow of true and lasting peace. If the mind is like a computer, it might be easy to think about a malware invasion having taken over the foundational elements of the device. Instead of ignoring the virus, discipline and determination are needed. The malignant habits of the mind can be hard to root out. It's not enough to casually affirm, "I am worthy of love," and close the door on self-help work. Instead, destructive thoughts require a strong hand in order to attain mastery over them. Think about it in terms of degrees. If a thought has a slight tinge of destruction, it will not require so much effort to cure the malady. But if a thought has deep patterns of hatred, violence, greed, and aggression, then it will require a powerful effort, mobilizing a multifaceted approach to root out the infection.

To combat negative thoughts, at least an equal amount of positive or skillful nature must be anchored in a very real and skillful way in the body and mind and in life. To succeed in balancing opposing forces, a new anchoring thought must at least be equal and opposite to the power and force of the negative, unskillful, or destructive thought. Working on the conscious level is difficult, tedious, and time-consuming. Updating the operating system of the mind is so powerful because it works on a foundational level and is more efficient and effective. The current framework of the mind is based on a systemic flaw rooted in the subconscious mind. Before substantive change can happen, we will need to perform a kind of utility analysis of the programming that runs at the under-layer of the mind.

One useful technique that can help reveal hidden programming is to consider the consequences of every thought. Reflect on how thinking that thought influences actions, relationships, and other interactions. Spiritual teacher Byron Katie encourages seekers to do what she calls "the Work." She asks people to question their thoughts in a series of directed introspection. She asks spiritual seekers to figure out how they feel and act when they think a particular thought. She then asks them to find an opposite thought that is equally true, in what she calls turning the thought around. It can be a useful practice to truly visualize and feel the impact that thinking destructive thoughts has on us. When we start off in a neutral space and then see how repetitive patterns of judgment, annoyance, self-criticism, hatred, anxiety, and depression actually feel in the body, it can be great motivation to change.

What becomes evident is that thoughts that feed patterns of negativity, rooted in fear or anger, do not lead to genuine, constructive growth. These patterns feed more of the same types of feelings. A common example to describe thoughts that is traditionally given in yoga is fruit. When choosing which fruit to eat, one naturally makes a selection of the sweetest and most pleasing fruit. If a food is not ripe, or worse, rotten, it is completely logical to throw that fruit out. Similarly, we are encouraged to work with our thoughts and choose only the sweetest, healthiest, and most pleasing thoughts. Just as there is no obligation to eat every fruit that falls off the tree, there's no obligation to believe or continue to think any thought, especially the ones arising from within our own minds.

Shifting to Solutions

The only detox we need happens in the mind. Thoughts are both solid and ephemeral, sometimes appearing as stubbornly enduring; at other times, dissolving like sandcastles in the waves. No matter how permanent a mental structure may appear, the truth is that the fundamental nature of all that passes through the mind field is emptiness. All it takes to change our thinking is a momentary shift in awareness. And that's a good thing. We can literally alter the trajectory of our lives, merely by learning how to think new thoughts. Emptiness is not a concept to fear. Instead, emptiness itself is full, rich, and resplendent, the silent promise of a blank canvas, like a becoming.

Problems and drama often present as solidified, immovable realities. Like noisy guests who arrive all on their own, uninvited, and move in, the difficulties of life can feel overwhelming. Repeated exposure to hardship hardens the mind and installs a pattern of deeply ingrained beliefs, based in the paradigm of the past. Changing our lives starts from within, and it is up to us to slowly shift our attention to the frequency of solutions. We can start by bringing what is working into greater focus. In moments of doubt, we can learn how to trust that an answer is on the way. When we find ourselves triggered, annoyed, or in a state of complaint, all the inertia of our emotionality seems to demand action. If we act in that moment, we will not act in love. When the momentum implores a reaction, we have to learn how to resist.

When you think you absolutely "need" to take action, press pause and give the urgency some space. When a compelling emotion arises that feels addictive, be patient and take a step back. Do not act when the inner circuitry runs hot. Any action taken from a state of reactivity increases the likelihood of even more reactivity.

The nitty-gritty reality of reprogramming is hard work. This effortful act could be called "the work" of awakening. Don't expect it to be easy. Whenever I start to do the work of changing an old pattern, the first place I feel it is in my body. Sometimes, just choosing a new course of action brings accompanying feelings of heat, shaking, disturbed breathing, and other physical manifestations of my process. Sitting with this discomfort is hard; the status quo is not designed to help us succeed. Sometimes, I am overwhelmed by the sheer inertia of the past that seems to pull me and even the most dedicated spiritual practitioners into cycles of suffering, over and over again. It can feel like we are all in a trancelike state, more than being truly alive human beings.

How can someone who lives in a trance wake up? We are advised to follow our bliss and trust what arises. But when the daily experience of life is like the walking dead, it is nearly impossible to discern the way forward. When every thought centers around a fundamentally flawed conceptual basis, then even what is known cannot be trusted. Challenging our own assumptions is the only way to shed light on the path. It is not easy to tell the difference between an act of love and an act of fear, anger, delusion, or hatred. The key in navigating through this complexity is to find our own place of truth. It would be impossible to walk through life without triggering anyone. It is enough of a goal to aim to find our own centers. Buddhist teacher Tara Brach teaches that people largely exist in what she calls a "trance of unworthiness," rather than living truly in the present moment. What this means is that most of us operate from our own flawed paradigms, rooted in rehashing the past or projecting in the future. Outside of the state of true presence, all our anxieties, triggers, and other negative emotional states take precedence above all else. Focusing too intently on other people's emotions, in an effort to please and appease them, is a form of tuning out. There are many ways to participate in the trance state, but a big one involves showing up in relationships in ways that perpetuate past suffering and hurt, while labeling the other as the enemy and, thereby, oneself as the victim.

To break the trance requires steady effort. Brach suggests that mindfulness alone is not enough. Instead, she teaches that only mindfulness tempered with compassion leads to a state of radical acceptance. This state feels like waking up from a bad dream but a dream whose reality and substance have been the foundation of our lives. It can feel tenuous and unsteady to wake up from the trance. We may not know who we are or what to do. It may feel like we are born again in some strange new life. In fact, we are. When we wake up from the trance of unworthiness, we are baptized to a new life in love. Just as a newborn child needs to learn language, body mechanics, and the ways of the world, so too will we need to learn how to operate in the new world of love and worthiness.

Some people mistake wakefulness with permission to do whatever they want. This is actually a delusion that feeds the original trance. While it is necessary to pause and listen, we are not responsible for other people's emotional outbursts or for processing their emotions. It is enough to do our own work. While the training of mindfulness encourages us to feel everything, the good and the bad, it would be a grievous misunderstanding to think that simply because we are mindful of negative thoughts that we now have permission to act them out. The process of awakening is not a devolution into chaos. Instead, it is an evolution to a new order of thought.

Love Is Who We Are

The choice to act in love begins with the discovery of an immutable center of deep connection to all things. Love is not only an act of self-validation. Without the lived experience of a seat for love within, all talk of self-love is merely talk. The old patterns will be stronger than any affirmations. The beginning of breaking the cycle feels like waking up from a nightmare or a confusing dream. The dream seems to repeat itself in different forms. Characters change but the basic plot remains unchanged. For moments, the promise seems new and different, but in reality, it never really changes—that is, until you change. The present moment is the vantage point from which change happens. It works best when we are grounded within the present. When we act in love, that action is rooted in a deep sense of worthiness and goodness beyond the physical form. In some ways, acting in love may be seen as an act of rebellion, an awakening whose ripples can be felt far and wide.

What we think matters, not just to the goals we set in life but to the world at large. The type of thoughts that make the biggest impact are unconscious, subliminal beliefs that have been programmed into the deepest layers of the mind. These beliefs often take root as preverbal biases that color our view on life. The only way we will ever change these deeply held assumptions is by bringing them out into the daylight of reality. The reason why these unconscious thoughts are so powerful and important to look at, deconstruct, and bring into consciousness is because they lay the foundation for the operational system of the mind. If left unattended, they will run on autopilot and gather momentum and "proof" for their validity. Soon, these thoughts will appear as evident truths, when, in fact, they are often systemic beliefs passed down from generation to generation, bearing the scars and wounds of the past. We think we are free, but, in reality, our thoughts are like chains. We think we determine our future, but repetitive cycles of thought trap us in a web of hurt. We think we see the "truth," but we see through thick, broken glasses that only show us a small piece of the puzzle. There is a way out of this muddled mess of the mind. It's the foundation of every spiritual tradition aimed at liberation. We have to do the work. It begins with us and then expands outward to include the entire world. Start deconstructing every thought—body, culture, education, work, beauty, family, history—and do not stop until every thought has been questioned.

There is no pass, no shortcut, no easy way around. It's hard work to untie the fabric of the mind and soul. Freedom—true ultimate spiritual liberation—is not something that happens with a snap of the fingers. A spiritual seeker has to be desperate to find the way out of the maze of misery. Spiritual questing is not a casual hobby; it is a lifelong commitment. If we want to tap into the freedom that is available to us in every moment, we will be required to make great strides against the grain of past thought. If we are to live from a place of universal, unconditional love, we must find that place within ourselves.

When we choose not to react, when we choose equanimity, when we choose love and forgiveness, we choose to step into the stream of well-being. We do this for ourselves, first and foremost. What works well for me is to keep a willingness to remain open-hearted in the real world, to get offline and out of chat groups, and to treat all beings in the same way that I would like to be treated—with respect, understanding, forgiveness, and love. Remaining neutral amid the pull of old patterns acts as a circuit breaker for the patterns of the subconscious mind. By remaining objective and refraining from acting, we stop cooperating with the past. If we start fighting against the past, the nature of the fight locks us into a vibrational holding pattern with whatever we seek to be free of. Instead, choosing not to act and just observing allows spaciousness to permeate tightness and opens the door to new possibilities. Neutrality gives space for responsive action, rather than reactive patterning.

We only really love someone else to the degree that we know and love ourselves. If we need to prove our worthiness and be perfect before we see ourselves as lovable, then we will demand that same standard from others—and from the world—before we love them. If we foster feelings of self-hate and unworthiness, then we will be more likely to treat other people as disposable and throw them out at the first hint of a mistake or a misstep. But we are not perfect. We stumble and we fall. We are not here to demonstrate perfection but to learn to love, despite our imperfections. The entire world is a confluence of opposing forces—agony and ecstasy, pain and pleasure, happiness and sorrow. If we want to be whole, we have to be willing to let it all in.

In order to build something new, we might have to tear down what we have. Or, at the very least, we have to stop conspiring with our old habit patterns. If we do nothing, it will at least stop the inertia that pulls us forward into a new cycle. It isn't easy to do nothing. It is even harder to craft a new foundation for action. To follow a new vision requires an unrelenting commitment to a course as yet uncharted. Big voices might try to stamp down the new sprouts. Friends and allies might sit by silently. There may be times on the journey when we feel lost, alone, and purposeless, as if we have failed. The night may feel long and dark, as though the promise of dawn is a lie.

But off in the distance, new voices from a new timeline will appear. A new story will unfold. The groundwork for a new set will be laid out. Seeds of new characters with fresh stories will take shape. There will come a time along our journey when we realize something important—it had to be this way. We couldn't bring the chains of the past into the freedom of the future. The ones who resist are caught in their own worlds, repeating their own cycles. To be a seeker is to commit to being fresh and new. And, like a snake that has shed its skin, seekers leave the outfits of the past with the past and carry only the new self forward. The process of spiritual rebirth is not without mourning or loss, but here it is.

Every living being is valuable beyond measure. If we accept the fundamental value of our own beings, we will instantly see that every being is valuable too—every human being, every animal, every creature, and every critter. All life is valuable. It can be overwhelming to tune in to the vastness of living beings in the world, but whether we think about it or not, we are connected to every single living being. And every single one matters.

In love, with love, all things are possible.

Meditation and Reflection Point

Enter the Operating System

Close your eyes. Bring your attention to your breath to establish a base level of mindfulness. Whenever thoughts arise, gently redirect your attention back to the breath. Keep practicing for at least five minutes until your mind drops down under the noise of thinking. Then, invite your conscious mind to unite with your body. Start with the physical body, and look for sensation on any body part that immediately comes into your field of awareness—perhaps your fingers and toes; perhaps your face. Be with your breath and body in a space of neutrality and nonjudgment. When mind and body unite in a space of awareness, you enter the operating system of the mind. Sustain and deepen this connection by exploring more sensations throughout the body, including awareness of the muscles, joints, and organs. Over time, with consistent practice, you will be able to feel the energy of the body, the kinetic potential contained at the subatomic level.

Mind Dump

Journal in a free flow for ten minutes. Hold nothing back. Allow yourself to roll down every alley of thoughts, unrestricted. If you feel blocked, use the prompts, "Today, I feel …" Read over your thoughts and question each one. What trends do you notice? What thoughts do you take to be true that are actually value judgments? What are your learned behaviors?

Chapter 4

From Suffering to Joy

> Most people have no clue why they are suffering—because they experience life in terms of 'me' versus 'the universe'. This means they are in constant conflict with creation, forgetting that they are just a small product of creation itself.
>
> —Sadhguru

Misery, like suffering, is both personal and universal. No human being I have ever met is truly happy all the time. People have both intensely individual reasons for pain and broader cultural sources of hurts, which are shouldered together. Two people with exactly the same experience can walk away with two radically different experiences, and both could be equally valid. One person might not be bothered by a course of action, while another might find that same course of action a source of suffering. The everyday aches and pains of living are sometimes unbearable and sometimes glorious. What is the deciding factor? Let's explore that together—it might just be love.

Spiritual seekers are defined by the spiritual nature of their inner quest. Suffering of one type or another plays a role in the initiation to the path. The spiritual aspirant answers the question of misery with a yearning to find the way out. That is perhaps the single most distinguishing feature of the teachings that promise liberation. It is, after all, liberation from suffering. And only those who are suffering, who are aware of their suffering and want to find the way out of their suffering, will be committed to the sometimes long and arduous road of awakening. Spiritual seekers have a soul ache that cannot be fixed with escapism, denial, numbing, or other qualities of a trancelike state of forgetfulness. Instead, the pain and anguish are real and sometimes overwhelming, leading a person to the edge of his or her being, in what could be considered a breaking point. Some people have been on a spiritual quest for their entire lives. Others wake up the spiritual quest at some point in their lives. And others might only ask deeper spiritual questions at the end of their lives.

No matter when a person turns to the spiritual path, it is almost the universal nature of suffering, as experienced on this earthly plane, which precipitates the turn inward. Whether it is the despondency of Arjuna, the acceptance of the necessary suffering of tapas, the Buddha's recognition that suffering merely is, or the passion of Christ, suffering is the pivotal moment that shifts the story of spiritual rebirth in many spiritual traditions. The acceptance of suffering is a basic tenet of every major spiritual tradition in the world. The New Testament describes "long suffering" as one of the fruits of the Holy Spirit. The Buddha says, "Suffering is." Yoga philosophy talks at length about the causes of suffering and details many methods of liberation from it. Tapas is a Sanskrit word for yoga's core belief that the acceptance of suffering leads to spiritual purification. The Torah details the usefulness of various levels of suffering, including suffering as a call to make atonement and return to God, the suffering of a righteous person (zaddikim) to rectify the human race or bring about the perfection of humanity. The Quran says that God uses suffering to test all (Quran 29:1–3). If there is one thing that is evident from the multitude of religious discussions regarding suffering, it is that suffering is a ubiquitous and omnipresent experience of humanity. What is not clear is the power of our own agency. By our choice, suffering can lead to either love or fear, and it can be used either as a means of generating more suffering or as a means of liberation from the chains of suffering.

No Material Escape from Suffering

Whereas spiritual and religious traditions teach a way out of suffering that often begins with its acceptance, secular culture sometimes promises a pipe dream of a life without any suffering whatsoever. Advertising imagery sells a narrative of utopian ecstasy built on escape from suffering. Whether it's miracle cream, magic tummy tea, crystal-infused water, the latest drop of must-have leggings, designer doughnuts, luxury accommodation, adventure trips to the moon, or some other product, experience, or object, the hidden promise is an end to the existential angst of life. The falsity lies not in that these things relieve pain and give pleasure but in the fleeting nature of the type of happiness that things provide. The culture of capitalism relies on the perpetual turning of the tides of the ever-insatiable consumer to continue to buy more things. The contemporary mindset of consumerism sometimes feels like a hungry dragon that constantly needs another hit just to settle down. It is too romantically anachronistic to say that in a bygone era, people bought things they needed and that was that. But what is certain is that we live in an era when what we buy is impermanent, both in its ability to provide lasting happiness for us and in terms of the nature of the consumer culture.

Sales culture is built on the notion that people need to buy things, even things they don't need. To accept suffering might mean the end of the next sales cycle, fueling corporate profits and shareholder dividends. The goal posts in capitalism are always shifting. There is always the apparent push to buy something new, with the idea that maybe this purchase will finally end one's plight and provide relief. The problem is rarely presented as one originating within. Instead, the advertisements seem to subliminally (or sometimes directly) suggest that the good life is available, if only the right purchase is made. The issue arises when human beings wake up to the ephemeral nature of the happiness provided by material objects. Everything is for sale, yet nothing really satisfies.

Materialism provides a momentary hit of pleasure that subdues suffering for a brief blip in the vast span of time. The fleeting nature of this pleasure ends up only fueling more craving and clinging because getting even a moment of relief feels good but leaves a void that yearns to be filled once more. It is a fruitless endeavor to pursue permanent happiness in material objects.

Some spiritual seekers eschew materialism for exactly this reason and take the extreme end of asceticism. I tried that when I first started practicing yoga. I shaved my head, gave away almost all of my possessions, wore organic clothes made by a tailor I personally knew in India, and ate food sourced directly from farms I could verify. After a while, I realized that this too was a kind of spiritual accoutrement, an outer form that I took on. The pendulum swung far in the opposite direction, yet I was still locked in a battle with material culture. My rejection was yet another form that I took on and not authentically me. After many years, I've settled somewhere in the middle on a path that I like to call conscious consumerism. It works for me, but it might not work for everyone. I encourage every person to find his or her own way to reconcile the spiritual calling with the material necessities of this world.

Tibetan nun Pema Chodron wrote a book titled *The Wisdom of No Escape*. I remember reading this book when I was searching for a way out of my own suffering. Her teaching resonates with the basic tenets of most spiritual teachings on liberation; that is, that there is no way out of suffering, but there is a way to make peace with whatever inevitable suffering happens to appear in life. Learning how to maintain the firm ground of a calm mind and an open heart amid the storms of life is the path that spiritual seekers walk. Traditionally, one crucial qualification of embarking on a sincere spiritual quest is intimacy with the suffering that follows all material interactions. Without this firsthand knowledge that the impermanent experiences of the world are not the foundation upon which to build a firm ground of peace and harmony, it is usually said that, at some moment, the spiritual seeker will find the hard work of liberating the mind too challenging and will quit. But that individual who knows there can be no permanent happiness in the material pursuit of pleasure and the avoidance of pain will accept the hardships faced on the path of awakening because, as Pema Chodron says, they understand that there is no escape.

To live life under the impression that no suffering should ever exist denies a basic truth; that is, that suffering is a part of life. It might sound depressing, but this realization is liberating. Living in a culture of pain aversion and pleasure addiction only fuels an endless cycle of yet more suffering. As long as happiness is dependent on a source outside of the self, such as material objects, exciting experiences, or anything other than the immutable spark of spirit within, then happiness is an endless rat race, where the finish line remains eternally just out of reach. Instead, find happiness in the here and now by rejecting the premise of the race and updating the operating system to a new framework.

The Greediness of Comparison

Not everyone will be the best at something. Not everyone will be the top sales performer in their company. We will not all be Olympians, let alone gold medalist Olympians. We are not all born equal. The teaching here is not about how to be the best but how to live in love. Love is not a competition or a zero-sum game. There is no "best" at love. There are no exclusions to the act of love. There is simply love. Whether someone is a billionaire or a barista, a starving artist or a wealthy benefactor, a CEO or a janitor, the path of love is about how to live in harmony and find happiness amid the reality of life, including both pleasure and pain, success and failure.

Social comparison limits the experience of love's limitless potential and fosters jealousy, competition, and a scarcity mindset. When the first thing that happens in a new human interaction is scanning to take stock across a variety of known benchmarks, then, consciously or subconsciously, an oppositional stance often takes root. While it's natural to make assessments, it's not always conducive to opening the heart and seeing without judgments. Chanting a competitive mindset requires vigilance and attentiveness while engaging in patterned behaviors, mostly off the yoga mat and meditation cushion, in "real" life.

A student of mine named Gina is a dedicated yoga practitioner. A big portion of her identity revolves around her commitment to the spiritual path and the accompanying lifestyle of love, inclusivity, and kindness. Yet each time she sees friends from childhood, particularly from the private school she attended, she falls into the same old tropes. She judges her former classmates by the stereotypical measures of size, shape, beauty, and wealth. It's hard for her to see the person standing in front of her because, despite her years of yoga practice, she reverts back to the childhood programming of one-upmanship. This paradigm prevents her from actually connecting with her old school friends, fosters a feeling of loneliness, and instills an unhealthy drive to achieve even more and "beat" her competitors at the game of life.

Life, unlike the *Game of Thrones* saga, is not a battle for a single iron throne, where it's win or die. Life is a beautiful tapestry of belonging that has space for everyone. But it's up to each of us to weave the pattern of inclusivity into our hearts. The unspoken truth about sizing up others is that it stems from a character feature that is difficult to admit to fostering—greed. To admit that greed lives in one's own heart goes against so many of the qualities of good personhood that are taught in religious and moral codes, and greed is not a quality that many of us would be proud of having. But greed is one of the fundamental driving qualities of market capitalism. Greed, perhaps more than any other character feature, is uniquely colonial and has its impact on the whole world. Unchecked avariciousness is perhaps the most destructive, antithetical, and corrosive quality of the status quo. But before we can uproot greed, we must first be willing to admit that we ourselves are greedy and jealous. We may hoard success, achievement, physical prowess, academic performance, financial wealth, real estate, cars, or things, or we may be greedy for approval, attention, friendship, or other soft values. But we are greedy and jealous nevertheless. Only by admitting and directly working with the shadow side of consciousness will there be any real chance of freedom.

Greed stems from craving and clinging, founded around the construction of the false self, sometimes known as the ego; that is, the source of I and mine. Achievement, as a paradigm, fuels ego-center city by telling a story that worthiness is earned and validated by performance. Tying self-worth to productivity, instead of to the inherent qualities of beingness, nurtures an insane push to constantly strive for better and more, simply to prove one's value. Greed is a natural tendency in a system rigged toward privilege and power and built on the foundation of ego and desire. Rapacity (extreme greed) may be one of the core tenets of contemporary capitalism. It is easy to point the finger at big, bad corporations and billionaires, whose wealth and power make them easy targets. It is harder to point the finger at oneself and explore how the paradigm of appropriation lives within one's own worldview. Unless we deal properly with our own tendencies toward avarice, all actions based on this core value will be relegated to the shadow side and covered up with false statements of equivalence.

The concept of greed thrives on the idea that success is a scarce commodity in a competitive zero-sum game, where one person's gain is another person's loss. In such a ferocious environment, it is only natural for human beings to assume guarded stances toward one another and remain distant. Accomplishment and attainment in this model rarely lead to lasting feelings of safety and security in the scarcity paradigm. Instead, one's own good fortune is a source of fear because a challenger to one's status could appear at any moment. The very thought of losing the attained success generates a whole cascade of anxious emotions, ranging from irritation to envy, desperation, and other attitudes of craving that destroy the foundation of compassion and whole being. There is no firm ground to stand on with this type of thinking. Instead, there is only a spastic winner-take-all gold rush toward endless accumulation, with little regard for the harm done to others along the way. Greed is a maladaptive program that seeps into the architecture of the mind and builds illusory walls of division.

The race of acquisition is destructive to all. Wealth disparity is at historic proportions, both in the United States and around the world. When 1 percent of the population owns more than half of the world's wealth, this is bad for us all. If the top 10 percent is calculated, then the top 10 percent owns nearly 90 percent of the world's wealth. No matter where someone is on the spectrum, taking a moment to contemplate the current predicament can bring up all sorts of emotions, from gratitude to rage, depending on where one sits on the spectrum. Yet no one is inherently a villain, victim, or hero, merely as a result of one's place in a larger socioeconomic structure. Instead, awakening is a process undertaken by each individual. The job of spiritual practitioners is not to "save" anyone other than themselves. Instead, by understanding and owning our personal shadows and prejudices, we can better shine that light on the inequities seen around us and ultimately be of service. No social-justice warrior will succeed while operating as the hero of a group of "them." We will all succeed when we operate from an "us" paradigm, expressed in caring and kind human interactions on a daily basis and a heightened awareness of the shadow side of our most powerful and impactful myths of personal development. Rather than a single-leader method, what an us paradigm might feel like is a collaborative process among equals. But before any true sense of sharing can occur, the paradigm of greed has to be unseated from within.

Jealousy Is a Paradox

Greed is not only manifest in capital accumulation. The feeling that nothing is ever enough is a form of emotional avariciousness that can be hard to identify. Sometimes, we are not interested in having large sums in our bank accounts. Instead, we may be filled with an insatiable desire for the next big adventure, the next tattoo, the next romance. Whatever it is matters less than that it is a next new experience that is hopefully bigger than the last. Sometimes, we may even crave the success of others and be burdened with jealousy.

Greed hardens the heart and skews the soul's course. An act of greed may even appear to be an act of love on the surface, but that is a lie. Greed says that there is a finite amount of all available resources, and those resources must be protected at all costs for one's own benefit. Operating from the paradigm of greed installs what is called a scarcity mindset; that is, resources, success, happiness, and all the attributes of the good life are just that—scarce—and need to be fought for in order to be attained. Life, according to this framework, is seen as a zero-sum equation, where there are a finite number of prizes to go around, and once they have all been given out, there is nothing left for everyone else. Once the scarcity mindset is accepted as reality, then greed and jealousy follow as natural expressions of desire and longing.

Competition in a dog-eat-dog world gets so deeply embedded within the culture of scarcity that no one is immune to its corrosive qualities. Office workers, yogis, and many more just fall into the familiar habit of judgment and comparison, craving and clinging. Even those who are at the top often harbor secret jealousy toward others. Having an abundance of money does not automatically make people more generous. As long as the measurement for self-worth is always located outside of oneself, nothing will ever be enough. There will always be a comparison to someone else that triggers a dive back into the "game."

If there is only a limited pool of happiness, success, and love available to go around, someone else's success or happiness can be seen as someone else's failure or sadness. Covetousness stems from the false belief that emotional states are like possessions, and when one person has it, someone else cannot have it as well. This way of thinking couldn't be further from the truth. But to be free from this type of thinking requires an update to the mainframe system of the mind.

The first thing to understand is this: jealousy works in the opposite way we think it will. The opposite of an envious heart is a joyful heart, filled with love. The insidious nature of jealousy has the potential to infect every aspect of the mind and heart. Jealousy eats away at the balance of the mind and works in the opposite way than one thinks. While obsessing about what other people have, the mind automatically also focuses on what it does not have. Attention is energy, and when time is spent obsessing about what other people have and what the present lacks, the scarcity mindset takes over. Time and attention are truly valuable resources that are potentially under our conscious control. But when the energy of our being is spent on a frivolous pursuit of obsessively jealous thinking, it is like burning good fuel for no purpose. Imagine a car with a full battery charge, engines fired up, stuck in a massive traffic jam until the juice runs out. This is jealousy eating away energy from the inside out; throwing away the valuable resource of attention.

There is nothing wrong with wanting to succeed. Jealousy, however, is something else. Coveting someone else's success is a spiritual implosion. No longer a source of inspiration, jealousy depletes the jealous person. Coveting someone else's success won't bring that success any closer. Hate and envy work in opposite ways; instead of bringing the hated person down, harboring hate and envy brings hate and envy to one's own heart.

A jealous state of mind is, like so many other negative states, rooted in the fear of the scarcity mindset. If there is only a limited amount of success to go around, and someone else has it, then it may feel like that person stole it. Bitterness and resentment are easy emotions to let fester from within the zero-sum game of life. The game of jealousy is unwinnable. The only way out is to stop playing or change the game.

Envy Sows Division

Carlos is a dedicated student of mine who has a jealous streak. Whenever he would see someone else achieve what we had been working hard on faster than he did, jealousy and pride would eat away at him. One day after practice, Carlos approached me and unloaded a deluge of negative comparison comments about his fellow yoga students—they weren't as good as he was; they didn't work as hard as he worked; his practice was so much better. On and on he went, disparaging and devouring his yogi cohorts. Depressed and dejected, he wanted to quit. One student in particular irked him—a male colleague named David, who was just about at the same place in the practice as Carlos was.

In my role as the teacher, I must admit that I tended to give David a bit more attention, not because Carlos was a bad student but because David needed more help. To the contrary, Carlos was one of my most capable students, and I had hoped he would become a teacher one day. I shared with him the praise that he had earned and hoped it would allay his doubts. Seeing his competitive nature encouraged me to use the tool of *asana* to facilitate an inner transformation. Rather than giving him more attention and teaching him more, I gave him even less attention than before. While this might seem harsh and unloving, I wanted to see what would happen when Carlos was allowed to stew in his own thoughts without too much external validation.

After six months, he seemed to be in more mental and emotional anguish. I was about to intervene, when one day, after practice, I saw Carlos speaking with his rival in a friendly manner. The untold side of the story is that David idolized Carlos. The next day in class, I could see something shifted. Carlos came up to me after class with a look of bewilderment. He was embarrassed by his jealous thoughts and said he would have to do some inner work. What Carlos ultimately gained from this experience was truly liberating. He learned that while he worked so hard to achieve success, he lacked a strong sense of internal validation. Most of his sense of self-worth was tied to the praise of people in positions of power or authority. When he didn't receive the approval he sought, or worse, when someone else received the approval he thought was his, the demons of jealousy kicked in. Then, Carlos realized that he was operating from a scarcity mindset, and instead of seeing his fellow humans as friends, he saw them all as competitors on a battlefield, fighting for a limited number of resources. Carlos had much to learn during this period of his spiritual path. Years later, I'm happy to say that Carlos and David are friends and that Carlos is a highly sought-after yoga teacher in his own right.

It can be hard to celebrate the joy of others when feelings of low self-worth appear. It is even harder when there is very little internal validation for one's efforts. The spiraling thoughts of jealousy are an easy temptation, but the spiritual path is not an easy one; facing the demon of jealousy is a necessary step along the route to liberating the mind and heart. Suffering of one type or another is seen not as something to be avoided but as fertile ground upon which to practice. Love is not grounded until it has been tested by the strongest demons. Only then will love take up residence in the bones, in the very DNA of the body.

Enemies of the Heart

Still, spiritual seekers often begin their quest by asking from where and why does suffering arise? Why do we act so far out of love, moment to moment, if love is who we really are and our nature is real love?

Well, let's look to traditional yoga practice for part of the answer. Yoga philosophy says that there are six enemies of the heart. In Sanskrit, these are called the *Arishadvargas*. They are kama (lust), krodha (anger), lobha (greed), moha (attachment), mada (pride), and matsarya (jealousy). Every human being can identify with having felt some of these states; I know I certainly can. The more actions that stem from these enemies of the heart, the harder the heart becomes. It is possible to be so blocked off from the capacity to love that all actions end up rooted in these enemies of the heart. Similar but teleologically different to the seven deadly sins, the six enemies of the heart line the path to suffering and the repetition of suffering. The premise of yoga is that the human mind, if left unchecked and untrained, will devolve into these negative states. It is all too natural for the mind to chase positive experiences and avert from negative experiences. It is all too difficult to train the mind to be aligned with God's grace and a heart full of love. But it is possible for everyone who practices. In fact, the entire spiritual path is a promise to all students that if the path is walked with diligence, sooner or later the heart will open, and the six enemies will be vanquished. In the meantime, we just have to keep practicing.

Suffering is considered to stem from a root misunderstanding about reality. Jack Kornfield says,

> Suffering is different from pain. Suffering is our reaction
> to the inevitable pain of life. Our personal suffering can
> include anxiety, depression, fear, confusion, grief, anger,
> hurt, addiction, jealousy, and frustration. But suffering

is not only personal. Our collective suffering includes the sorrows of warfare and racism; the isolation and torture of prisoners everywhere; the unnecessary hunger, sickness, and abandonment of human beings on every continent. This individual and collective suffering is what we are called upon to understand and transform. (Kornfield 2021)

For each person to be free from suffering requires the necessary truth that each person recognizes, understands, and accepts his or her role in the creation and continuation of suffering. The degree to which people wake up to the truth about themselves and the world is the degree to which each person is liberated. The degree to which people are deluded about themselves and the world is the degree to which each person spreads more suffering. No amount of prayer and lip-service salvation can wipe away the truth of personal responsibility. Waiting around for a savior to appear and make a clean slate turns adults into children, waiting for their parents to show up and save the day. Operating from a paradigm that denies the reality of suffering is not only untrue, destructive, and pacifying but a fundamental misunderstanding of the truth about life here on earth.

Take a cross section of any human community; it will be evident that there are people suffering. Both human and nonhuman beings suffer. Understanding and making peace with both our personal suffering and the suffering of the world is a necessary step on the journey to act in love. Without the acceptance of suffering, love will seem two-dimensional and shallow. But when love is big enough to embrace suffering, then liberation is possible.

The spiritual wisdom of the East, including the teachings of yoga and that of the Buddha, says that you cannot end suffering by fighting against it. Instead, through pure observation, suffering inevitably changes. Instead of trying to make the world free from suffering, the teaching advises adepts to cultivate the state of equanimity so that their inner states of peace cannot be disturbed by it. Stop the war with suffering and instead just experience life for what it is in all its fullness. To act in love, moment to moment, is to dispel the root of suffering, but it requires great sacrifice of oneself, both in terms of what is given to the practice and in application to life.

After a ten-year break from silent meditation retreats and a difficult period of my life that contained much suffering, I signed up to sit for a three-day meditation. During this time, the course maintained the Buddhist principle of noble silence, called *noble* because the vow of silence is taken to facilitate the inward turning of the mind toward spiritual practice. At the start of the course, I was nervous about the intensity of the practice, and my mind was unsteady. It felt like I could no longer meditate, but I sat there and did the work. All the mistakes and pain of the past arose with crystal clarity and, like anything else, also passed. But there was one experience that I simply could not understand. I would begin the sitting period with good intentions, and then, somehow, I found myself slouching down. I did not recollect choosing to slouch, but there I was, hunched over, feeling I was more in a position to binge-watch Netflix than to meditate. I straightened up as soon as I noticed, but it kept happening, over and over again. Feeling rather desperate to understand what was going on, I made a commitment to search for the sensory experience in my body in the exact moment before I slouched. I had to cultivate a hyper-vigilant state of awareness. And then, I saw the pattern that I had been reacting to unconsciously; big surprise—it was pain.

In the moments before my body went into a slouch, there was the hint of a burning sensation around my right hip and lower back. My body seemed to react without my conscious mind being aware of it, and my body was pulled toward this slouch. Up until that moment, I was unaware that I was even in pain; I had just "found" myself slouching. But this realization of the pain as the source of slouching was astounding. Not only did I realize that I was in pain, but I also realized that I was unconsciously and repetitively avoiding pain. There was a deep habit pattern of pain avoidance programmed into the very fabric of my mind. In order to break free of it, I would have to sit with it.

There is something so utterly liberating about being willing to sit with all your pain. Not only did I sit with my pain, but I learned to love

86

it with it, and love it. When I let the pain in, without being overwhelmed by it or allowing it to cause hardness or bitterness, something in me changed. Whether that pain is physical, emotional, financial, or spiritual, understanding and becoming intimate with my own pain created the space for love. I began the work of changing the paradigm there and started to unroot the six enemies. Whereas in the past, I had acted in hatred or lashed out as a response to pain, my choices would be different going forward. It would be hard work, but with pain as my friend, I was ready and equipped to do it.

What Doesn't Kill You

Life is sometimes very hard—unfairly hard. Of course, life is also beautiful, sometimes overwhelmingly so. There are ups and downs along this journey. Some valleys are so deep and dark and contain so many pitfalls and missteps that the experience may be qualified as traumatic. The American Psychological Association defines trauma as "an emotional response to a terrible event like an accident, rape or natural disaster" that often includes shock, denial, unpredictable emotions, flashbacks, strained relationships, and even physical symptoms, like headaches and nausea. Traumatic events are those that cause physical, emotional, spiritual, or psychological harm and leave the person with unresolved feelings of anxiety, fear, sadness, anger, and other debilitating emotions. The mind and body are impacted in trauma, which can be acute, chronic, and complex. Anyone at any age can experience trauma; understanding the symptoms and implications of trauma create a trauma-informed perspective. The National Trauma Council states that 70 percent of adults in the US have experienced some form of trauma—over 200 million people in this country alone. Globally, the statistics could be even higher.

Psychology is now able to document three potentialities that can occur after a traumatic event. In post-traumatic stress disorder, the individual who experiences the trauma returns damaged and tracks below the level of happiness and functioning prior to the event. The Veteran's Association reports that seven or eight of every one hundred people will have PTSD at some point in their lives. To put it into perspective, that amounts to about eight million adults in the US who have PTSD in a given year. This is only a small portion of those who have experienced trauma. In other cases, the individual is observed to return to the same level of functioning and happiness as before the traumatic event. But a few outliers are documented as flourishing in the aftermath of a traumatic event. This is called post-traumatic growth (PTG) and was first documented by Richard G. Tedeschi and Lawrence G. Calhoun at the University of North Carolina at Charlotte in the mid-1990s. In the case where individuals experience PTG instead of PTSD, they actually have more resilience, success, and happiness than before the trauma. They are able to embody and feel more love. Those who are able to attain PTG are highly functioning individuals who have been able to turn the most difficult and challenging circumstances into something positive. They have touched the root of suffering itself and have emerged with love.

Studying cases of PTG is useful in offering a path toward meaning beyond the suffering of trauma. There is a promise in PTG about transcendence and hope, as though the stories of these flourishing individuals who were able to turn their trauma into growth are trailblazers on the path. They light the way for others to follow. Of course, when reading stories of PTG, it can be only natural to wonder why we couldn't have been the outlier and why we haven't yet found a way out of our suffering. But the purpose of sharing the potential of PTG is not to shame or condemn those who haven't yet found the path toward flourishing after trauma; far from it. Instead, PTG is a kind of empirical proof that a shift in the paradigm of the mind can bring about miraculous changes. It is perhaps only love that can truly turn experiences that would otherwise be debilitating and overwhelming into a catalyst for major positive life change.

Sympathetic Joy

That on which we put our attention says more about us than almost anything else. Spend a few moments with another person, and listen closely for signs about where that person's attention gravitates. If something is always wrong, if there is always a complaint, if nothing is ever good enough, if the first thing seen is the annoyance, which tells its own story. But if the opposite is true, that also tells its own story. Someone who always sees the good in things, who looks for the light in the darkness, who sees the best, who is easy to smile and laugh—these qualities tell their own story too.

We all have qualities of light and shadow. We are both people in the example above, on different days or sometimes on the same day. The magic of the spiritual path comes from a conscious shift to a purposeful life, where instead of being dictated by happenstance, actions are chosen. See the light, or see the shadow. Both are always present. Deny either one and the act of resistance strengthens the very thing that has been rejected. Energy works in a paradox. Cling for it to stay, and it goes. Cling for it to go, and it stays. Accept the inevitable coming and going, and there is a chance of finding a place in the flow of life.

Attention has the power to create whole worlds. Emotions are powerful drivers of focus and ones that few people master. Instead, emotions often run rampant, like an out-of-control roller coaster wreaking havoc all around. But there is a way to get back into the driver's seat and gently guide the force of emotions toward a more productive—or at least a conscious—outcome. Every human being has felt joy, love, and peace at least a few times in their lives. And every human being has felt anger, sadness, and anxiety at least a few times as well. Imagine if, instead of a few rare instants of joy sprinkled throughout a sea of adversity, there was the potential to live in a state of limitless, childlike joy, wonder, and love. Does this sound like a fairy tale? Well, keep reading …

The standard Western dictionary states that joy is the notion of great delight or happiness, often caused by something exceptionally good or satisfying, success, keen pleasure, or elation. But yogis are encouraged to look deeper than that. The spiritual teaching of yoga is rooted in the ancient languages of Sanskrit and Pali, both of which use the word *mudita* for joy. Mudita is presented in Patañjali's *Yoga Sutras* as the state of mind that the yogi cultivates in response to other people's pleasure, happiness, and success. To the average Western individualist, this may seem counterintuitive. In order to fully express the spiritual concept of mudita, most translations add a qualifying word—instead of simply joy, mudita is often translated as sympathetic joy or pleasure stemming from delighting in the success of others. The most common example used to explain the concept of sympathetic joy is that of parents sharing in the success of their children.

Rooted in selflessness, mudita is a state of joy that is free from self-interest and that is consciously cultivated. The active practice of celebrating others' success works to eradicate the chains of ego. While it may be easy to see how a parent would experience true sympathetic joy for the happiness and success of their children, it is sometimes baffling to understand how someone could be happy for the success of a stranger or, even worse, an enemy. Yet that is exactly what the practice of mudita asks of spiritual practitioners.

Mudita is a truly powerful teaching, rooted in the truth of the human spirit. There is no end to joy. It only grows. Celebrating the success of others multiplies that joy and brings it closer to one's own heart. Mudita is paradoxically the most selfish thing that can be done. Instead of waiting for personal successes, the practice of sympathetic joy allows everyone to share in all the joy that the whole world has achieved. Jump on the joy bandwagon without the hard work of producing the results by relishing in the success of others. While it may feel like something is lost when another person wins, that is just a remnant of the scarcity mindset. Changing the paradigm to a joy-abundance mindset is a monumental shift in the control center of the mind. To shift from selfishness to selflessness is perhaps the most revolutionary shift that can happen. By practicing mudita, not only for oneself and those in the inner circle but for all beings, friends and enemies alike, the capacity for joy is exponentially increased.

And just like happiness, the magic of multiplication means that joy is truly limitless. Moreover, when the experience of joy and happiness are unlinked from the attainment of material objects or specific goals, more joy naturally flows. And of course, in the state of ease and flow, the power of attraction is magnified. Remember that it's not about what is achieved or the accumulation of results; it's about the state of mind that pervades along the journey.

Switching the paradigm is not like switching a light on and off. It's not about being joyful and happy immediately but inviting more joy and happiness into the heart and mind over a time. Reworking the grooves of the subconscious mind requires steady effort and perseverance. As the work is done, deeply held repetitive patterns rise to the surface. Applying the teachings to daily life demands a high level of consciousness in every thought and action, which can be challenging, exhausting, and daunting. When jealousy, hate, bitterness, depression, or other unwanted emotional states arise, recognize that this too is the fertile ground upon which to practice. Only by integrating these states and transmuting them will the radical change fully take root. All it really takes is the willingness to show up and put in the work day after day.

The door to the inner world lies just inside the heart. Each moment offers a potential to be a bridge toward the mysterious realm of the spirit. There is always a choice, even in what appears to be a choiceless place; that choice is the work of mental training and discipline. The conscious mind is only a fraction of all thoughts. Working with both the conscious and subconscious mind turns every spiritual seeker into a conscious co-creator with the universe. A stream of joy and well-being seeks every living being. Ancient yogis found the secrets to access this fountain of liberation. Some in our present era refer to the illusive state of flow as being in alignment. No matter which words are used to describe the teaching, the benefit of reprogramming the mind with deliberate intention is enormously positive, both for oneself and for the world.

Make good use of the technique; learn to celebrate the success of others, especially those deemed enemies or competitors, even though it seems counterintuitive. Even one small act of love can be a revolution. Even one tiny instant of joy can open the door to a wellspring of goodness.

1. Meditation on Suffering

Start in a comfortable seated position. Take a few moments to tune into your breath and body. Notice any places of discomfort and allow yourself to accept what is as it is. Notice your own suffering—the achy tenderness in your heart where you may be in emotional pain. Perhaps there is intense physical pain in the body. Sit with it for a few moments. Practice being present with whatever pain or discomfort is present, without trying to change or eradicate it. Practice sitting with your pain, whether that pain is big or small, physical or emotional. Notice how the pain feels, once the habituated pattern of reactivity is attenuated. Simply staying present with whatever pain is present has the power to retrain the mind and establish a new way of responding. Claiming the seat of neutrality is itself a new space in the fabric of thinking.

2. Reflection

Identify a particularly difficult period of your life. Reflect on the level of happiness and functioning that was present prior to the event. Then, notice the shift that happened, days, weeks, and years afterward. Identify the impacts still occurring in your life, and see if you notice signs of PTSD, PTG, or a return to a level of functioning similar to prior to the period of difficulty. If you have never experienced PTSD or PTG, then spend some time thinking about the trajectories of public figures, and see if you can identify at least one example of PTSD and PTG.

3. Exercise

Replace jealousy with sympathetic joy. Think of someone toward whom you harbor feelings of jealousy. Perhaps it is because of that person's status or success. Identify the emotional state that you think accomplishing what he or she has accomplished will give you. It might be relief, respect, joy, happiness, acceptance, or love. Ask yourself if you can give that to yourself right now by celebrating that person's success. When you celebrate the success of others, you piggyback off their work and move directly into the good feelings for which they've worked hard. Watch as the ego resists the celebration of sympathetic joy, and then carefully plant the seeds of mudita in your heart, and invite the emotional state of success into your present experience right now.

✳

Chapter 5

Stepping Off the Emotional Roller Coaster

> If her past were your past, her pain your pain, her level of consciousness your level of consciousness, you would think and act exactly as she does. With this realization comes forgiveness, compassion, peace. The ego doesn't like to hear this, because if it cannot be reactive and righteous anymore, it will lose strength. When you receive whoever comes into the space of Now as a noble guest, when you allow each person to be as they are, they begin to change.
> —Eckhart Tolle (2003, 92)

Romantic love is the stuff of legend and myth. Each and every human being craves intimacy and connection, even those who say they don't.

Love, or the pursuit of it, has led great heroes, world leaders, and people like you and me to great heights and great lows. From the face that launched a thousand ships to Shiva and Parvati to Romeo and Juliet, romantic love is a great driver of human action, for better or worse.

Finding peace and happiness in romance is one of the greatest mysteries of life to solve. Without it, there is heartbreak and misery. With it, even the perfunctory activities of housework can seem to sing with a heavenly joy. It is in our romantic relationships that we are also perhaps at our most vulnerable and volatile. They challenge us utterly and relentlessly to keep seemingly impossible dialectics—love but don't smother, respect boundaries (yours and your partner's), give but don't enable, hold but don't try to control or possess; this list goes on and on.

There is no official training in the school of romance. Most people learn, through a kind of familial osmosis, how to pattern roles in relationships. We take in the behavior that our parents model for us as caregivers and as lovers joined together, however successful or unsuccessful they may be. Perhaps even more problematic, we learn from movies and sitcoms that tell stories of impossible love. We buy into a carefully crafted narrative of romance that no actual living relationship—let alone how we ourselves might show up in a relationship—could ever fulfill. We, like so many people, are left dazed and confused, navigating the waters of romance with a faulty compass, lost and looking for love in all the wrong places.

So what is the "right" place to look for love? First, love begins with oneself. Love for another person can only be fulfilled to the degree that self-love exists. Otherwise, what may sometimes feel like love may only be a chimera of the real thing. The depth of love is limited by the depth of self-love. Self-rejection blocks love not only for oneself but for others.

Love, especially romantic love, is often conflated with possession. The casual usage of the word *love* makes it hard to distinguish what love really is. After all, we may "love" pizza and "love" our favorite shirt, but this love is not the boundless love that will set the soul free. A pizza or a shirt simply cannot be loved in the same way that you love another person. To objectify love is to limit it. To use the auspices of love to try to control another person or a situation is to limit love. Love is, by its nature, limitless. Control and possession are betrayals of love.

Love does not control. If control or manipulation is at hand in the situation, actions are most likely separate from the deepest source of love. Control is not in the nature of love. Control is rooted in fear, hurt, blame, and shame. It is also rooted in the ego, the false idea that outcomes can be manipulated according to individual will. Love cannot be a command; a person cannot be forced to love. Love is rooted in faith, with an understanding that the outcome of any situation is in the hands of a higher power. Love is responsible and generous; control is greedy, jealous, and often untruthful. Yet it is sometimes easy to mistake love for control.

The flowering of love between two people is a gift from God. It's the same type of gift that spring is each year, that the sunrise is each day, and that new life is each time it's born. Love cannot be produced to order or standardized to fit the mold. Love is alive and vibrant and filled with potential. Real love, whether love of oneself, romantic love of another, or the love of God, has an element of fear in it. It is this fear that makes control and manipulation so tempting when faced with the daunting nature of love's overpowering greatness. With equal parts excitement and awe, love conjures up the feelings of otherworldliness, an adventure of unparalleled proportions, where we are asked to risk it all and be dissolved into something beyond our known world.

There is danger in love because when the risk is the dissolution of the false self, the ego will fight for survival at all costs. There is so much magic in love that it is bigger and grander than any one being, but it also *is* the core nature of every being, including the entirety of the universe. Love as a state of beingness, however, is not taught in the standard operating system of the mind. Love is the loss of self, the renunciation of personality, a kind of destruction that breaks apart the mind, a flood that pulls all into heaven on earth. This immersive love is what each of us tastes in moments of ecstatic connection with another. It's this drop of sublime elixir that drives us to insanity when we lose it. The spiritual path is about finding the fountain of love as an eternal wellspring within.

Emotions Are Your GPS

Feeling is the gateway to love. The murky world of emotions is what clouds the judgment required to navigate the terrain of love clearly. Yet love is also an emotion. So in order to truly understand that intoxicating pull of romantic love, we have to dive deeper into the psychology of feeling, being, and relating. We have to start with understanding our own emotions.

Most of us have not received much formal training in emotional self-awareness; at least, I surely never did. Instead, we are trained to downplay our feelings in favor of the realm of mind and reason. We learn one technique or another to repress or hide our emotions from others—and even from ourselves. Yet the raw power of emotions is the foundation of the vibrancy of our being. The act of denial, however, fails. Suppressed and repressed emotions have much more power over us than feelings that are felt and processed. Instead of emotional suppression, working with emotions can be liberating. Instead of emotions running wild in the depths of the subconscious mind, unprocessed and unresolved, there is a path that leads to emotional self-regulation. Instead of emotions being dirty little secrets, emotions can be seen as helpful signposts from the inner world. Emotions are part of our internal GPS, and by learning to navigate our emotions, we gain access to an intelligence far beyond mere intellect.

Romantic relationships are the place where very deep patterns are often held and where the raw power of emotions often surfaces. We get caught in chasing intense highs and lows and become addicted to the drama of what we think is love. In truth, what frequently happens is that we look for validation and affirmation in our romantic partners. We look to someone outside of ourselves for wholeness. Unfortunately, looking for wholeness outside of oneself is a recipe for failure. Wholeness begins within and then is expressed in interpersonal relations.

Romantic relationships operate within the paradigm of the mind's assumptions about oneself and the word. Almost every relationship begins with the feelings of hope, joy, and happiness. Anyone can fall into a honeymoon state for a short while. Over long months and years, however, the deeper patterns start to surface and the shadow side appears. After that initial glow abates, if blame and shame appear on a regular basis in a relationship, which is a good indication that the relationship is rooted in a flawed paradigm. The operating system of the mind includes all the assumptions and thoughts that are held about oneself and the world. What we think are love relationships are sometimes rooted in a paradigm of hate and rejection. Before lasting happiness flourishes in a relationship, the deeper patterns of the mind have to be updated. Otherwise, all searching for romantic love merely perpetuates the same old stories that have led to suffering and heartbreak.

You Are Responsible for Your Own Emotional Well-Being

My student Penelope walked into class one day, appearing shy, tenuous, and shaky. Low self-esteem oozed from her every move. Although she wanted to try yoga, she was nearly trembling when she described herself as weak, inflexible, incompetent, and overweight. She was not blessed with natural flexibility or strength, but yoga is not a game of ableism. I was confident that regardless of the physical shape of her body, the practice would be beneficial for her and that she could practice yoga. I encouraged her to practice—and practice she did. There was a big change in Penelope's overall presence, and there was a true transformation in the way she inhabited her body. About two years after she started practice, Penelope stayed after class to speak with me. She told me that practicing yoga had increased her self-confidence and that she felt so much better about herself. But, she said, there was one area of her life that still felt off—her relationship. She and her partner, Georgia, fought a lot. Whenever they would argue, Penelope felt like the victim of Georgia's temper. Although they had been to therapy, Penelope kept on waiting for something to change in Georgia so she would be happy in the relationship. But, she said, that wasn't working. Even when her partner did try to apologize or change in the ways that Penelope wanted, it wasn't enough. Penelope's emotions were out of control. Penelope, like so many other people in unhappy relationships, was waiting for Georgia to say the right thing before her emotions could regulate.

What I shared with her that day perhaps wasn't what she was expecting. Rather than simply take her side, I shared what I've learned through the spiritual path—that is, that every single person is responsible for his or her own emotional well-being. Life is a mirror that reflects what's in our hearts. While we have to be realistic about whether or not someone's actions cause harm or cross a line, if we are not able to regulate our own emotions, nothing will ever be clear. If we need people in the world to be a certain way before we are good, then goodness will always be held hostage to the changing winds of the world.

We see in others what is really within ourselves. Change always begins within. Happiness and peace start from the inside out. Complaining or ruminating won't work. We are each responsible for our own happiness and emotional well-being. It's that simple—and that excruciating. That includes the wisdom to know whether another person's actions cause us harm or are simply annoying, and we are the ones who need to relax. The lie is the paradigm that assigns the locus of happiness to anything outside of oneself. Believing the lie locks in cycles of sadness, self-rejection, and even abuse. Unlearning the lie is the work of liberation and spiritual awakening. The degree to which emotional well-being is located within oneself is the degree to which wholeness can be experienced, both individually and in a relationship. External circumstances change constantly and cannot be controlled. There is no perfect situation, and there is no perfect relationship. Love of oneself cannot be dependent on the approval or the mood of someone else. Instead, love of oneself must be the root of every single action taken in life.

Participating in the framework of self-rejection condemns us to try to manipulate others in order to feel better about ourselves. We think that we will be happy when we hear the right words, receive the right gift, and are treated the right way. But so often, even when all the boxes are checked off our list of dreams, happiness still evades us. Even when our partner tries to say and do all the right things, there is still something missing. That something can only come from within, as a self-evident expression of wholeness, as love manifest inherent to the state of being. No other person has the secret to happiness. Love is unlocked from within. We are each responsible only for our own emotional well-being. If we wait for the world outside of us to be in a particular way before we are at peace, then the locus of control shifts to a realm where we will always be out of control. Feelings of empowerment, peace, and resolution arise when the locus of control shifts to an internal realm.

Emotional well-being is a tool that anyone can learn. While self-care has been relegated to images of days at the spa and other privileged expressions of leisure, true emotional self-regulation is a life skill that can be learned by and benefit every human being. Holocaust survivor and psychologist Victor Frankl said that human freedom lies in the space between stimulus and response. Self-acceptance starts with becoming intimately aware of all responses to all outside forces and influences, whether positive, negative, or neutral. Life is a ceaseless onslaught of stimuli that register as positive, negative, or neutral. The body produces endless signifiers of comfort and discomfort, whether hot or cold, sleepy or energized. The world is constantly changing, sometimes to your liking, sometimes not. The only thing that any being can truly control is how to respond to these ever-changing stimuli. It is an act of love to care for one's emotional well-being.

Yoga, meditation, breathing, walking in nature, exercise, positive self-talk, silence, affirmations and visualizations, guided therapy, and journaling are just some of the tools that I use for my emotional self-regulation. Understanding what triggers the emotional system and working with methods that calm the nervous system is the foundation of emotional self-care. There is a path that works for everyone. Some people choose art, motorcycle riding, laughter, cooking, cleaning, building, and more. The paradigm shift uses awareness to recognize that the foundation of emotional health is within oneself. Feel emotions as what they are—navigation points on the path that work like a GPS. When a warning signal arises, instead of waiting on a hero to arrive, waving banners of salvation to redirect the route, use the tools of emotional self-regulation to autocorrect. Then, it will be easy to follow the signs of emotional well-being toward a path of wholeness and love.

The Drama Triangle

In order to be free to regulate the emotions, it can be helpful to unpack a common power dynamic that prevents real love from showing up. The actions that show up in cycles of manipulation and low self-worth can frequently be traced to a pattern labeled as the victim-hero-perpetrator triangle, referred to as a "drama triangle."

The drama triangle was developed by Dr. Stephen Karpman (2015) more than forty years ago. The drama triangle concept is a dynamic model of human social interaction and destructive conflict. The triangle is composed of oppressors, victims, and rescuers; the roles are fluid and changing and are deeply held in the subconscious mind. The drama triangle is an insidious subconscious pattern that often masquerades as social activism, whistleblower righteousness, and victim-centered anger. As long as this is the paradigm from which one operates, freedom, peace, and love are impossible to experience. Within this framework, love appears as an illusion but actually is a kind of exchange for services rendered.

Often learned at a young age and programmed deeply within the subconscious mind, the victim-hero-perpetrator triangle can be hard to spot at first. But once seen, the act of awareness helps to move beyond the triangle. In the drama triangle, three roles are tied together. The victim has been hurt and abused by the perpetrator and seeks a hero for salvation. When a person is in the role of hero, he or she is loved by the victim. But if the hero missteps or acts out of accordance with the standard set forth by the victim, he or she will be cast out as the perpetrator. The role of aggressor is played by the perpetrator, but the perpetrator can easily shift toward the role of the victim. Victims too can shift and become perpetrators, especially when they believe they are entitled to a course of action.

The perpetrator can be the actual harmful actor from the past or can be generalized to the present or future to include other people whom the victim finds triggering or generally disagrees with. The hero's role is also fungible. Heroes are called into action to save the helpless victim and stand up to the aggressor. Both the hero and victim roles contain an element of moral superiority that increases the dysfunction. Each identity has just enough power to make it seem intoxicating enough to want to hold on to it. But the victim-hero-perpetrator triangle is a downward spiraling cycle that leads only to codependency, unclear boundaries, and more hurt and pain.

> Under their 'helpful' exterior, rescuers feel like victims. What they do in order to stop feeling like a victim is to try to rescue another victim. They find someone who is just a little bit weaker than they are, a little bit more needy. This is where codependency emerges. Each person/role becomes dependent on the other to satisfy their emotional needs. The rescuer is dependent on the victim to remain helpless. The victim is dependent on the rescuer to take care of him. These dependencies may not be observable to the untrained eye. On the surface these people may look happy and fulfilled. (Zimberoff 2011, 6)

The shifting roles of the drama triangle are mind-boggling. Reflect back on Georgia and Penelope. They were engaged in a perplexing but very common interpersonal drama-triangle relationship. Penelope cast herself as the victim of Georgia's temper but also looked to Georgia to be her hero. When Georgia failed to perform in the role of hero, Penelope lost her emotional balance and lashed out. In a sordid twist, Georgia then felt victimized by Penelope's lack of emotional balance, and she cast Penelope as a perpetrator. With each argument, they turned the wheel of suffering once more, spinning the drama triangle.

The roles switch so that the rescuer suddenly feels like a victim, the persecutor transforms into a rescuer, and the victim empowers himself or herself to the role of either rescuer or perpetrator. Triangulation is the foundation of this pattern. The solution comes from an update to the operating system of the mind that challenges this power dynamic, where individual boundaries become very clear.

Victimhood is at the core of the drama triangle, regardless of which role is assumed. People enmeshed within the drama triangle get addicted to the game—the drama itself. When the victim personality is in full force, it often manifests in cycles of addiction, sexual or physical abuse, and psychological manipulation. Not only will these patterns appear on an individual level, but they appear on a societal level as well.

Victimhood is powerful. Once the victim identity is solidified, there are often accompanying entitlements, such as certain behaviors, that would otherwise be off limits due to social norms. For example, while in the role of the victim, one may feel that one has a right to yell, scream, attack, or otherwise treat others unfairly. Victims may feel little compassion or empathy toward those who have been identified as perpetrators. Victimhood can be worn as a badge to ward off all criticism and control the behavior of others. Letting go of this false and addictive power can be scary, but it is the only way that leads to healing and true love.

It is highly likely that we all have participated in some form of this drama triangle at some moment in our lives. There is no reason to feel shame about it. The drama triangle is not something that has been developed privately. The victim-hero-perpetrator triangle is written large into societal structure. It would not be an exaggeration to say that the victim-hero-perpetrator triangle is a systemic issue within society. The downtrodden often search for a hero upon whom to attach their salvation. Once the knight in shining armor presents himself or herself, all hope is cast onto this "great" person to save the day. Whether the leader is a political candidate, a religious icon, a yoga teacher, or some other figure, once the mantle of *hero* has been assumed, the identity of the victim and perpetrator are also locked in. If no obvious enemy exists, the search for the necessary evil-doer will begin, consciously or subconsciously. The politics of fear, unfortunately, are highly effective at manipulating the human psyche. Any challenger that seeks to be victorious over such a power dynamic must break free from the fundamental psychological paradigm, lest the cycle simply repeat with a new hero/perpetrator/victim. There are many examples of the victim-hero-perpetrator triangle in society. Start looking, and they will appear ubiquitously. From missionaries to zealots to extremist political parties to white saviorism to cancel culture, the drama triangle lives and breathes in the broader sociopath/political context as much as it does within our romantic relationships. Challenging this triangle has the potential to heal not only relationships with potential partners but also the very fabric of society itself.

Breaking Out

Once the drama triangle is revealed, it may seem like it's everywhere (and it might be). No doubt, the next logical question that arises after seeing this familiar trope play out in one's personal life and on a global scale is the question of how to get out. How are we supposed to break out of the triangle?

David Emerald Womeldorff presents an alternative to the drama triangle that recasts the roles of victim-hero-perpetrator in a new perspective. In his book, *The Power of TED*, Womeldorff outlines what he calls "the empowerment dynamic" that is now used in transactional therapy, as well as in large corporations, to facilitate healthy teamwork and increase productivity.

The role of the persecutor is seen not as a manifestation of cosmic evil but simply as a challenge that offers the potential for personal growth and evolution. The role of the rescuer is seen not as a flawless angelic being but as a coach whose actions restore one's own agency. The role of the victim transforms into a conscious creator, focused on outcomes and solutions rather than problems.

At first, the differences may appear to be subtle, but recasting the roles of the main act of one's life can spark the process of dismantling the whole system upon which the drama triangle is based. Breaking out of the drama triangle is part of the work required to install a new software on the hard drive of the mind and heart. Playing by the old rules of the drama triangle cannot lead to liberation, just like working on old computer software cannot lead to the next big tech breakthrough. The major update needed to break out of the drama triangle begins with reconceptualizing the root of each role in the drama triangle system and digging out the root of fear.

Instead of resting on fear, installing love as the basic motivator of every action, word, and thought necessarily moves beyond the drama triangle. Operating from the paradigm of oneness and connection means that those old tropes simply don't compute anymore. After the shift, when the drama triangle arises, it will feel like trying to run an old software program on a new system—it just won't work. It's not that these roles will just disappear; far from it. The drama triangle may be even more evident, but its power will be diminished. The power of the drama triangle is its subconscious nature. Once the dynamic is revealed, the power drains from the drama triangle to control the flow of energy in relationships.

Seen from the perspective of positive psychology, breaking out of the drama triangle allows for post-traumatic growth in many areas of life. Romantic relationships will most likely be the first sphere to get a massive upgrade from the shedding of the old skin of the drama triangle. Resist the urge to judge yourself or others, and instead, work on updating the software of the mind. Just reading this chapter may be enough to crack through the layers of subconscious patterning that sabotages romantic relationships.

I was caught in a drama triangle for many years. I looked to my husband as my hero, and I gave him the keys to my emotional well-being. Not only was this an unsustainable path for me, but it was unfair to him. Placing the burden of my happiness on his shoulders was unfair, and whenever he didn't succeed in making me happy, the roles shifted, and suddenly, he was the perpetrator. It took all the tools at my disposal to see through the painful old tropes and break out of the drama triangle.

Looking back, I can see that the road I walked was tough and seemed insurmountable at times. I couldn't bring the chains of the past into the freedom of the future. Each time I resisted my own potential for growth, it was not something I did wrong but a chance to revisit the pattern and learn how to break out of the cycle. Once the drama triangle lifted, it felt all fresh and new. That's what a paradigm change feels like. Like a snake that has shed its skin, the outfits of the past remain with the past, and there is a kind of emptiness that awaits the unknown future. Big change does not come without mourning or loss, but when it happens, there is a chance to be reborn with more compassion. For me, it felt like a sudden shift that happened internally, paired with the hard work of actualizing that change in the material substance of my life. The shift was instantaneous, but the work to make it real was not.

Drama is small and diminishing. When drama disappears, there is the freedom to act in love. When there is no longer a role to be played, there is only the authentic self left to be expressed. Love is not something that has to be possessed or controlled. Love itself is the possessor, the only true owner of itself. All we can do is surrender, trust, and allow love to be what it truly is.

Real Love

Love, as it turns out, nourishes the body in a similar way as the right balance of sunlight, nutrient-rich soil, and water nourishes plants and allows them to flourish. The more a person experiences love, the more the body and mind open up and grow, becoming wiser and more attuned, more resilient and effective, happier, and healthier. Love helps human beings grow spiritually as well, making it easier to see, feel, and appreciate the deep interconnections that inexplicably tie us together and foster bonds within the grand fabric of life.

Just as the body was designed to extract oxygen from the earth's atmosphere and nutrients from the foods we ingest, the body was also designed to love. Love—like taking a deep breath or drinking a glass of water—not only feels great but is also life-giving. Regularly tapping into the feeling of love is an indispensable source of energy, sustenance, and health.

Love is not only in intimate relationships, nor does the equation of love with intimate relations tell the whole story. Instead, something else defines what love really is. Love is not dependent on a particular person, but it does depend on connection, whether that is with another human being or with another living being or even a cosmic presence. We all long for love, whether we're single or coupled, whether we prefer to spend our days amid a boisterous crowd or in quiet seclusion. Love is an essential nutrient of the heart. Giving and receiving love in balance and harmony is the essence of the promise of liberation. To break free of unhealthy dependencies and awaken to the true purpose of life is the goal of the spiritual path.

In order to know what love is, the state of love must be delineated from dependency and other counterfeits. Where love liberates, dependency manipulates and controls. Love is healing, while the phantom of love destroys. Love is kind, patient, and giving, while stepping away from love permits cruelty, hastening, and taking. Love is an action rooted in fearlessness and built on honesty and protection. Striking against love stems from fear, relies on deceit, and leads to exploitation. Love is endless and forgiving, and it never fails. The illusion of love eventually and inevitably fails.

We all instinctively know real love. No matter how twisted the mind is, the memory of our true state of being remains intact. There may not be an actual memory, but there is a visceral feeling of what a world and a life based on love should or could be. It is the dream of utopia that is never far from idealists. This is not only on a personal level but also on a global or societal level as well. And one thing is certain—if we want to find a way to a better world filled with happy relationships, it begins with finding a path to wholeness within ourselves.

1. Meditation and Reflection Points

Identify one public drama triangle of which you are not a part. It could be a political group or a relationship that you view from the outside. Note who plays which roles most often and how easily these roles shift. Did the drama triangle ever shift in this instance, or is the cycle still in action? Next, identify at least one instance where you have been in the drama triangle in your own life. Are you in it now? If so, what is your main role? What role are you most comfortable in, and what role are you least comfortable in? How are you benefiting from your role in the drama triangle, and what is stopping you from breaking free from this triangle? Ask yourself if you are willing and able to do the work to recast the roles of the drama triangle and set yourself free.

Chapter 6

Love and Hate

If we could read the secret history of our enemies, we should in each [person's] life sorrow and suffering enough to disarm any hostility.

—Henry Wadsworth Longfellow

In the midst of hate, it is almost impossible to feel love. While it might be desirable to move quickly from love to hate, more often than not, it's just too much of a shift for the mind and heart to handle. Instead, a more modest goal might be to refrain from actions whose roots are tied to hate, whether that hatred is self-directed or focused toward another being. In the midst of hate, rage, and aggression, the nervous system is triggered toward generating more hate, rage, and aggression. The flood of intensity generates a cycle that gathers momentum and power. Actions taken when hate is present tend to pile on the hate and set the conditions for even more hate. Clear thinking is obscured when hatred courses through the veins. The first step out of hate isn't love; the first step out of hate is non-hate.

When I first stepped on to the spiritual path, I thought that everyone who practiced yoga and meditation never got angry. Wow, was I wrong. Just because individuals practice yoga, meditate, or aspire to raise their vibration doesn't mean they will never be angry again. Some spiritual aspirants have a guilty conscience about feeling hate sometimes. Well, that only compounds the problem and makes it linger even longer. In fact, the process of awakening can involve getting in touch with repressed anger that has transformed into bottled-up resentment. What we refer to as the process of enlightenment is rarely a unicorn-filled fantasyland, where cotton-candy clouds float on the horizon, and ethereal music plays a tune of only love and light. Instead, personal growth is often messy and gritty. Hands get dirty while digging around in the garden of the mind in search of old stubborn weeds. The lotus flower only appears in the hands of one who is prepared to be covered in mud.

Practically, the instruction about hate presented here is a kind of emotional sliding scale that begins with the admission that we all have the seeds of hate within our hearts. If we never acknowledge that the heart harbors hate and the seed of aggression within, then we can never be free of it. Good villains play the role so well that the audience truly hates them. The villains in our lives often play their roles all too well. Casual comments spark outrage within us, and the fire in our eyes blazes, sometimes uncontrollably. Learning how to take good care of anger when it arises is an important step on the path of spiritual learning. Without understanding the root of anger, why it arises, and the intelligence contained within it, anger feels like a noose around the neck, suffocating and squelching out the life within us.

In the midst of hate, it is almost impossible to feel love. Yet paradoxically, we can sometimes hate the people we love the most, especially if they're engaged in an activity we find annoying or displeasing. Love and hate are not light switches that click on and off. Emotions are more like a sliding scale, and shifting them is more like an elegant dimmer than a simple flipping mechanism. What often works for me when I'm in the midst of hate is not to try to tap directly into love; instead, I aim for a more modest goal. I try just not to hate that person so much. Even if I still hate them a little, I place my efforts on not hating them so much; or if I want to be a little more ambitious, I could set my target for neutrality. But really, even just softening the hard edges of hate weakens the pattern and gives a little space to breathe and be. That small space precipitates even more space and makes room for what might end up being a miraculous shift. That little extra space is a benefit to all. Remember that when hate flourishes, it taxes the body, mind, and nervous system. It is in the hater's interest to process those feelings and perhaps even let go of the negativity. At the very least, something I find useful, which helps me lessen the cycle of hate, is to refrain from making any major decisions or taking any big actions while I'm boiling with rage. This might seem obvious, but hate is cyclical and addictive, and it gathers momentum. Once the fire is ignited, it's hard to stop. Learning how to abstain from acting in hate is an important first step on the journey of learning how to truly act in love.

One of the most liberating things that has come from my spiritual practice is the subtle change in what bothers me. Before I started on this long journey toward my own liberation, everything (or at least, it seemed like that to me) annoyed me. My mind was filled with complaints, judgments, and disappointments about myself, others, and the world at large. All the self-help sweet talk that directed me to love myself fell into an abyss. Not only did it feel inauthentic, but I just couldn't make the valiant, heroic switch in one fell swoop. Instead, the work I did centered around claiming the seat of neutrality. I tried, with persistent effort, to hold neutral thoughts about all the things that pushed my buttons. I focused with intensity on the things that didn't drive me up the wall. Gratitude would have been too much of a stretch, so instead, I directed my mind toward small things that were perhaps not positive but neutral, such as the fact that the annoying person was not present in the room with me. It seems inconsequential, but the reality is that life would have been more irksome, had the being I had labeled as annoying been physically present. Neutrality is a kind of beginner mountain to climb on the path. It's hard work too, and it gives you all the tools for the steeper climb toward love. If the technique isn't established in neutrality work, then the mind is as ill-prepared for an advanced hike as a novice hiker would be at the base of Mount Everest. It takes discipline and practice to gently pull your foot off the accelerator when the engines of hate start revving up. Just like the gears of a car shift, emotions can be consciously shifted as well. And just like working a vehicle, there's a bit of finesse required, especially if the car is an older model with a persnickety nature.

The sustained seat of neutrality opens the door to forgiveness, understanding, and, perhaps one day, compassion. A big mistake many well-intended spiritual practitioners make is rushing the steps that lead toward compassion. I've known students who felt guilty about not being able to love their enemies. The reality is that most people have a hard time with that step. Praying for people who persecute others is ambitious and often risks retraumatization or, at the very least, reigniting the cycle of hate. There is always a reason why people do things that make others suffer, and it usually has to do with their own misery, unconsciousness, or hurt. Those who hurt others often are hurting themselves. While this is not an excuse for their behavior, this fact can be useful in generating compassion. In a relationship that has deteriorated into spiteful dialogue, both parties are hurting.

Neutrality is the middle ground, where meeting is possible. In order to trust the space of true objectivity, it's a good idea to be able to sustain it for a few days or even a few weeks, not just a few hours. As long as the fires of hate burn, the smoke obscures clear thinking. While the most effective place to act is when the heart is filled with love, neutrality is good too. When the charge of negative emotions dissipates, everyone can relax a little.

Abraham-Hicks, teachers of the law of attraction, present emotions as a kind of ladder that can be consciously worked from one step to another. They affirm that the switch from hate to love, while possible, is too gigantic a leap for most people. Instead, they suggest working step by step and feeling the way modestly from one state to another—from hate toward neutrality, from neutrality toward appreciation, from appreciation to love. This process might sound easy, and intellectually, it is easy to walk through the emotional sliding scale. But reality can be so much harder. We are up against all the patterning and inertia of the past.

Unconscious Anger

The majority of thinking happens in the subconscious mind. At most moments throughout any given day, the subconscious mind goes on thinking, feeling, and reacting with very little conscious awareness. There is what could be called a veil between the conscious and subconscious mind. To a large degree, the subconscious mind holds our deepest thoughts—the ones that form the framework for what we think reality and life really are. And since these thoughts are so deeply programmed and happening nonstop, the danger is that we assume our view of reality to be "the truth," when, in fact, it's just a bunch of deeply programmed, unquestioned, unconscious thoughts, many of which were laid during traumatic events or through socialization.

To make any substantive life change, the subconscious mind needs to be reprogrammed. If affirmations, goals, and visualizations circulate only in the realm of the conscious mind, the past will still dictate the future. Only by diving deeply into the innermost caverns of the mind, body, and soul will change happen in the most powerful part of the mind. I don't mean to say that the subconscious mind is bad. It's not bad; it's powerful. Anything so powerful that it controls 95 percent of your thoughts needs to be respected. Mastering the subconscious mind unlocks deeper levels of mastery in life.

Avoiding or ignoring the power of the subconscious mind eventually sabotages the conscious effort placed on life transformation. The body shows telltale signs of the unresolved inner world, and the fruits of whatever seeds are being sown in the subconscious mind will eventually materialize. This pattern can be surprisingly hard to identify, though. Most people, myself included, pop around from one interaction to another, hoping that things will get better and that this next chance will be their big break. In a chaotic frenzy for success, we are driven forward to the promise of a better day in the future. We deploy all the tools of modern-day self-help culture, spiritual wisdom, and life coaching, while we remain essentially caught in the same old cycle—that is, until the cycle reaches a crescendo and explodes or, perhaps more correctly, implodes on itself.

I was an angry yogi, and I didn't even realize it. While I projected an aura of positivity and happiness on the surface, I was angry deep down inside. What's more, the culture with which I surrounded myself revolved around a fundamental rejection of anger. All my rage was repressed, and when it came out, it did so in volcano-like explosions that had drastic repercussions on me, my livelihood, and the people around me. Anger festered, turned to hate, and twisted into balls of self-directed negativity and bitterness toward the world. This was the knot at the center of my being, one so deeply held and tightly wound that it had defined nearly every moment of my life. The most shocking thing was that I didn't even realize it was there. Sure, there were signs; I can look back now and see how they pointed to the existence of this central tension at the core of my sense of self. Nothing I did—no spiritual practice, no list of positive affirmations, no amount of material success, and no amount of external love or validation—would ever bring me lasting joy until I dealt with and faced this fundamental issue buried deep within me.

Fuel for the Fire

When I first embarked on the spiritual path, some teachers promised liberation through an unconventional path. Instead of working to train the subconscious mind, the teaching was the opposite. These teachers encouraged their students to have whatever they were attracted to. The only way out of desire, they said, was to fully give oneself over to it and exhaust the impulse. People who follow this immersion-oriented pursuit will go as deeply into a desire as the desire takes them. For example, if individuals are obsessed with chocolate cake, then they are directed to have so much chocolate cake that, one day, they will be so full, so sick of chocolate cake that whatever knot initially tied them to that particular desire will break.

When I first encountered this teaching, it felt too good to be true. In fact, it might just be too good to be true. The tricky side about allowing passion to drive life is that it is likely to lead to only more desire and intoxication. Few people will pursue the teaching to its full end of dissolution of desire. It's one thing if it's chocolate cake, but if the pattern is something more injurious, then it can be problematic. Imagine allowing all emotions to run full force. Being triggered already feels like an emotional hijacking, whether passion, anger, depression, rage, or anxiety. Neuroscience already shows that the more an emotion is felt, the easier it is to feel that emotion. Intense emotions are like drugs that pull even the most dedicated spiritual practitioners into a maze; many enter and lose themselves in it. Throwing away all the rules might seem seductive, especially to those who tend toward extremes, but in my experience, the middle path has the most wisdom to lead us out of the jungle. In order to integrate all the disparate parts of the self, sitting with what arises is more humble but perhaps more effective than lashing out or lashing in.

The more an emotion is felt, the easier it is to feel that emotion. Each time the charge of an emotion courses down a neural pathway in the brain, that pathway deepens, like a groove. Neuroscientist Donald Hebb said that neurons that fire together wire together. Not only does the pattern of feeling a particular way get more familiar each time an emotion is experienced, but the body's biology becomes hardwired to accommodate the behavior and to hunger for it in the future.

Some emotions have such a powerful charge that they are addictive. Adrenaline courses through the body and inflates one's sense of self. Anger, for example, is addictive. The more a person gets angry, the easier it is to get angry. Outrage generates more outrage. The body, once acclimated and accustomed to the high of anger, will actively search for the next excuse to blow up.

While repressed anger isn't the answer, neither is actively practicing anger on a regular basis. Just like any addiction, outrage addiction sets the stage for an even greater explosion in the future. The ball of energy at the root of anger never gets truly processed. Instead, the root gets fuel for the fire. If honoring rage simply means reacting to it by spewing and vomiting angry thoughts outward, then, unfortunately, there is a misconception of what it means to honor a feeling. The feeling called anger is not something outside of oneself. When the first reaction to the presence of the feeling of anger is to send it outward, there is actually very little acceptance of the feeling within. If the actual sensory reality of anger leads only to generating fuel for outrage, that essentially throws the feeling out like garbage into the world. Much online outrage is essentially throwing anger around from one side to the other, trolling for the next high. This pattern is not liberating consciousness. This pattern is intimately connected to the drama triangle and engenders more oppression and suffering.

So what to do, then? Instead of denial or acting out, there is a more subtle training that can teach the body and mind to sit and be present with the sensation that is at the root of anger. Once the energy of anger is neither repressed nor fueled, that energy will cycle through the body and become whole. Tension in one area of the body might migrate to other parts of the body before it finally integrates. There may be heat, discomfort, tingling, or a host of other sensations. If these feelings and sensations are allowed to run their course without any acts of denial or reaction, then, eventually, the energy will run its course.

When the seed of anger is activated, the central nervous system can get hijacked. In the throes of anger, a person is no longer of sound mind. Instead, the neurological state of the fight-flight-freeze response runs the show. Action taken while in the heat of that cycle adds more fuel to the fire. Depending on how the fires have been fueled, the emotion may need numerous cycles to calm down. It will eventually calm down, as long as no more fuel is added to the triggering thoughts.

A good strategy for interrupting triggered anger is to disengage. Do anything that gives some space—go for a walk, watch a funny movie, listen to relaxing music, practice yoga, meditate, journal, do some gardening, cook an interesting meal, clean the house. Let the activity be focused enough that it breaks the repetitive cycle of thinking and involves some change in the physical and emotional state. It is hard to walk away from a heated argument because the body's biology is gearing up for a confrontation. Pressing pause is different from what is called *spiritual bypass*, a concept we will discuss in chapter 11. Pressing pause does not gloss over the inner conflict. Instead, pressing pause allows the emotional hijacking to calm down and waits for clarity to return. Then, once the emotional dysregulation returns to a more coherent state, it is possible to reengage and continue the dialogue.

There is a tenuous line to walk between repression, acting out, and true processing. Action taken in a heightened state of arousal has been documented as less than ideal. Words spoken in the heat of the moment are often not what we truly mean, once the emotions of anger have been cleared. But if anger isn't allowed to cycle, it will eventually curl back up into a ball of repression and wait for another chance to arise from dormancy. This destructive cycle of either lashing out or repressing creates harm in every direction. When the cycle of anger is in full force and the action taken is either repression or acting out, those repetitive actions create an addictive pull that generates more of the same behavior, even if the conscious mind claims to want peace.

The direction I have received in my yoga and meditation practice has always led me toward a path of full embodiment. For me, the spiritual path is about feeling everything; not always acting on all that is felt but always feeling everything—the light and the shadow, the yin and the yang.

There is an intelligence in rage that must be honored. When I was uncomfortable with my own anger, I was also uncomfortable with other people's anger. When someone else was angry, I did not know how to act or react. All I wanted to do was jump in and diffuse their bomb. But that creates codependency and deprives the person who is angry of the right to process and feel his or her own emotions. There was anger within me that I hadn't dealt with. Raw, unprocessed anger has a kind of magnetic power. There is a dark, seductive mystery around the animal nature of pain. Understanding this is crucial to integrating the lessons of anger into the spiritual path. There were times, despite my conscious mind being committed to peace, when I would act out, lash out, or otherwise act in anger. While appearing powerful for a moment, these actions were not actually true sources of power for me. Screaming in rage at someone is only a temporary way to feel powerful, whether that involves raising one's voice or writing comments online. Once I agreed to step onto the battlefield, all victory was lost. There is no real vindication for acts committed in hate;

at least, there wasn't for me. Hurt, separation, and pain are the results of actions committed in hate. Even the victor loses in a war of the mind. Once the chemical high created by intense emotions fades, what remains are the broken pieces of the heart to put back together and start again. What's more, there is a residual craving for anger, created by the vacuum left in the rubble.

Remember, anger is not the culprit. Anger is as valid as joy and bliss. Destructive actions are something else. No emotion lasts forever. When anger arises, the teaching is simple: return to the breath and body. Don't repress or suppress. Just be with it. Like waiting out a storm. Sooner or later, the sky clears, the rain stops, and there may even be a rainbow. Every emotion can be a powerful teacher but only if we truly understand how to work with, process, and be present with all our sensations.

The question for spiritual practitioners is not how to remove anger but how to process anger and truly act in love. The task at hand is teaching about how to feel everything and not throw it out or repress it. The operating system of the mind is predisposed to war. Updating the system breaks the cycle of addiction to repressed emotions and charts a course toward freedom. The meditation technique presented at the end of this chapter is a tool that can be deployed whenever a trigger arises. Embodying and feeling emotions as pure energy helps give space to whatever emotion is present to run its cycle within the body. The journey is toward embodiment and out of repression. More importantly, the technique teaches how to insert a pause between the triggering incident and any action that might be taken. Just integrating this one teaching has the power to change so much in life. It changed mine.

Yogi Case Studies in Anger

A student of mine named Carol arrived at one of my classes, distraught and nearly in tears. At first, I thought something really tragic had happened, but then, once she started speaking, I realized that her distress was over a parking spot. While parking and road rage can be really annoying, it is a lesser difficulty in the big picture of things that can go wrong in life. No one died, no limbs were lost, and, in this case, no one even yelled at one another. It was just stressful and triggering.

After a long day, Carol wanted to meditate as the sun set before coming to an evening yoga class. She arrived at the parking lot with what she thought was ample time to get a spot, but after thirty minutes of idling, she said it seemed like no spot would ever open for her. To make matters worse, she missed a few open spots that other people seemed to swoop in and get. She looked at a van and thought it might leave; instead of trusting her instinct, she passed the spot to put herself in what she thought was a better position. As it turned out, a man walked out to the van to vacate the spot, but when Carol circled back to get the spot, another car already was in place. Moved by a sense of proprietary ownership of the spot, growing impatience, and worry that she wouldn't get a spot in time to meditate and make the class, Carol decided to plead her case to the other driver. She got out of the car and said she'd been waiting for a long time. But the man was not having it; he said that it was his spot, and he wouldn't move. She had no choice but to drive away.

What happened next was interesting. Triggered and trembling, Carol was overwhelmed with rage. All her old stories of failure were activated. At first, she directed her rage toward the man who wouldn't give her the spot. She felt like this wasn't fair, that it was her spot. With her mind racing, negative thoughts proliferated until she was caught in a spiral of blame. She asked herself why she couldn't have just followed her instinct and stayed in a better place. She also couldn't believe she had confronted another driver about a parking spot. Then, just as she was beating herself up, she found a spot. But her emotions did not settle. Even though she found another spot and was able to get to the sunset and meditate before class, Carol still arrived triggered and filled with rage.

Carol and I had talked about her anger before because it had come up in yoga class a few times. So when she arrived at class, displaying all the signs of anger, it seemed like a sign to dig in a bit more. Carol wanted to complain and launch into a rant about how life was unfair. Instead, I directed Carol to breathe and feel her body. I asked her to validate her feelings and what was arising in the body, while being brave enough to just sit with it and not need it to go away. Once she was able to feel and accept her own rage, things shifted. First, she felt the anger as energy and watched it move through her body. It seemed to start around her hands and shoulders and then ball up when she tried to deny it or judge herself. But when she just watched and allowed the energy, it moved down through her legs and swirled around her head. After a few cycles, it was gone. Instead of seeing it as a failure, a stroke of insight arrived. Whereas in the past, she always felt like the universe had everyone else's back but not hers, this incident showed her that the universe *was* looking out for her. Not only did she get confirmation that her intuition was spot on (the car she thought would leave *did* leave), but when she appeared to have lost out on the spot of her dreams, another one immediately opened up. She suddenly saw how she was both guided and blessed. When this thought arose, she breathed a sigh of relief. She could forgive herself for speaking to the other driver. She saw her response in a new light. While Carol did engage with him, she wasn't angry and didn't raise her voice, and she let go of what wasn't hers.

While it might seem like a trivial incident, these small moments of success and failure in the emotional realm build up. Thoughts multiply easily, and the mind can be caught in a spin, faster than we realize. Carol's process took just a few hours, but it is also possible that a process like this could take a few years. In between the triggering moment and the long, deep sigh of relief that signals a return to home, we are often caught in a trance, frozen and locked in old patterns. The tools of the spiritual path teach and guide practitioners to shorten the time between the trigger and the relief.

Anger in Relationship

Nonviolence often requires more courage than violence. Anger, as a pattern, is easy to learn and hard to break. Anger in intimate relationships requires double the effort because two people bring two sets of patterning to the table. Romantic love brings out the best and the worst in us. Anger, aggression, and violence build with the inertia of two parties whose emotional high fuels the storm with double the power. From a neurobiological level, the molecules of anger cue up a temporary high, followed by a low to which both parties can become addicted.

Anger in intimate relationships breeds a particular type of abusive pattern that often generates real harm, whether psychological or physical. Chris and Lisa were a married couple who were committed to their daily practice of yoga, meditation, and personal growth work. Chris was a mechanic and Lisa was an insurance agent, and they came to me as yoga students during a particularly difficult period of their lives. Despite their shared values of nonviolence and their regular practice of both yoga and meditation, their marriage was brutally abusive. While they never engaged in acts of physical violence, their arguments were verbally abusive and regularly crossed the line into unchecked rage. In the midst of a heated argument, neighbors called the police out of fear of domestic violence. The more they argued, the more they argued. Both held tightly to their positions, and neither was willing to back down. Anger, in this case, only led to more anger.

Lisa approached me one day after class and asked how yoga could help them heal. Committed to one another and to their yoga practice, Lisa told me that in the most heated moments of their arguments, neither of them cared whether their words hurt the other or if their actions were in alignment with their moral code. They only cared about being right and making the other pay. But since both were spiritual practitioners, they held deep shame about the tumultuous nature of their relationship. They both felt like failures and, while they were not immediately able to see it, they equally bore the responsibility for their pain.

I shared with Lisa that the anger cycle was a pattern and that there was a way out. She was committed but didn't know where to start. Yoga, in this case, was not enough. In order to heal their broken marriage and break the pattern of anger, Chris and Lisa found a cognitive behavior therapist who helped them navigate the destructive pattern of anger and abuse. They both recommitted themselves to the spiritual ideas that were important to them. Healing the negative cycle was not an easy task, but they kept at it, and they kept practicing yoga. Over the course of a few months, I saw a change in their demeanor. Their process was not easy, but through regular therapy sessions and guidance in empathy and compassion, they broke their cycle of negativity and returned to the love that had brought them together. They changed their mode of operation from fear and hurt to love and compassion. Thanks to the discipline of their spiritual practice and the help of a good therapist, they slowly shifted the dynamic of their relationship back to being an act of love.

Buddhist meditation teacher Tara Brach says that once you experience an emotional high like anger, the pathways in the brain that lead to that emotional state not only open but actively search for the next chance to fire. Yet angry speech and lashing out in the midst of an argument with your spouse will almost certainly lead to regret later. Shame, blame, and guilt get planted in the heart, and the anger cycle repeats, in search of a new high and temporary relief from discomfort.

Two long-term students of mine, Lenny and Sam, seemed like they lived in a perfect relationship. From the outside, everything looked great, but on the inside, there was another reality. While Lenny appeared to be happy and easygoing, he was quite critical and had a hard time managing his anger. While Sam appeared to be successful and even fearless in a professional capacity, he was not nearly as confident as he appeared.

I first noticed this behavior while the couple was on retreat. One day, I walked down to the yoga space after class to pick up a sweatshirt I left behind. There, I found "easygoing" Lenny yelling at Sam, and Sam profusely and tearfully apologizing. While I'm not a relationship counselor, when they both saw me there, something must have clicked because they both looked at me and said, "We have a problem." I directed them to seek help from trained psychologists, and they did. Once their treatment was over, they shared their epiphanies with me.

Lenny's angry outbursts provided both the seeds of negative growth and traumatic experiences for Sam. Due to his commitment to personal growth, Sam was able to grow from these troubling experiences in many ways. But in one way, Sam's growth was always stifled. He wasn't able to share negative feedback with his partner, and he felt both uncomfortable and disrespected by Lenny's anger. Whenever Sam brought up even the slightest negative thing, Lenny's anger took over and flipped the argument back to Sam. After years of this type of behavior, Sam not only stopped sharing the negative, but he also adapted a coping behavior that deprived him of freedom. Sam no longer shared the constructive criticism needed for his partner's growth, which deprived them both of a relationship between equals. All the while, he internally blamed Lenny for his anger. Sam apologized at the first indication that his partner was angry. He did this before he even reflected and considered what was wrong. This apology was false and controlling. He assumed responsibility for his partner's emotional balance and created an unhealthy codependency that locked them both into cycles of negative growth.

In order to break free so that both could flourish, Sam needed to adopt a new behavior and to set a firm boundary with Lenny. In order to do so, Sam needed to learn to get comfortable with anger—both his own and his partner's. Sam needed to make peace with the crouching tiger within himself so that he could make peace with the crouching tiger within us all.

With the help of a therapist, Sam learned how to process his anger and share negative feedback with his partner. More importantly, Sam finally stopped trying to process Lenny's anger. When Lenny was angry, Sam learned how to sit with his own discomfort and let Lenny be angry without needing to solve it. Lenny learned how to sit with his own anger instead of lashing out. Lenny also learned how to listen and be more respectful of Sam's boundaries.

They both continue to practice yoga today and share a life together. I was so grateful to be a part of their learning experience.

Yoga teachers often say that they see themselves in their students. I can certainly see myself in Sam's behavior. For years, I would immediately apologize and assume responsibility for things that weren't my fault, just to make someone else's anger go away. Since I was not in touch with my own anger in a balanced way, I feared the volcanic explosions that I instinctively knew were lurking just below the surface in many situations. I traded my own self-respect, just to end a perceived conflict. I share this with you so that you understand that I'm a fellow traveler on the spiritual path, just like you. I still get triggered by all sorts of things. I still get angry. The difference now is that my triggers do not operate in a world based on fear or separation.

The False Apology

Sam and I shared the tendency to be uncomfortable with anger and to use the maladaptive coping strategy of apologizing to make the problem go away. I call this behavior the false apology. It appears to keep the peace, but it sets up all parties involved for a downward spiral. Behavioral psychologist Marc Cordon teaches that positive or negative growth can happen after both ecstatic or traumatic experiences. This is important because arguments between couples can register as traumatic incidents, as it did for Sam. If one party in a relationship is unwilling to allow the other to experience his or her own pain, then that party deprives the partner of necessary steps needed for growth. In the end, both parties end up languishing, and the relationship lacks the depth of intimacy that is its true potential. Anger is the core passion that gets stifled. What happens after an intense experience has the potential to spark change, positive or negative. But if intensity is kept at bay and is artificially controlled, then growth is limited. It requires courage to be honest and share negative feedback with someone who has a temper. It can be even harder to be around someone who flies off the handle at apparently random times. But the only way that persons with an anger problem will ever face it is if they are left to experience the ramifications of their own actions. In the false-apology scenario, the person being yelled at apologizes for the aggressor's actions and assumes responsibility for restoring the peace. However, the price that is paid will be both self-respect and authenticity.

In order to create a meaningful life, Cordon teaches that we need a mixture between purpose (eudemonia) and fun (hedonia). If a person pursues only temporary hits of pleasure, his or her life will become hollow and lack depth. If a person is too driven with purpose, he or she will miss the joy and spontaneity of life. In the case of a relationship with a false-apology codependency at play, it is unlikely that either party will find true fulfillment together. They may distract themselves with play here and there or pursue goals together, but if their fundamental power dynamic is left unresolved, both parties will end up seeking their moments of flourishing outside the relationship.

Many people have a false-apology pattern. For children of addicts or victims of abuse, it can be all too easy to assume responsibility for the emotional well-being of others. The world is filled with many peacekeepers who bite their tongues and hold back from saying what is truly on their minds. This is a disservice to both the world and the upward potential of growth that is possible, both individually and globally.

Here is a set of guidelines that helps me whenever a triggering situation arises and I feel the urge to immediately apologize. Press pause. Take no action; make no statements until there is time to reflect on what is going on. It's OK not to act immediately. Ask questions, listen with an open heart, and tune in to how the body is feeling. After a period of contemplation, if there is something to apologize for, then offer a heartfelt apology. If not, then simply sit with the discomfort of the situation.

Take time to search for a true apology. An apology is an admission of guilt. If the only apology that can be mustered sounds something like, "I'm sorry that you're upset," what actually gets expressed is closer to pity than a true apology. True apologies begin with "I'm sorry that I did ____"; express both remorse and the desire to change.

Navigating the space of anger means getting comfortable with discomfort. We are only ever truly responsible for our own actions, yet we bear the impact of our actions on the world, at least to a certain extent. It's tempting to alter oneself in an effort to appease others, yet that leads to inauthenticity. Instead, it is always possible to listen without taking any action or making any statements. Just listening without defending or reacting can be enough.

Someone else's bad mood is no one's responsibility. Just because someone is angry or upset doesn't necessarily mean that anyone else has done something wrong or that fixing the aggravating circumstance will make the other person happy. Anger belongs to the person who is angry, and only that person can truly solve and work with his or her own emotions in a way that is constructive. No matter how righteous a claim someone else's anger is, that person's emotional reality can only be handled by him or her. If there is an urge to apologize and diffuse someone's anger, which may not necessarily be the path that leads to the most spiritual growth for all. Instead, anger can sometimes be a powerful fuel that needs to burn inside someone for a good while to spark a course of action. Being present to anger may bring up insightful moments of self-reflection that lead to a true apology, but emotions have to be processed by the person who feels them. Taking on emotional labor and processing other people's emotions can lead to codependency and other less healthy mental states.

Love Our Enemies

Anger is one thing; hate is another. The decision to hate is the total rejection of a common bond. Hate designates a person as an enemy and normalizes violence. Anger can sometimes be an expression of love. When hate drives action, the battle is lost before it begins. When anger is present, there may still be a path to love. Anger and hate live close to each other but have key differences. Both emotional states multiply. Anger, if left unchecked, leads to hate. Rather than harming the one who is hated, hate harms the one who is hating. The object of hate, whatever it is, has power over the one who is hating.

Hate sucks a great deal of energy out of things. Hate is maintained with a high level of attentiveness; it constantly needs to be reactivated or it will wither away. Hate requires regular feeding cycles to sustain itself. All emotions have a shelf life, after which they will dissipate unless they get new energy. For anger to turn to hate requires a constant influx of thoughts and experiences. Unfortunately, we live in a highly polarized world right now, where the center is unpopulated, and opinions and beliefs easily become moral absolutes that function as litmus tests. In hate-fueled exclusionary thinking, beliefs are just one slippery step away from actions that seek to eradicate other people who do not fit the mold. When everyone who doesn't think or act a certain way gets canceled, unfollowed, or banned, the echo chamber created fosters even more extremism. Soon, everyone who thinks differently is an enemy. Dividing the world along lines of friends and enemies, followers and unfollowers, or us and them is so far away from everything I understand to be the heart of the spiritual path. If it's about loving all beings, then that has to include the ones labeled as enemies—those we would want to block, cancel, ban, exclude, or silence.

One of the most revolutionary spiritual teachings of Jesus Christ is his instruction to love our enemies. While this may sound either impossible or like a spiritual bypass, this one teaching from the Christian tradition has the power to change all of our lives. Christ suggested that working to foster love for one's enemies breaks the cycle of hate. Since hate itself is a chain, loving one's enemies is freedom from hate. Plus, the one who loves is the one who actually has the power, whereas the one who hates is locked in by hate. The decision to love instead of hate is all about personal freedom.

Jesus tells his disciples not to "resist an evil person" and to turn the other cheek if they're slapped (Matthew 5:39 NIV). He continues, "If anyone forces you to go one mile, go with them two miles" (Matthew 5:41 NIV). And then, Jesus says, "But I tell you, love your enemies and pray for those who persecute you" (Matthew 5:44 NIV). The sun, he says, shines on all equally, and the spiritual path of Christlike discipleship aims to embody the love of all.

The reality is that most people have no idea how to love their enemies. I certainly didn't. Most people are unwilling to admit that they harbor hatred or ill will toward another. Yet the path to love from hate must start with acknowledgement of the hate that is currently harbored within. Truth is the beginning of any spiritual journey. Acknowledging that rage, hate, and anger lives within one's own heart allows light to shine into the inner darkness.

Along my own journey, I had to be brutally honest with myself about the degree to which these fiery emotions ruled my inner world, especially the subconscious inner world. I only considered trying to love my enemies as a last resort, when hating them actually failed. Learning how to love an enemy is the most magical alchemy of the spiritual path, the process of transmuting the energy of hate into love. Like all energy, things can shift, but this process must be done from an awakened heart, one that sees clearly and is willing to move deeply into the reality of anger and rage. Simply giving lip service to the idea of loving one's enemies turns the heart into a place of denial or repression. If love is only superficial, then statements of love will further deepen the false delusion of peace that keeps misery in place. The second meditation given at the end of this chapter is an introduction to the incarnation of love as an antidote to hate. It is a way through—not around or out but straight into the heart. Sending love to one's enemies can sometimes be triggering, so proceed with awareness and sensitivity. Love breaks the chain of hate, liberates one's own heart, and leads seekers farther down the path of Christlike awakening.

Other spiritual paths offer a similar message. Buddhist teacher Jack Kornfield says,

> The opposite of aggression is not passivity, it is true strength. When we have lost a sense of our innate nobility, we mistakenly believe in fear and weakness. We try to be strong through hate and aggression. When we release aggression, we discover true strength, a natural fearlessness, the courage to face our griefs and fears, and to respond without hate. (Kornfield 1993, 218–219)

Maintaining an ability to love fully, despite the ups and downs of life, is what yoga is about to me. It's easy to be wide-eyed and filled with wonder when everything is easy, before life has had its chance to beat you down. But to stay innocent, open, and free, even after the heart has been broken and dreams haven't come true—well, that's something else entirely. Yoga is a path of awakening, a rebellion against the chains of the mind that bind the heart. The spiritual path is an inner revolution that has the power to change the world.

I don't ever want to live in a world that is beyond hope. I don't ever want to stop believing in the dream of love as the most powerful force in the universe. In the story of my life, I will always hold on to the idea that if it's not OK yet, it's not over yet. Yet I don't believe we will always be happy and cheerful, that no more tears will ever be shed. We will be angry, hurt, disappointed, heartbroken, divided, and ready to fight. This will all happen. Yet I have faith—faith in basic goodness, an unwavering belief that the common ground that connects us outweighs the divisions that separate us. My faith only needs to be the size of a mustard seed to move the mountain of doubt.

It starts with a crack. In the darkest moments of life, amid even the most charged and heated arguments, there is a heart underneath that remains capable of love. There is always a path that leads back to the truth. There is a distant song playing in the background, like a call to prayer. This soulful music carries the tune of a long journey home. What opens the heart to the quest is the very resonance that brings the heart back into harmony with all that is. Love is the beginning, and love is also the end. The moment the heart starts searching for love, in some ways love has already been found. Love is the call, the music, and the hope.

1. Meditation One—Process Your Anger

Start with the breath and body, and allow yourself to sit for a few moments of mindfulness. Call up anger, or, if you're already triggered or angry, be aware of your anger. Locate the feeling of anger in your body. Be careful not to judge it. Just feel. Close your eyes. Let it process. Feel the texture, smell, and taste, and see the raw energy. Let it move through you. Notice if there is an epicenter, a knot or like a ball that surrounds the anger. Repeat this process as many times as needed. Ideally, stay for at least five minutes or possibly twenty to allow the full cycle of anger to process in your body.

2. Reflection

Count how many times you apologize or say *sorry* today. Notice if it's a habituated response or if there is truly something for you to apologize for.

3. Meditation Two—Love Your Enemies

Start off in a comfortable seated position, either on the floor or in a chair. Bring your attention to the breath and body, and allow yourself to sit for a few moments in mindful presence of the feeling of the incoming and outgoing breath and any sensations that arise in the body. Then, allow the heart to tap into an infinitely loving presence. It could be a parent, a teacher, or a spiritual figure such as Jesus, or it could be a more general feeling about the goodness of the universe. Feel the flow of unconditional love toward you, and steep in that for a few breaths. Next, call to your awareness someone you love dearly. Send that person unconditional love. Call to your awareness people in your outer circle, perhaps the people in your neighborhood. Send them unconditional love. Call to awareness all beings in the world, human and nonhuman, recognizing the same basic desire for happiness in all. Send all unconditional love. Finally, call to awareness someone with whom you have a grievance; someone you would consider as a source of evil. Recognize that this difficult person is just like you; this person is on his or her own path. Cover this person in unconditional love. If that is too challenging, then simply pray or send a blessing to this person to come out of his or her misery and for the seed of true spiritual realization to be awakened in his or her heart. Bring your mind back to your own heart. Sit with your breath, and feel the softening of your heart.

Chapter 7

Love Your Body

You can't hate yourself happy. You can't criticize yourself thin. You can't shame yourself worthy. Real change begins with self-love and self-care.

—Jessica Ortner

No one is born hating his or her body. It's a learned behavior. We pick up on social cues that sing a song of our unworthiness and then personalize the tune. We buy into the cultural story of one particular version of beauty, sold to us in images that are often far from our reality. We blame our bodies for not fitting the mold, and we internalize hate as deep self-rejection. The seed of body hatred manifests in different forms for us all, and it often shows up strongly when we are down and most vulnerable.

When feelings of loneliness and isolation dominate, it is hard to be satisfied with the image reflected in the mirror. Instead of seeing beauty, it's all too easy to see ugly. Instead of focusing on what works, the mind tends to focus on and exaggerate perceived flaws in a tragic kind of dysmorphia. There have been many times when so many of us, myself included, have looked in the mirror and rejected our own images. Each time we look at the image of the body and sit with disgust about what we see, it hurts. Each of these moments solidifies a narrative of self-hate. Operating in this paradigm, the body is not a friend; the body is an enemy to be vanquished. But the good news is that we're here now, and we are in the process of reprogramming the mind together. Speaking from experience, I can say that it *is* possible to learn how to be friends with your body. After years of hating my body, I learned how to love it, and I know we all can too.

The current framework of the body, written large in society, is rooted in self-hate and self-rejection, but it's starting to change—slowly. New norms are being established in every corner of the media and in every corner of the mind. I have written this book so that we can change the root from which the relation with the body springs forth. I am here to light the path of peace and show the way to befriend the body.

What Is a Body, and Why Do You Need One?

Our relationship with the body is the longest relationship any of us have here on earth. The body is with us from the first breath we take and stays with us until our very last breath. Even when we work against the body, it never stops working for the good. No matter how many times we yell at the body, get mad at the body, or hate the body, it never stops giving. There is no more reliable, steadfast friend than the body! If we treated a dog with the same disdain that many of us treat our bodies, even the most loyal dog would, sooner or later, skulk away.

No matter what size, shape, age, or color your body is, let's begin by understanding the vast intelligence and magnificence of the body itself. There is no other piece of machinery in the world that can simply be put to sleep, and it regenerates. If something is wrong with the body, the best thing to do is give it rest, and it will begin to work wonders. Whether the body is sick, injured, stressed, or otherwise hurt, resting the body triggers miraculous cycles of regeneration. Imagine if cars performed the same activity! When the check-engine light turned on, instead of bringing the car to a mechanic for service, we could simply put the car to sleep overnight, and then the next day, it would work again. Maybe one day, someone will invent a car that fixes itself while in sleep mode, but until then, we are bound to the auto repair shop.

The body, however, is in a league of its own. Each human being has a gifted piece of physical machinery, the likes of which not even the most brilliant scientists can understand or emulate. This collection of material substance works continually for the owner's service. Compared to the great benefit of having a body, there is very little required to take care of the body—eat, drink, sleep, move a little, clean a little, and expose the body to fresh air, and it will flourish. Not appreciating or understanding the great blessing that it is to have a body relegates these activities to just another laborious task that we'd rather avoid. Even worse, it is also possible to abuse the body or neglect these basic functions.

Even though each of us is incarnate, we are not our bodies. Each and every human being is not bound by the physical. Each human being is made of light and energy. While we do not need a body to live, we have a body while inhabiting this dimension of life. And that is a great blessing. Without the body, we would not be here on earth, nor would our thoughts and experiences be filtered through this field of mind and matter. Without the body, the spirit that each human being *is* would be only pure thought and energy, moving at a very rapid pace. The spirit without a body can be everywhere at all times, and there is no limit to the cycles of thoughts. Every living being is composed of the divine spirit. Without the body, the energy is free to roam wherever it may, and there is no division between a thought and its impact or actualization. That is both highly freeing and highly problematic. If thoughts are positive and joyful, then being in the realm of pure energy is blissful. But if thoughts are filled with hate and anger, then being in the realm of pure energy is torture. Having a body is a kind of field of experience. The mind without the body moves so rapidly that it is almost uncatchable. By incarnating in the physical form of the body, the mind and all its thoughts and emotions have to slow down and be processed in the very hard material substance that the body is. This is actually very useful for the work of the spiritual path. By slowing down the rapid-fire intangible cycles of thought and emotion, the body gives the spirit in the body a chance to actually experience which patterns are present. Embodiment is just that—the bringing into physical form the substance of the immaterial. Not only do we all experience physical sensations throughout the body, but thoughts, emotions, and the patterning of repetitive thoughts, emotions, and behaviors take root in the body.

For this reason and many others, the body is a great gift, best used as a learning tool in this classroom called earth. Without the body, none of us would be equipped to learn the lessons of this plane of existence. A spirit with a body is more powerful than a spirit without a body, not the other way around.

Whatever state of being practiced while embodied gets amplified when a spirit moves to a state without a body. Some of us spend vast amounts of time envying other people's bodies. We say, "Oh, if I just had this person's body, then I'd be happy." But none of us knows what it's like to be in another body. Each body has its issues, limitations, blessings, and gifts. We are not often aware of it, but we each have chosen, accepted, and been given this particular body because it is best equipped for the learning available to each of us in this particular cycle of life. This body that is present today, right here and now, is the perfect body for the lessons of this life. It contains all the hidden secrets that will best support the spiritual journey. This very body has within it the keys that will unlock all the mysteries of this very life. If the bodies could somehow be switched, journeys and life experiences would need to be switched as well.

The body is the vehicle for the journey of life. Just like driving on a road in a car, holding an antagonistic relationship with the body doesn't help. In the midst of a flood of anger and hatred, it is hard to navigate optimally. While it might be possible to exchange an old car for a new one, it's not possible to do that with the body. As such, it makes no sense to go on hating the only vehicle we have. The journey of life includes all the pain, suffering, illness, and injury. True depth appears on the dark side of the moon of consciousness. When anger, hatred, bitterness, and all other knots of negativity untie, only then will the line of sight be truly clear. The body is the reservoir for all the most private, deeply held thoughts. A crucial step for every seeker is the act of communion and harmony between body and mind, or spirit and incarnation, and that is what we are here to do.

Meet the Body

Most of my new students in yoga are body-foreign. I was body-foreign when I first started practicing yoga too. The feeling of foreignness is a feeling of not belonging. Many people feel estranged from their bodies for any number of reasons. Body awareness is not taught in schools. Instead, we spend hours learning grammar, mathematics, history, and other subjects. Biology is mostly intellectualized but rarely a lived experience. To know and become intimate with the body is something else entirely.

One of the main premises of yoga practice is the reintroduction of a relationship between body and mind. While some people see the intense poses and think that the goal of yoga is a handstand, the reality is that the poses are just tools to help yoga practitioners feel their bodies. When yoga requires students to feel their bodies in complex twists and folds, students develop what is called *kinesthetic intelligence*. Kinesthesia is a kind of knowledge derived directly from the body that includes an awareness of position and movement of body parts by means of the senses and proprioception in the muscles and joints. Yoga is, in many ways, a process of learning to speak the body's language. If we cannot speak the same language, we cannot communicate. The body's language is not held in words or thoughts but in the vast realm of sensation. To listen to the body is to learn how to feel.

When a person is body-foreign, there is no way to truly become acquainted with what the body needs, is capable of, and truly is. Worse yet is the combination of internalized self-criticism with estrangement. Few people naturally meet their bodies from a foundation of love and acceptance. It takes both unlearning and reeducation to come to a place where the foundational principle between the mind, heart, and body is love. Unless someone is a professionally trained athlete or is practiced in some other physical discipline, it is rare that any individual, prior to yoga or some other form of mind-body awareness practice, has put in the work required to truly meet the body. Even athletes, performers, and dancers, who may have "met" their bodies in a highly trained form, may not have learned to truly love their bodies. Using the body as a tool for performance is something other than truly meeting, loving, and accepting the body as the blessing that it is. Learning to be friends with the body requires walking together as friends, in the full scope of what friendship truly means. Becoming acquainted with and befriending the body is an act of love.

Scientist Barbara Fredrickson writes in *Love 2.0*:

> Self-love first requires safety and connection. Beating yourself up with the continual harshness of self-criticism is no way to make yourself feel safe in your own company. Likewise, if your self assessments are unflappably sunny, unhinged from reality, or otherwise blind to your ingrained bad habits, you can hardly feel safe either. A true friend, after all, is one who is the truth. (Fredrickson 2013, 137)

So many of us do not think much about the body unless something is wrong with it. Training in education in the Western world (North America and Europe) is geared toward training the mind—go to school, get a good job, pay your taxes. People walk around like large brains plopped on top of an annoying and cumbersome unit, charged with dragging the head around. The motions that comprise daily duties and responsibilities rarely leave time for subtly tuning in to the realm of the body. Yet if wholeness and liberation are part of the path, we will need to learn how to do exactly that.

A language that the body speaks is one of emotions and sensation. Unlike the mind, the body never lies. The pure, honest truth of the body's intelligence is always speaking. We, however, often are not listening. Not because we are bad or because we don't want to, but many people are not listening because of two things: we simply don't know how to speak the body's language, and we have been indoctrinated into a culture of body rejection.

Let's change that! The first step is unlearning the culture of body rejection. Then, once the armor of self-rejection that sits on the body and compresses or harms it falls away, we can begin the work of truly meeting the body and learning its beautiful language.

Unlearning Old Body Hate

A safari of stuffed animals sits on a floral bonanza bedspread. Madonna gives her sultry look from a worn-out poster on the wall. A young mixed-race girl sees her image in the mirror, reflected back to her from behind her bedroom door, and feels a sense of otherness. She wishes her thighs were thinner. She wishes she looked more like the models on the covers of magazines. But here she is, young and beautiful, already indoctrinated to the ways of self-hate.

That little girl was me and maybe was many of us, but I hope it won't be our daughters. For every moment I wasted on wishing my thighs were thinner, I hope the next generation of young people spend loving whatever size and shape their bodies are. Buying into the false equivalence of thinness with worthiness and beauty is an act of self-directed violence, inherited from a culture built on subjugation and oppression. Although I've spent over twenty years on a spiritual quest for liberation, the childhood obsession with thin thighs was not an easy habit to kick.

I never valued, loved, or appreciated my body. I was taught at a very young age that my mind was the key to my success. While I am quite intelligent, I find it a rather ironic turn of events that I am now a yoga teacher whose claim to fame is built, to a large degree, on my physique. I'm sharing my story with you because I have a feeling that maybe we all, to some degree, have been caught in a loop of self-hate or at least harsh judgment about our bodies.

There's probably at least one body part with which everyone has a difficult relationship. So many of us have looked at our bodies with critical or even hateful eyes. It might not be the legs. It might be hips, belly, nose, hair, or something else. Those rejected, unloved, and unwanted parts of our bodies offer the greatest opportunity for healing. In fact, choosing to love the body can be a kind of personal revolution. This very body, the one we have looked at with judgment or hatred and wished was something else, is the best friend, a door to liberation, a pathway to peace, and the way back home.

How we each think about the body really matters. When we think we're ugly, we plant seeds of unhappiness. A feedback loop happens when we look down and think we are not attractive. Sometimes the results are instantaneous, and sometimes they are delayed, but the results almost always manifest. Sometimes, it's just an uneasy feeling of discomfort in the skin. Other times, it could be an urge to look down and judge the body as flawed, over and over again. Worse, the impact could be a compulsion to escape those dark feelings by escaping, zoning out, or generally engaging in behavior that leads to the body feeling worse. Body hate is a destructive cycle that cannibalizes itself.

Here's a formula that shows how body hatred is a self-generating loop that builds negative inertia. Rejecting the body leads to feeling uncomfortable in one's own skin. Feeling uncomfortable in the body leads to actions taken to avoid sitting with the discomfort, such as overeating, using drugs, compulsive shopping, and other destructive behaviors. Engaging in these behaviors produces feelings of guilt, shame, and even more discomfort in the body. The increased feelings of discomfort prompt yet another cycle of escapism and addictive, uncontrollable behavior, which leads to feeling even worse and engaging in even more severe forms of self-loathing. This is a cycle that can be broken, but it requires great effort to break the inertia.

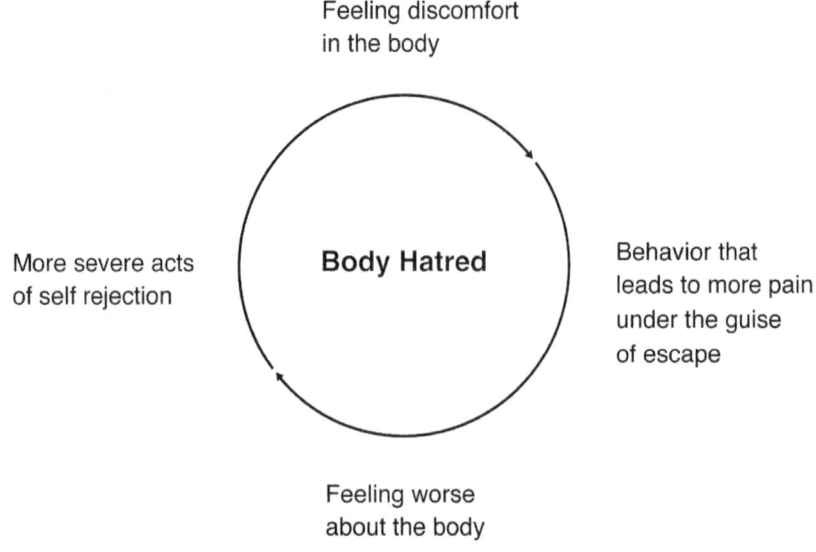

Feeling discomfort
in the body

Body Hatred

More severe acts
of self rejection

Behavior that
leads to more pain
under the guise
of escape

Feeling worse
about the body

Body hatred leads to feeling discomfort in the body. Feeling discomfort in the body increases the potential for behavior that leads to more pain under the guise of escape. The result of escapism, denial and defense is yet more body hatred, feeling even worse and more severe acts of conscious or subconscious self-rejection. There may be a brief pause until the cycle begins again and builds inertia.

I experienced this cycle one day during a meditation retreat. It was a cold autumn in the American Midwest, and the retreat center hadn't turned the heating on yet. Maybe the locals weren't cold, but I, being a native Floridian, was freezing. I put on a pair of thermal wool leggings, but the fabric wasn't very stretchy and was very itchy. That combination brought up a familiar feeling of wishing for thinner thighs. The leggings seemed too tight over my thighs, though loose at the waist and way too long. So when I got back to my room and pulled them off, I looked down and felt hatred toward my thighs. Instead of blaming the leggings for their ill-fitting design, I blamed my body for its shape and size. I said to myself, *fat thighs*, and I knew what it meant. That thought meant that I was unlovable, unworthy, ugly. Then, I changed my clothes and carried on with the day, ready for the next meditation sit.

During the next group sitting, I began to practice mindfulness, as instructed. Within a few moments of introspection, an itchy, creepy feeling crawled over my legs. I can only describe it as extreme discomfort. Since I was in a meditation retreat, I was able to remain equanimous and observe, instead of identifying and reacting, as usual. That's when it became clear to me that the self-directed negative thoughts were actually manifesting as feelings of discomfort in the very body part toward which I had sent hate. My thoughts were manifesting on my body. The more I hated my body, the worse it felt. The worse it felt, the more likely I was to engage in actions that would lead to more body hatred, such as compulsive eating or destructive behavior, like drug use. After those acts, I would feel even worse, increasing the likelihood of even greater acts of self-rejection and lowering the likelihood of good self-esteem. I had the unique chance to break the cycle of self-hate during that meditation retreat.

We all can apply this lesson in our lives today, even if we have never spent a minute in meditation. All it takes is a simple shift in awareness. Stop and observe the discomfort, instead of running from it. Healing cycles of body hatred is a little bit like weeding out a garden before planting something new. Old negative thoughts are like weeds growing in a garden. If a brand-new fruit free and a bed of roses are going to flourish, we will need to weed out what's taken root before we begin planting. If the new seeds are planted amid a bed of thorns and weeds, they won't grow or take root properly. I'm probably not the only person who has said to love the body. In order to truly love the body (and ourselves), we each will have to get real about the places where we hate the body (and ourselves). If not, then all those affirmations will only sink to a frustrating surface level and not penetrate deeply into the subconscious mind. Each of us can only heal and transform what we are strong enough to reveal in the light. What remains in darkness remains hidden from view, like the roots of weeds planted deep in the soil. Only once we see clearly the destructive pattern of our own negativity will we be in a good position to plant new thoughts.

Love is a feeling, a lived experience, more than a concept. There is a visceral response to being in love and being filled with love. The whole body relaxes with warmth and openings. The heart may actually expand, as though it is stretching out wide enough to embrace another being. There is a kind of magnetism that pulls us closer to those we love. To learn to live in love, we will have to become present to the cycle that prevents love from flourishing within. The journey of liberation starts with being willing to sit with and feel pain, without running away from it. Thoughts have a vibration; they are alive in the realm of the inner being. When there is a history of thinking negative thoughts, it is not as simple as just running positive thoughts. The precursor to positivity is processing and healing the patterns that have been rooted in the subconscious mind. Processing means being willing to feel it all first and choose a new reaction pattern without rejecting anything. Instead of avoiding, escalating, or zoning out, the learning is about how to choose the nurturing state of presence. This is the deepest work on the spiritual path, the kind of work that changes the habit pattern of the subconscious mind. What's more, it's a constant work in progress. To shift the mind requires discipline and vigilance, a daily discipline of love and devotion to slowly shift the status quo away from the reactionary patterns of the past and into a conscious place of wholeness. No one will execute this task perfectly. We will all slip and stumble, but that is part of the process. There is learning in failure too.

Love is also a skill that takes practice and action. If the goal is real, true self-love, don't expect to achieve it with a snap of the fingers and immediately bubble over with self-love. Instead, look for opportunities to practice self-love, and stay grounded in the reality of what truly is good (there's so much that is really, truly good!).

Someday, When

Pradeep, a US-born son of Indian immigrants, walked into a beginner's course on yoga I was leading in Miami. Yoga was part of his heritage, and he was familiar with the benefits. But he, like many interested people all over the world, didn't think he was ready to start practicing. With much hesitancy, Pradeep suggested that the course wasn't for him. In fact, he told me he had no intention of practicing that day, despite his appearance at our yoga center. Pradeep just wanted to meet me after seeing my videos online and get a sense of what I was all about. When I asked him why he didn't think he was ready to practice, he said that he was waiting to lose some weight before starting yoga. Well, I've heard that line before, and I encouraged him to get on the mat and just start. Without too much prodding, I convinced Pradeep to just get on the mat and try. A few years later, he's still practicing.

This type of thinking can be referred to as "someday when." It is the idea that the current state deems us unworthy of the wonderful activity that others find beneficial. So the answer is to say that we will do it someday when. Many people think that yoga is only for thin people, so they say that they'll start yoga someday, when they've finally lost those few extra pounds. These are incorrect assumptions. Yoga is not only for thin, able-bodied youngsters. Yoga is for everyone, no matter what size or shape you are. Very often, the people who can benefit the most from it are the ones who feel the least qualified.

"Someday when" pops up often in relation to body image. Diet culture sometimes centers around the mythical fairy tale ending, when all the weight is finally gone, and now we are ready for life. So many people will not allow themselves to do things they sincerely want to do because they are waiting for that someday when. This refrain might be all too familiar, as either we or a friend may have said, "Someday when I lose a little weight, I'll wear a bikini and go to the beach"; "Someday when I get a little thinner, I'll go shopping and buy a new outfit"; "Someday when I've dropped a few pounds, I'll start dating again."

Diet culture profits from feelings of unworthiness. In truth, dieting doesn't really work. Based on the notion that we are not good as we are, the diet mentality trains us to be on alert for bad behavior. Debunking the paradigm of dieting requires a radical shift in thoughts about the body and embodiment in general. The first step is dropping the thinking that achieving the perfect weight signals finally being good enough. Paradoxically, we have to start with the premise that we are good enough as we are. It may seem daunting to practice love and acceptance of things exactly as they are, but that's where the paradigm change begins. So much dieting is done as an act of hate, as a rejection of the body. In order to be free of the chains of that way of thinking, we need to start with a new thought—a thought rooted in love.

Diet culture is often the internalization of self-rejection. So many people live their lives ping-ponging from one diet to another. The diction and syntax used to speak about the body tells a story of deep self-loathing. Spoken in an unconscious trance of self-rejection, words tell a story of a body cast in the familiar terms of the animal world; that is, wild and unruly and needing to be tamed and trained to fit into a box. The phrases "thunder thighs," "elephant legs," and "tree stumps" are not any one person's creation. These comments, spoken casually, are internalized words of hate. All sizes and shapes of people participate in this dialogue of division; they spout the lies of body dysmorphia and, in doing so, codify the dialogue of misery in our bodies.

Many people make casual comments on other people's bodies, sometimes meant as a compliment: "You look so good; you lost weight. Good for you." While often well-meaning and benign in intent, comments like this often serve to codify the equivalence of thinness with beauty. Saying that individuals look good, now that they've lost weight, implies that they looked worse before, when they had a little more weight—the assumption being that thinner is better, prettier, more desirable. Weight-loss culture is never-ending. There are always a few more pounds that can be lost or a few more parts of the body that can be toned. The goalposts can always be shifted farther and farther away. Well-meaning intent does not erase the hurtful impact of casual comments. Instead, what is often expressed in these easy-breezy daily interactions are the subconscious patterns of a culture geared to reject a certain body type and to perpetuate a particular standard of beauty. To reject that and claim one's independence is to launch a revolution. Each comment from apparently innocent bystanders can feel like missiles launched from the enemy that threaten to destroy hard-earned intellectual and emotional freedom. Comments about size and shape, even ones that are meant as compliments, often register as micro-aggressions that codify a culture of privilege, subjugation, and discrimination. These concepts might be confusing or triggering, but hear me out.

What we talk about signifies what we value. When we comment on a person's size or shape in a way that prioritizes thinness, we glorify a mainstream aesthetic that has been spoon-fed to us from magazines, movies, and retailers. These images are emblazoned on our psyches as signs of a happy, successful life. We have been told a story that skinny, rich, and successful all go together. The obsession with thinness is part of the culture of *more*, which profits from the story that we are not good enough as we are. When comments and thinking operate within that universe, those words enable the people in charge to maintain their position of power. Yes, this may happen subconsciously. Yes, it may stem from an innocent intention to give someone a compliment. Yes, people might mean well.

No, not everyone who is enmeshed within the unconscious culture of bias is a bad person. Nevertheless, this is a wake-up call to join the revolution. Anyone engaged in the act of spiritual development is already a part of the critical mass of consciousness change that I hope will save the planet. I've written this book to bring the often-unspoken transformation that happens in the hearts and minds of spiritual practitioners on the leading edge of culture change to the forefront of the conscious mind. I'm counting on all of us to be willing to show up and do the work of deconstructing deeply held personal, cultural, and global assumptions about what it means to be happy, successful, and worthy of love. Ground zero for the next war of independence is the body—my body, your body, every body. Let's start by blowing up the false equivalence of thinness and beauty.

The time in my adult life when I was thinnest was after my father passed away. My dad was an epicurean, and he loved food. There wasn't anything he wouldn't eat and enjoy. After he died, I lost my appetite because whenever I saw food, particularly anything that might taste really good, I thought about how he wasn't there with me to enjoy it, and I couldn't eat. I lost a lot of weight. People made comments about how good I looked. I was grieving. Since my heart was heavy, and I lacked the social filter that a stable mind has, my reply was often brutally honest. I said, "Thanks, but I lost my appetite after my father passed away." There is no conversation-stopping comment more powerful than the death of a family member or loved one. When I said those words, people were visibly shocked. I didn't care at the time because I was grieving. But as I reflect on it now, I think that maybe what shocked them was not only the fact that my father had died but that my statement of simple truth also challenged the cultural assumption that thin is equal to happy. For me, thin meant sad, grieving, and unhealthy.

My body likes to carry just a little cushion. I'm healthier and stronger with a little bit of fatty tissue distributed around my thighs and midsection. If I starve myself to expose six-pack abs or get thinner thighs, all I'm doing is starving my body of nutrition and my heart of the happy feeling of enjoying time with friends. I've never been morbidly obese or even what one could call fat in my entire life. Yet I've lived with the fat phobia and the body dysmorphia that told me I was at risk of being fat if I ate normally.

Health, fitness, and beauty are used interchangeably but have very different meanings and implications. Many apparently well-meaning comments aimed toward bigger-bodied people are really fat phobia and thin privilege masquerading as health concerns. The truth is that we don't know why anyone is the size and shape they are. Comments about size, shape, weight loss or gain, or other related things are neither friendly nor welcome. I am kindly asking everyone reading this to refrain from commenting on anyone's physique, using the paradigm that weight loss is always good. Instead, change the operating system. Comment on how happy, healthy, or vibrant someone looks. Comment on how kind that person's heart is and what valuable contribution he or she may be making to the world. Leave the discussions about health to the doctor's office because we don't know what the circumstances are regarding anyone's weight or health situation.

Someone, somewhere—usually a large, multinational corporation—is profiting from self-rejection. It's the diet, exercise, fitness, fashion, and beauty industries that play up feelings of low self-esteem, only to sell the next fad. The stakes of self-rejection are higher for some groups in society than others. When the narrative of otherness is internalized by members of nondominant groups, it creates real damage to the souls of living beings. If one of us sees ugly in the mirror because we have never felt beautiful in the eyes of the mainstream, that's not our fault. The arbiters of culture sell a story that profits off our insecurity. The more we feel less-than, the more we buy products that pander to our desire to feel loved and to belong.

I don't know about anyone else, but personally speaking, as a human being who hasn't always fit the mold of mainstream iconography, I am ready to say, "No more of this." Maybe joy—real, embodied joy—is the revolution for which we have been waiting.

Find the Root

People are afraid that if they accept themselves with all their rolls and folds, wrinkles and stiffness, and pains and aches that they won't be motivated to change and evolve. The truth is more of a paradox than we think. Remember that the root bears its fruits, and sometimes it takes years to see the relationship between the root and its fruit. By making a radical decision to love and accept things as they are and to love and accept the body as it is, the root is changed, and in doing so, the fruit is also changed. Whether there are any changes in body weight is secondary to living a happy, healthy, and fulfilling life. Choosing health and vibrancy in a way that embraces our vital life essence is an individual path that each of us must find for ourselves. Not everyone's path to optimal health and vitality means fitting into a size 2. In fact, for most people, it won't. Size and shape are not indicative of a happy life. Instead, a heart filled with love for oneself and one's body is the way out of the cycle of body hatred.

Yes, we want to be healthy. Yes, we want to be attractive. This is not unreasonable. But when "healthy" becomes a mask for thinness and when there is a zero tolerance for fat, cellulite, or other all-too-human characteristics, our desire is not for a happy, healthy body but for something else entirely. What we are craving is not a balanced state of being. What we crave when we yearn to be something other than what we are is acceptance and love. Looking in the mirror and feeling less-than, we think that if we succeed at bending and molding the body into the right size or shape that we will finally be lovable and get the success we so desperately think we need.

Exercise can be a form of punishment and feed into fat phobia and thin privilege. We can come to our yoga mats, or put on running shoes, or hop on a bicycle for the sake of health, to burn calories, to tone the body, or a mix of purposes. The intention brought into the exercise routine determines what the result will be. Just as a seed determines what type of fruit will be born; the thought that drives the goal sets the tone for the outcome of one's actions.

If anger, self-rejection, or irresolution is the motivator to move the body, then that will color the result. But if peace, self-love, and health are the motivators, then the stage is set for an entirely different outcome. Negative emotions are inverted potential. Instead of leading toward flourishing, starting exercise with a punitive mindset fuels the cycle of low self-esteem. This hidden fact is the reason why so many people often fall out of their well-intended plans to "get healthy." Latent within the conscious desire for health is a cover-up for the old, familiar equivalence of thin and pretty or desirable. I speak not only for heterosexual women, but for all genders, including nonbinary. Men of all sexual orientations, nowadays more than ever, fall victim to the same body shaming tropes as do women of all sexual orientations. The farther away from the mainstream dominant notions of sexual orientation a body may be, the easier it is to hate the body and manifest that in unhealthy diet and exercise regimens or other more destructive actions.

When are we going to see it's not our bodies that are the problem but the hatred we carry within our hearts? Instead of the next new fad diet that hides eating disorders and body hatred, there has to be a wave to truly love and honor the bodies that we have. This is the work we are being asked to do today.

Unlearn Hate; Practice Acceptance

Feelings about the body and embodiment in general are learned behaviors. What we have learned, we can unlearn. There is a story for every scar, a birthmark for the new self, born from pain, rising up and healing. When we stop cowering in fear of rejection and stand up for who we are, then we can be proud of every scar, the mottled threads of which contain the magic of transformation, rebirth, and renewal. Let the body tell the love story that starts with looking in the mirror and saying, "Hey, beauty; hey, handsome. I see you shining back at me."

In order to access self-love on a daily basis, it is crucial to learn how to create a sense of safety within the body itself. Methodically divest from the old stories of self-hate and harshness, but keep your feet firmly planted in reality. I find it useful to avoid delusional self-deception and tell myself the truth about what is happening, even if it hurts. If I am willing to be authentic, vulnerable, and honest with myself and truly meet the being that I am, where I am, it all feels so much better. Honor and respect walk hand in hand with absolute unconditional love.

No human body is perfect. Even supermodels have what the system calls "imperfections." With Instagram filters and beautifying apps, everyone can airbrush their imperfections away. But what if, rather than hiding behind technology, we decided to love the scars, the cellulite, and anything else labeled as an imperfection? It takes effort not to fall for the industry built on selling the promise of a better version of now. Masquerading as diet, targeted fitness courses, the next shipment of our fave leggings, or a magic tummy tea, there is a daily onslaught of products designed to tap into subconscious self-rejection and self-hate. Putting our scars on full display is a defiant act of love, and it can ruffle some feathers.

If love is to unlock all the barriers, it has to start with a soulful embrace of the body. Flaunting insecurities instead of hiding them shows the world what humanity really is. Relentlessly embracing what *is* with a deep peace doesn't mean that we will never work for change. In fact, radically accepting what *is* lays the foundation for change to be an act of love.

We must learn to define beauty for ourselves. Do not drink the serum being sold for billions of dollars—that beauty is one-size-fits-all. Mainstream media often plays directly into the standard model of beauty. It's changing now, thanks to the active work of so many people who demand change from the largest companies in the world. Still, thin, mostly white, able-bodied cisgender men and women appear in so many ads. Their image is held up as the gold standard of achievement. Yoga and wellness have a particularly tricky relationship with imagery and profitability. One could argue that big business, owned by mostly white men in the United States, profiting off India's culture with the use of thin, able-bodied, white women is an act of cultural appropriation and neocolonialism. The yoga business relies so heavily on the wisdom of the East and needs to learn how to honor, not appropriate, India's cultural heritage. There's a kind of proprietary mindset at the heart of an industry that seeks to sell yoga practitioners clothes and products, based on the idea that they will gain access to a coveted aesthetic (or spiritual) realm of beauty when they can finally fit into the right size. Some big yoga brands don't even make sizes that fit the average American body type.

It's hard to love the body and see beauty when there aren't clothes that fit. Just because someone starts practicing yoga doesn't mean that he or she is immediately free from the same old cultural mythology. It is, after all, a practice, and we are all at different stages of our journey. It can sometimes be heartbreaking to realize how many acts of aggression we commit against our bodies every day. The hope lies in the idea that we can break free. We each matter, and we each have great power. Our freedom of mind could be seen as an assault on the powers that be. Love is a kind of inner rebellion. Sometimes it's loud and can be heard across the globe. But sometimes the rebellious act of love can be quiet and intentional, like learning how to truly care for the health of the body. Rather than chasing an impossible standard of thinness, acting in love toward the body means that every interaction with your body is rooted in love.

True love unlocks beauty. Something is beautiful because we love it. Even the most aesthetically pleasing object can be made ugly by use and context. Perhaps people become beautiful when we love them, not the other way around. We don't love people just because they are aesthetically beautiful. It is our love that illuminates the beauty within others.

The Body as Belonging

My grandfather was Japanese, and he spent the most time with me while both my parents worked. I was five years old before I remember meeting another Japanese person, when my grandfather's family came over to visit from Japan.

My mother, a Japanese American, grew up in a time when it wasn't trendy to be Japanese. In the post-WWII South, kids in school beat her up, called her names, and told her she was ugly. Teachers paraded her in front of classrooms to reinforce the Asian stereotype of top achiever (she was always at the top of her class). But years later, the remnants of systemic racism still live on. Sometimes, she tells me, she thinks to herself, *Maybe they were right.*

When I dyed my hair blonde for the first time, it unlocked something for me that I hadn't found before. I guess I looked less like an Asian American and more like the "average American girl" stereotyped by media outlets. The dominant culture fetishizes and normalizes Eurocentric definitions and images of beauty, and I always felt separate from that. But with my blonde hair, questions about my ethnicity no longer led every conversation. I felt like I stuck out less, and, truthfully, I was more accepted. Suddenly, I benefited from the dominant culture's narrative about being a member of the blonde world. A young, blonde, thin female appears to be worth more in men's eyes and maybe in other women's eyes too. Hair tells a story about who we are and where we belong. Changing the color of my hair was a way for me to try to fit in with conventional American stereotypes. Letting my roots grow out was a way for me to reject the mold that I made myself fit into.

Body is belonging. To reject the body is to reject oneself at such a deep and fundamental level that no true peace is possible until that knot is untied. We will be free to the degree that we have untied the knot of hate and learned to love the body with each and every act. A miraculous act happens when we transform the mundane into the sacred by loving, honoring, and accepting the truth of who we are. The body is not separate from the spiritual beings that we are. The body is deeply integrated as a manifestation of the infinite within each of us.

If the body has never been truly loved, honored, or appreciated for itself as itself, to do so feels foreign and awkward. Yet with practice, this too can become second nature. Just as it feels so easy to criticize, words of forgiveness and love can come to replace that old, negative inner dialogue. The paradigm can be shifted from one of hate to love, and, in doing so, all boundaries and limitations to awakening the full human potential can be transcended.

Meditation

Start off with a few moments of mindfulness by bringing your attention to your breath and drawing your mind into the body. Scan through the body, starting at the top of the head. At each point of contact, say the words, "Hello, my body; nice to meet you." Once you get down to the tips of your toes, scan back up, and say the words, "Hello, my body; I love you." Hold your attention at your heart center; feel your breath moving in and out. Say the words, "May I love, honor, and accept myself fully. May I love, honor, and accept my body fully." Repeat three times and as needed, perhaps daily, until it rings true in the fibers of your soul.

✳

Chapter 8

Rewiring Your Mind for Work

It is easier for a camel to go through the eye of a needle
than for a rich person to enter the kingdom of God.
—Mark 10:25 (NLV)

Think of how much time, in every twenty-four hours, is spent doing things related to work. Whether commuting to and from work, working more than one job, thinking incessantly about work, failing to fully unplug when finally done for the day, or working far more than the standard eight hours a day, work and all that is done in service of work occupies perhaps the greatest percentage of the average human day. In some ways, it could be argued that many human beings worship their work. This is not to critique the obsessions with work; individual priorities are something each of us must decide for ourselves. Instead, work and the business associated with it offer a unique platform to assess and potentially reprogram some of our most entrenched beliefs.

Since work requires dedication, discipline, and effort, sustained over long periods, the patterns installed in the hardwiring of the brain carve deeply through the neurological pathways. The sheer repetition in which each of us engages when involved with work illustrates just how habitual the entire activity really is. Neuropsychologist Rich Hanson reports that one-third of what he calls *inner strengths*, which are positive traits hardwired into the biology of the brain, are genetic, whereas the other two-thirds are learned behaviors (2016, 6). Reassessing the underlying pattern of how and why we work may be so impactful that it may radically change the foundation of one's life, especially for workaholics, whose lives seem to revolve around work.

Labors of Love

The best work brings purpose and meaning and is not done simply to maximize profit or pay the bills. The best work is a true labor of love. When work is passion, done through actions rooted in values and integrity, work expresses the highest potential of the human spirit. On the other hand, toiling away at a job that one finds meaningless or, worse, is misaligned with one's values can be deflating and depressing. In an increasingly capitalist world, where it can sometimes feel like the world of work is a competition to the top, to reconnect to one's work as an act of love may feel naive and overly idealistic. Who, it might be asked, really loves being a plumber or a grocery clerk? Some people think that loving one's work is a domain for the privileged, and few get to live out their passions with financial freedom.

I am not going to say that the magic trick is saying a few affirmations every day, and then someone will knock on the door, offering up a dream job. That's probably not going to happen. There is a way, however, to change our thinking about how we work and where our purpose is found in what we do. The first thing to address is a type of thinking based on the idea that there is a finite amount of success out there and that if we don't fight, claw, and do whatever it takes to step on the other people vying for the same position, we won't succeed.

Whenever actions are based on the idea that only a limited number of successful opportunities are available and only to a select few, this type of thinking can be referred to as a *scarcity mindset*. Operating from a scarcity mindset frames life as a game of survival, where every living being is competing against one another. This type of thinking assumes that there is a set number of resources, and it encourages competition as a basic mode of conduct. After all, if there are only a few spots at the top, allocated to a small select group, then, at least on one level, it makes sense to push, fight, and battle to get there. The story of the self-made millionaire as the hero of rugged capitalism perpetuates the idea that life is a zero-sum game. Many people think that if you don't get out there and claim your prize, someone else will.

Operating from the paradigm of scarcity is a recipe for feelings of loneliness, jealousy, unworthiness, insatiable desire, and guilt. Scarcity mindset exacerbates the gap between the rich and the poor, prevents charity and generosity, and prioritizes short-term personal gain over the long-term good for all. There is, however, another path. But before we get there, let's take a look at some of the ways that scarcity mindset shows up.

Spiritual Poverty

My husband and I ran into an old yoga teacher friend one day named Daniel. He trained with us in India, but we hadn't seen him for a very long time. We were walking along a popular shopping street in Miami Beach, where we live, and Daniel drove by in a big, fancy, new BMW sports-utility vehicle. Waving at us from behind the shiny door of his eye-catching car, his initial happiness at seeing us quickly shifted to a look of embarrassment. As we walked over to say hi, Daniel's first words were about how he got a good deal on the car and that he was sorry the seats were leather. While I personally didn't judge him for his choice in cars, the guilt our friend Daniel felt at reaping the fruits of his own success highlights a common dilemma in spiritual communities. Financial success and spiritual pursuits often seem to go in opposite directions. When a spiritual person is financially successful, people assume that person has sold out in some way. A spiritual teacher is generally frowned upon for driving fancy cars, flying business class, wearing expensive jewelry, living in a big house, investing in the stock market, or otherwise participating in capitalist enterprise. Even more, some people argue that yoga, meditation, and the tools of spiritual liberation should be free.

Theoretically, that's a nice idea. But unless a spiritual teacher has taken a vow of renunciation and a yoga center has a wealthy benefactor, they will have the typical cares and concerns of a householder or business in present-day society. The electricity, internet, water, gas, tax, phone, and other bills need to be paid. Some independently wealthy yoga hobbyists with another source of income offer classes for free without giving a second thought to how to pay the bills. But most yoga teachers live hand to mouth, working as a labor of love, without the necessary business acumen it takes to run a thriving business.

Andrea was a student of mine who progressed quickly in the practice. She dove deeply into the spiritual journey and spent time studying with me; she even traveled to India to follow the same path that I did. In a casual conversation, I picked up on a comment she made about credit card debt and inquired more. It quickly became obvious that she had funded her trips to India and all her yoga studies through credit cards. The debt was weighing over her head; she was unable to make the payments and was at risk of going bankrupt. Unfortunately, this scenario is all too common for yoga teachers. What was even more troubling was that Andrea was not only my student but a yoga teacher, working at our yoga center. While she was being paid at the top end of our teacher rate, it wasn't enough for her to account for all the past expenses. It was so bad, she said, that she was considering quitting teaching yoga to get a "real" job. I counseled her in some practical things, like debt consolidation and financial planning.

But the deeper issue was related to the poverty mindset. Andrea resisted the idea that she could be financially successful and be aligned spiritually. She said she didn't want to think about money because thinking about money brought her away from the heart of yoga. There would be months where she didn't check her bank accounts or open letters from the credit card companies to whom she owed a great deal of money. For Andrea, it was as if money really was evil. In order for her to break free of that thinking, she had to break away from the scarcity mindset and challenge the false equivalence she had made between spirituality and poverty. I'm happy to say that Andrea is now debt-free and a successful yoga teacher entrepreneur who owns her own flourishing yoga center. She supports herself without compromising her values; what's more, her financial success means that she can keep teaching.

I am a yogi/business owner, so I know all too well the criticism that can be levied from a circular firing squad of my fellow yogis. I've been called a series of names in public-comment threads, private messages, blogs, and articles that range from politely critical to misogynistic trolling. Some people assume that because I'm successful, I must have stepped on someone to get where I am. There are those who critique my success and ambition just because I have it. As the founder of two successful businesses rooted in the world of yoga, I am conscious of the paradoxical nature of being a spiritual entrepreneur and the need to adhere to spiritual ethics, not only profitability. I am not perfect. I've made some mistakes along the way, just as everyone does in their practice. But I am committed to the process of learning and breaking the mold of the past.

Poverty is not a badge of authenticity in the yoga or spiritual world. There are certainly larger patterns of financial inequity based in the entrenched power hierarchies of race, religion, and class. There is something that could be called the "spiritual industrial complex"—a collection of businesses that profit from yoga, meditation, and spiritual teaching. Yet even those with immense privileges can fall into the trap of internalizing the belief that money is the root of all evil, and they end up living in poverty. Money is not evil. Business is not evil. Business makes one's true values evident through systems and actions. Money is a magnifier for the morals and proclivities contained within one's heart. Money is power. And power has the potential to corrupt even the best of us. The wanton, reckless pursuit of power and money, without a firm foundation in ethics, leads down a road of suffering for all. But if only the individuals without ethics have money and power, then the world will be run by the worst of us. Instead, imagine a world where the most powerful leaders of corporations are guided by the sound principles of ethics and whose daily actions are grounded in the philosophy of yoga, meditation, and deep ethical principles of care for the common good.

Coming to terms with our financial health may either resonate or push some buttons. Either way, trust that this message is likely exactly what is needed right now. We all have some resistance to financial success. It's time to let that go. Each and every one of us is worthy of being financially successful. There may be a thought that assumes that everyone who is successful has harmed others. It's time to let that judgment go. When we succeed, we model what success looks like for others. The more spiritual entrepreneurs who blaze a path of abundance based on sound ethics, the easier it will be for others to follow that path.

Be Humble and Know Your Worth

When I first started teaching yoga, I took my résumé around to more places than I can remember. Most rejected me. I had a standard email that I sent out with my yoga résumé and bio, along with some photos. If I sent out fifty emails, I'd get a reply from ten. Of those ten, nine would tell me no thanks, and one would suggest I might come in for a meeting. Most often, I would meet the general manager, but that person would turn me down.

I kept reaching out to different places until one or two put me on the sub list. From the sub list, I eventually made it to having a class that paid me five dollars per student, with no minimum. If no one showed up, I didn't get paid. It took me a while to build a small following of local students who enjoyed my class.

I felt like I had to say yes to every opportunity that presented itself. My persistence paid off, and after nearly a year of presenting myself to my local community, I was teaching twenty-three classes a week with no days off. Some days, I drove all around South Florida to teach four classes a day. With the five-dollars-per-head fee and no minimum guarantee, I wasn't getting rich. I was barely making enough money to save for my return trip to India to continue my studies. After a few months of this crazed schedule, I lost my inspiration to practice. There was a period when I just couldn't look at the mat. I would teach a private lesson at 7:00 a.m., a public class at 9:00 a.m., and be home at 11:30, with enough time to squeeze my practice in before leaving at 2:30 p.m. to drive around town for my evening classes. I remember standing on my mat, alone, wondering what I was doing. With a fair amount of effort, I managed to get through twenty minutes of practice before deciding that I wanted to go for a walk instead. I'm glad I went through that. It was a kind of trial by fire. After almost a year of that hectic schedule, I had enough money to spend six months in India. But I was also exhausted, worked to the bone, and uninspired to do the thing I once loved—yoga.

Saying yes to everything embodies the scarcity mindset and operates from fear rather than love. Taking everything that comes without discrimination stems from less-than thinking and leads to exhaustion, frustration, and burnout. Less-than thinking is also a profit scheme that fuels addiction to material products by selling the idea that an object can bring a sense of wholeness. Less-than thinking is a cycle that pushes us farther down the rabbit hole of worshipping work. The self-deprecating mentality that is willing to accept whatever comes has a certain element of honorable humility, but unless the actions are rooted in love, the cycle of suffering continues. While working hard is an accomplishment, if I could go back in time and offer myself a piece of advice, it would be this: don't overdo it. You don't need to say yes to everything; be humble and slightly choosy. It's more about finding what fits than shotgunning the whole community and being everywhere. This is actually a lesson I'm still working on today.

When I sat on a panel of expert yoga teachers, we were asked to speak to the business of yoga. The first question came from a newly minted yoga teacher, fresh out of a two-hundred-hour training. He asked us what advice we had for new yoga teachers. The moderator directed the question to a well-known colleague of mine, whose teaching had been featured in yoga magazines and whose teacher trainings were always full. My colleague's response was, "Market, market, market." Yes, any successful business needs good marketing. And yes, yoga teachers are essentially entrepreneurial gig workers who need to market themselves. But as the foundational advice for a new yoga teacher, marketing was the last thing on my mind to give. Instead, what I shared was more like, "Practice, practice, practice." It's no secret that yoga teachers often end up sacrificing their own practice for their teaching. Yoga teacher burnout is real, and many inspired new teachers end up deflated after years of talking people through the correct way to do Downward Dog. While I agree that marketing is important, it's not the foundation of what makes a good yoga business.

I think those same rules apply to any business. Manufacturing a sleek image will only get a business so far. Instead, working on the solidity of value of what is offered and focusing on the reason and purpose of the product or message leads to lasting impact, both for the business and for the world. Quality versus quantity is a question that every business owner I have ever met sits with.

Finding a job can be an act of love and an expression of one's own self-love—or lack thereof. As I ran around town, going from one teaching gig to another, I wore myself down beyond a reasonable point. At a deep and fundamental level, I didn't believe I was worthy of the good teaching jobs, so I took anything and everything I could get, regardless of class time, attendance, or pay rate. Later in my teaching career, after I was already a highly respected yoga teacher, I did not have as many issues with requesting a high minimum rate. While I still offer lots of free classes, scholarships for marginalized communities, and students with financial need, I no longer operate from a paradigm of feeling less-than. Instead, I strive to remain humble while believing in my work. If I'm honest, I do still get a little shy when people ask me what my rate is for a class or a private lesson. But I own my worthiness much more than ever before.

Humility and pride work in an inverse relationship. Too much pride blocks opportunities that would otherwise be available. Too much humility, ironically, also blocks opportunities that are for the taking. There's a middle path, one rooted in love, which seeks to bring balance to work.

Corporate Greed

Stories of corporations pillaging pristine communities for resources are the stories of the history of humanity. Whether it's drilling in the Arctic, multinational companies lobbying for laws in their favor, real estate moguls who pay zero dollars in taxes due to depreciation loopholes, or Wall Street CEOs with golden parachutes, there are an abundance of villains in the capitalist system. It's easy to think the world is stacked against the average person. Truthfully, the system upon which our society is based is unfairly formed. It is hard for those without immense privilege to rise up, yet the myth of the self-made millionaire is ubiquitous. Anyone operating from a foundation of ethics and morality will often be outperformed by those unbound by similar ethical principles.

The dynamic in the business world of wellness and spiritual circles is also the story of capitalist conquest, with hints of colonialism and cultural appropriation. Surveying the owners, CEOs, and boards of the largest yoga and wellness corporations reveals that mostly white men maintain positions of power and leadership, and they steer the helm of billion-dollar corporations that often place profitability first and foremost. It's business, after all. There are even US-based yoga clothing companies that seek to usurp the voice of yoga in the world from yoga teachers and students themselves.

But the reality is that corporations are not beings on the path to enlightenment. Rarely are corporate behemoths led by spiritually oriented individuals, who themselves are on a path to enlightenment. Even those few companies run by well-intended people can so easily fall into the common traps of capitalism, which is problematic when a company is profiting from a spiritual system that seeks to teach and instill ethics. While there are unicorn stories of change, it is quite often the same old story of power hierarchies at play in the wellness world. As soon as there is money to be made in any industry, there will be those who seek to mine that sphere for all it's worth. In an act of plunder, the capitalization of the spiritual heritage of countries like India that have preserved the sacred teachings of spiritual liberation runs the risk of being turned into McMindfulness

Inc., trademarked and owned by for-profit companies whose aim is far from the heart of spiritual awakening. There is powerful work being done by the Desi community, both within India and throughout the diaspora to reclaim India's cultural heritage and safeguard the most potent aspects of the yogic path. But there is much more work to be done, and it begins with dismantling the structures of power within the mind itself.

When yoga, meditation, chanting, sound healing, energy work, essential oils, juicing, plant-based diets, intermittent fasting, and all that relates to one's health in the body and soul are all just marketing ploys, then it's more of the same old pattern in a new form. When the corporate entity that sells products isn't run by individuals who walk the talk, it is a kind of abuse and violence against the indigenous cultures that protected these teachings and against the consumer or would-be student who is too easily duped by the polished images.

This is not a cause of despair but a rallying cry for each of us to do the work of awakening. The system is broken, but the system is not outside of us. It's easy to point a finger at all that's wrong out there when, in fact, that same system of corporate greed lives inside our minds. In order to change the world, we must start with changing the operating system of our own minds.

Consumer capitalism is an old paradigm that needs updating—or perhaps hacking. Updating the operating system of the mind demands deconstructing the operating system of the business of the world in tandem. All consumers need to question their roles as consumers and reclaim their own power and agency in the process. Decolonizing the mind and changing patterns of thinking disrupts the old rules in the world. There is a revolution at hand, and revolutions are rarely neat and tidy. Now, I'm not suggesting that changing the operating system of your mind means taking up arms against governments and corporations whose actions are harmful. Acts of direct warfare and aggression play right into the system of division and conflict. Remember that to act in anger locks oneself into a bind with the object of anger. To fight oppression and the oppressor with the same violence and tactic of conquering is simply to perpetuate the same old cycle. What I see is more subtle, yet more radical—a rebellion that begins in the domain of the mind, the soul, and the spirit and reverberates outward and takes root as real change.

There is a place for righteous rage and justified anger; we will delve into that later. Working within the system of capitalism to update the model requires patience, determination, endurance, and a bit of creativity. One person's role might simply be to model and live a life based on a new paradigm of love. Another person's path might be that of an activist; still another, a public figure or leader in a new type of corporation. Regardless of which role we each play, the change is afoot, and conscious consumerism is a powerful tactic to thwart corporate greed and foster a shift. Business monitors spending habits, and once a critical mass changes direction, business has no choice but to follow suit—that is, after all, the nature of capitalism.

Hack the Algorithm

Operating from a scarcity mindset, it might seem like the goal of work is to claw back some of that percentage of wealth in a Robin Hood mindset of social redistribution. Looking at the balance sheet of the world's richest companies, it is easy to question whether or not good people ever end up on top. But simply paying out dividends to the 99 percent won't change the core belief system that runs the world. Instead, change has to start with a personal revolution of consciousness. One day, perhaps the foundation of business will be something other than maximization of profits for short-term shareholder gain, at the expense of the long-term health of society and the planet. We are here to hasten the tipping point.

There is a way to run a business that is rooted in love, where the paradigm of success is not solely based on short-term self-interest, but it requires a shift in the hearts and minds of the leaders of corporations, employees, employers, and consumers. More than an ethical code, operating from the paradigm of love resets the system.

Not everyone who is successful and wealthy did it by harming others. Understanding that it is possible to run a financially fruitful business on a foundation of love and care changes the paradigm. We can take care of ourselves, take care of others, and take care of the planet while still turning a profit. What's more, the fruits of our labor will be long-lasting in the physical and spiritual sense.

Conscious consumerism is a way that every single human being can vote each day for the type of world that he or she wants. Even in the absence of financial wealth, each of us has something infinitely more powerful—attention. Data accumulated by global technology companies surpassed oil, gold, and other assets as the most valuable resource in the world. Facebook, Google, Amazon, and other tech giants trade in human futures, and you are the holder of one of their most prized assets. Each of us, in the role of consumer, viewer, and user, holds the power.

When life offline is dictated by algorithms, unconscious programming is at work. Online behavior is manipulated by an echo chamber designed to foster extremes of thought and action. Algorithms best serve the powerful interests, who can afford to buy the ads that are seen and to pay the most-watched influencers and who will ultimately profit off the viewer's attention. But the algorithm can be hacked by changing your paradigm and changing a few key behaviors.

We live in a mindset of accumulation and instant gratification. The idea that more is better in any circumstance fuels the endless cycles of consumerism that drives GDP. Sociologists have called this the "culture of more." More clothes. More money. More stocks. More information. More photos. Bigger. Faster. Better.

The culture of more is built on the premise of scarcity. While generating more of everything, the actual result, paradoxically, is less happiness, security, and peace. Contained within the subtext of the shiny advertising messages that sell the onward-and-upward message of infinite upgrades is the dirty little secret that no one is ever enough as he or she is. The need to buy something new is based on the idea that no person ever has enough, no matter how much that person has. All this "more" is sold as a filler to stuff inside an inner void. The problem is that no amount of external stuff can ever replace a sense of true wholeness. Nothing, not even other people, can be a substitute for the realization that the spirit within each of us is enough, exactly as we are.

The true spiritual path offers an alternative paradigm, if it isn't co-opted for financial gain. Instead of accumulating more, the spiritual seeks to accept who they are, where they are, and what they have or don't have. This attitude of contentment is called *Santosha*, derived from two Sanskrit words: "Sam," which means complete, altogether, entirely; and "Tosha," which means content, satisfaction, acceptance, being comfortable. As such, Santosha means completely content with, satisfied with, accepting and comfortable with. Included in the *Yoga Sutras*, under the list of Niyamas, the concept of Santosha is a foundational principle of yogi life. Yoga practitioners are not expected to arrive at the practice in the state of Santosha. Instead, it is the practice itself that cultivates the attitude of contentment with all the varied circumstances in life.

Some people come to yoga and import the culture of more to their yoga practice. This, unfortunately, leads well-intended students to fall for the common trope that associates more poses, deeper stretches, and higher lift-ups with advanced yoga practice. When the goal of yoga is rooted in an accumulation of physical forms, there is the risk of making an "ass-ana" out of the practice. If the goal of yoga is just to go deeper, do more, and collect more poses, then the culture of more has infiltrated the yoga practice. Students who make the false equivalence of poses and depth often end up sacrificing the health of their bodies to achieve certain poses. The reality of the physical body, however, is that no matter how much we try to control it, the body changes. A yoga pose may be done one day but not the next. Or a yoga pose may be possible for a decade, and then it slips away. Even more confusing, some students can naturally do a pose, while others may practice for many years and never attain it. All this pose-oriented focus is meant to be a laboratory for life experience. Life, like yoga, is constantly changing.

Some of us toil our entire lives for very little success. Others seem to fall easily into lucky streaks. Some people are born with great privilege and squander it. Others are born with no advantages and seem to rise far beyond their potential. Some people have all the money in the world and are still miserable. Others have next to nothing, materially, yet seem so happy. Some days are sunny. Some days are rainy. Sometimes the car breaks down. Sometimes airplanes are delayed. Life never goes according to plan—well, at least not our plan. If we think happiness in life only comes from a steady linear progression toward the goal of accumulation, then the unfortunate truth of change will one day become self-evident. No matter how much anyone may try to prove otherwise, life is uncontrollable. The spiritual path of yoga challenges the culture of more with a culture of Santosha.

Learn to be at peace with things as they are. Learn to accept what *is*, rather than trying to force what *isn't* into being. Practice an attitude of complete and total acceptance. For people who are indoctrinated in the culture of more, this feels scary, like quitting. When I first heard this teaching, I thought that nothing would ever happen if I lived in a bubble of contentment and didn't push for it forcefully. But the opposite is usually true. No material circumstance will ever bring about permanent happiness. We can either learn how to be happy right now, as we are, or we will find ourselves no happier, even if we succeed at accomplishing all that our sights are set on. We will be the same person, just with a bunch of stuff or a series of checks off our to-do lists. Yoga says that happiness begins right here, right now, by radically accepting what is.

We often think we need to launch an attack to elicit change in the world. Unfortunately, this paradigm can generate only more division and polarization. Approaching difficult circumstances with an attitude of Santosha doesn't mean that no work will ever be done for positive social change. Instead, it means that every situation is grounded inside a willing, peaceful heart. It is often said that people wait to understand a person before they can love that person, but love comes first and opens the door to understanding. Santosha is a way to express unconditional love, both in your relationship with yourself and in your relationship with the world.

Reflection Points

Hack the Algorithm

Since social media is such a powerful interface with the influence of capitalism and business, this exercise targets your relationship with the online culture of mental programming.

1. Turn off all notifications on all your devices.
2. Consciously choose to like and reshare positive stories and experiences. Pause before sharing incendiary stories, and research everything you read before believing.
3. Refrain from going down the rabbit hole by not clicking on any ads or recommended videos.
4. Go radical. Turn your phone on airplane mode for twenty-four hours. Notify friends and family beforehand, and give them a way to reach you. Go on a fast from the internet.
5. Practice Santosha. In the silence and emptiness left by the voice of an internet-free space, observe what is in your life today. Actively practice being content with what is.

Chapter 9

How to Love through Trauma and Shame

> Being traumatized means continuing to organize your life as if the trauma were still going on—unchanged and immutable—as every new encounter or event is contaminated by the past.
>
> —Bessel A. van der Kolk

We have all done things that, in hindsight, we regret. There is, quite simply, no perfect human being. Whether due to ignorance, adrenaline, incompetence, or willful acts of harm, every human being has harmed another. This is the unfortunate reality in which we live and is the cost of incarnation. Yet each misstep has a purpose. Each grievous act has the potential to awaken us.

Our faults and failures are how we learn. For a time, it can be useful to review life events and question one's motives and the results of one's actions. From this retrospective vantage point, once the heightened emotions of the event have passed, it is often possible to see much more clearly into the intricate details of the inner workings of the mind. Details arise that were not evident at the time, and clarity often comes with time. There is a moment when the mistakes that were made become obvious, and the impact of one's actions on others is unavoidable. We all learn at different paces. Some people may see quickly, while others need years or lifetimes to process. Regardless of the speed at which we work through stumbles and falls, there will come a time when the learning is complete, when we have gotten all that we can from that situation. Once the learning is complete, there is no more reason to rehash the past. Cycles of shame, blame, and guilt drive the subconscious mind into destructive patterns that lead to deep irresolution, rather than the growth we are here to achieve. When we reject the parts of ourselves that committed those heinous acts in the past, we prevent ourselves from learning and moving on. When we hate ourselves for the mistakes we've made, we doom ourselves to repeat them.

Many people think they cannot forgive themselves for the mistakes of the past because they think that if they let themselves off the hook, they will make the same mistakes again. Instead of accepting imperfections and celebrating the growth potential and the learning, so many of us hold on to shame, blame, and guilt far beyond what is necessary. There are, of course, others whose shame, blame, and guilt are so repressed that they will need to wait many years before coming to a final reckoning of their actions. In the balanced scales of life, everyone's actions are held accountable, not by courts of human law but by a power and logic whose unparalleled wisdom and love guides each and every one of our actions. We all will have our day of atonement. The question is whether we will play an active part in the process or it will happen by chance, inadvertently, at the end of our lives.

No human being is without a conscience. I believe that somewhere in all of us, even in the most sociopathic individual, lies a heart waiting to be awakened. Perhaps the wounds of this lifetime are too deep, and the heart will be opened in what lies beyond; nevertheless, the soul remains intact in even the most apparently irredeemable among us. The question on the spiritual path is whether we move toward growth and learning in the short term, or we have to wait decades to go through the process of evolution. But evolve, we all will, as surely as the cycles of the sun drive the seasons forward. Each and every one of us is on a path of awakening, and we, collectively, are walking on a long journey home.

The Vestiges of Trauma

We all have experienced things that were problematic, hurtful, and perhaps even traumatic. The National Council for Behavior Health states that 70 percent of adults have experienced a traumatic event at least once in their lives (National Council, November 2020). Trauma is defined as an event or circumstance to which a person responds with intense fear, horror, or helplessness, leading to extreme stress and being overwhelmed. The word *trauma* comes from the Greek, literally meaning "wound." A traumatic response can be immediate or delayed, as in post-traumatic stress disorder (PTSD). Trauma can be acute, resulting from a single event; chronic, resulting from repeated and prolonged stress; or complex, stemming from multiple sources. There are many sources for trauma, including medical, environmental, physical, sexual, economic, familial, communal, societal, cultural, historical, generational, genetic, and more. There is a high likelihood that spiritual practitioners are trauma survivors. Statistics show that 90 percent of behavioral-health clients have experienced trauma. I am writing this paragraph for a reason. Whether we or someone we know is on the road to healing, the teaching presented here may assist us along the journey, provide sustenance for the soul, and help answer some deep questions that may keep us locked in a perpetual negative spin.

Let me be clear: without the support of medically trained professionals who can guide us through qualified treatments, healing can be difficult. I strongly advise everyone impacted by trauma to seek guidance from therapists, psychologists, counselors, or others who may assist the process of reconciliation. This teaching is meant as a supplement, not a substitute, for qualified medical guidance.

Trauma is often a source of deep shame. It was for me. I am a childhood sexual trauma survivor, so I know, deeply and personally, the process of working through the impacts of abuse. Before I started to work on the spiritual path in earnest, if someone asked me whether I was ashamed of anything, I would have said no. But the truth is that I carried a deep sense of shame with me. Those early experiences of abuse triggered a downward spiral of self-loathing and shame that led to deep feelings of insecurity and victimhood. I, like many others, did not tell my story for many years—it took me nearly twenty years to speak the truth about what happened to me because I was ashamed of what happened.

Not only did those early incidents of sexual trauma plant a seed of shame in my mind and heart, but they retarded my emotional development. Years were lost in telling the story of how everything that happened was OK. Emotions buried deeply in the sea of the subconscious drowned the right to say no and obscured healthy boundaries. Somewhere in the inexorable aftermath of trauma, the me that is deemed authentic, true, and real by the world was shelved to obscurity—that is, until I found the way back to myself through the spiritual path. Walking the road of my own awakening for more than twenty years has lessened the torments of the past, but they do sometimes still haunt me. Liberation is not won in one sweeping moment, but in a series of small steps whose persistence wears down the buttressed fortress of ego. Light seeps through the cracks, like dawn peering in through the smallest fenestration.

Trauma can feel nonsensical and confounding. Hardship and difficulty sometimes seem irreconcilable with a belief in the goodness of the world. Like the story of loss written in the book of Job, devastating loss and suffering make even the most devout of us wonder what we did to deserve this horrible reality. It doesn't seem fair that good people suffer or that we can do everything right and still have it all go wrong. We might decide to hate or blame the world, or we might decide to hate or blame ourselves. But it doesn't have to be that way. Remember Victor Frankl, who found meaning through immense suffering and those who found a way to flourish in post-traumatic growth? We can be that person too by discovering the wisdom of our pain. Our work is about walking the path that leads to just the right moment, when it will all make sense and the pieces of the puzzle fit together. The work of awakening is messy and personal. Every spiritual seeker answers a clarion call, much like a seed answers the call to sprout when given the right conditions. Working with trauma can feel like stepping into a wild, overgrown garden. Before the seed can sprout, the weeds of the past often need to be removed. Each weed extracted might feel like a gaping wound at first but is actually just the shape required to house the next iteration of beingness—a life where love is the foundation and firmament of every action.

Most people fail to see the empty crevice of their souls' wounds as the fertile ground of awakening. Instead, shame takes over, like a fungus that rots the soil before anything can grow. Whether shame spawns from abuse, trauma, body size, ethnicity, handicap, religion, economic standing, culture, intelligence, or some other ignominious feature, shame spins in a vicious cycle. Shame, at its core, is self-rejection and self-hatred. Yet no matter how much or how long the period of self-denigration runs, there is always a stable core within that yearns for belonging. No matter how silenced that voice may be, it nevertheless cries out with a desire to be loved and for a recognition of intrinsic worthiness. Part of the artillery of ego, the shamed shelf does not believe it is worthy of love as it is. The great act of falsehood and chimera begins in a deceit and deferment of truth. Instead of being oneself, shame demands the adoption of a persona. Some choose people-pleasing; others choose bullying; more still choose victim, hero, or perpetrator, but the act is for naught. No life built on shame fulfills purpose. Rather than the achievement of acceptance and honor, actions rooted in shame lead to more shame. This happens even with actions that have a genuinely good intention. This is the corrosive way that unconscious patterns work against us. Remember that you can harness the power of the subconscious mind for positive change, once the operating system of the mind is updated. That is the work we are doing here.

The shamed self believes that what it has done or what has been done to it makes it irredeemable and unworthy of love and acceptance. The seed of shame is a core belief, the patterning of which spins like a violent whirlpool in the sea of consciousness. Disrupting both the surface and spiraling far below, the pattern of shame devastates even the strongest conscious commitments to change for the better. Positive affirmations spoken over a heart filled with subconscious shame do not penetrate deep enough. It is the root that must be removed before those gentle seeds will grow.

Forgiveness Is the First Step

Mike was a student of mine who began practicing yoga at the prodding of his sister. When he showed up to class, it was evident to me that he had very little self-respect. His posture was slouched, and his casual disposition glossed over an underlying hostility. It's hard to explain the way the body's language in yoga reveals what the conscious mind cannot. Speaking about himself, Mike only said positive things about how "awesome" he was. Yet his actual inner state was far from the exterior mask that he presented to the world. Disheveled and uncoordinated, he fumbled through the basic movements and was more interested in how he looked without his shirt on. I share his story not to disparage him but because many of us are just like Mike—wanting to be awesome yet so very not awesome. We reject the part of ourselves that we think will be rejected—the beginner, the vulnerable, the less-than, the shameful. As it turns out, what was hiding under the very thin veneer of false confidence was a deeply abashed person worthy of love.

After a few months of practice, Mike started sharing some more personal details with me—that there were parts of him that he hated and wanted to change. When I asked him to explain, he demurred at first but then shared a convoluted story that illustrated the cycle of shame. Like many people of our contemporary era, Mike got caught in a web of his own actions and thoughts. He would engage in behaviors that he knew were not ethical and then berate himself for his actions. Using an anonymous handle on social media, he would post words of vitriol and vituperation against those who disagreed with his beliefs or otherwise irked him. Mike was, he said, an internet troll. He felt so low in the aftermath of his tornado that he would swear to himself that he would never again engage in those actions. But then he would take the bait, and the cycle would begin again—except with each cycle, he sank to new lows. Rather than finding a way out, Mike was only digging himself in deeper.

When friends and family members confronted him on his actions, he would lash out and defend himself. He admitted to only feeling good about himself when he had torn someone else down, but that high was so temporary and fleeting that its fix left him even more depleted than before.

Bound by forces that seemed beyond his control, Mike bravely shared with me that he had contemplated ending his life. More than anything, he said, he wanted to press the reset button on his life. Raised as a Christian, Mike said that he had let himself down, more than anyone else, but could not find the way out.

I told him that what mattered was not the past but that he was here now, putting in the work. The way out of self-hatred and shame isn't blame. The way out of shame starts with love and forgiveness.

Where desire resides often defines the course of action that is taken. Desire points to the true north of any given situation. Unfortunately, unconscious desires often drown out conscious desires. As long as the shamed self is activated, unconscious desire will carry everything else in its powerful tide. Desire to be free from shame leads to compromised values, as well as both intentional and unintentional blindness. Mike wanted to fit into a group of people, and so he engaged in the grievous act of online bullying in a bid to please others and fill a hole within himself. The more rage he shared, the more certain groups egged him on. We have all been there. It is easy to ignore warning signs when a deep emptiness appears to be fulfilled. The soul's thirst cannot be quenched with falsehoods. The desire for popularity is a portal that opens to darkness, slowly reeling you in along the fishing line of shame. The only way to break free is to directly confront the demon with love and firm boundaries. We need equal parts love and discipline; otherwise, we will be right back in the shame cycle. We can only truly be effective from a place of love.

Mike thought he was unforgivable and that he needed to be punished, but spiritual learning does not work like that. As long as shame blocks healing, the self-hatred cycle will continue. The only way out is to work directly through it. Let go of the concept of fault, blame, and punishment. Don't obsess about who did or didn't do it. The suffering itself is like a virus that plagues the whole world. The cure has to work from a totally different paradigm. The punishment of any act of harm is contained within that act itself. In order to evolve beyond the paradigm of shame and blame and embrace the paradigm of love, we all need to learn how to do something that seems strange; that is, we need to learn how to fail up.

The voice of shame is like a heckler who screams obscenities from within the arena of the mind. When even a bit of progress appears, the voice of shame hits the sore spot and pokes at all the vulnerabilities and weaknesses. It is tempting to get off the podium and tangle with the heckler, directly engaging in conflict or argument, but all that does is turn the inner world into a war zone. Then, the fight ensues on multiple fronts—feeling unresolved within while simultaneously battling the forces in the world without.

An act of love in the moment that shame comes up does not run away or respond with hate. An act of love in the face of shame looks like kindness, forgiveness, and clear boundaries. The impetus of shame has the same seed of devotion and determination. Instead of carrying the torch of shame, it is possible to learn how to carry the torch of goodness. It's the learning that matters. It's the healing that makes the world a better place. When the shame cycle breaks, the world is lighter, brighter, and happier. Without the burden of shame, energy and insight appear that would otherwise be out of reach. It is our ability to love and accept ourselves unconditionally that breaks the cycle. When we finally forgive ourselves and all the other actors at play in our traumas, we are free to act in love. To stand on the other side of shame doesn't feel like a triumphant victory; it's tenuous. It feels detached and unidentified, yet peaceful, glorious, and humble.

A Core Knot Unravels

From the time I was a little girl, I have always hated the way women are treated in the world. The word *hate* is both strong and purposefully chosen because it's how I felt. Under a veneer of happiness and what some people would describe as a smiley personality, I hated the femaleness of who I was. On a deep and largely unconscious level, I resented being born as female.

There is systemic, subconscious, and overt violence against women in the world today. While, in many ways, this is the most comfortable society yet to inhabit the earth, we have a long way to go before we make this world a truly safe space for women, let alone women who sit at all the intersections of humanity.

In this life alone, my female body has experienced enough trauma to account for my feelings of rage and resentment. Childhood sexual trauma had a lasting impact on my sense of self, but it was more than that. I felt it long before the sexual abuse occurred, perhaps subconsciously, prelinguistically, as a kind of unexpressed, unprocessed, and unverbalized angst. I can only describe what existed within me as an existential knot tied up at the center of my being. The Gospel of Thomas says, "If you bring forth that which you have within you, it will save. If you do not, it will destroy you."

The rage internalized within me expressed itself as unchecked ambition, angry activism, self-rejection, toxic relationships, unconscious sexual encounters, drug abuse, opportunistic business actions, long-term depression, and suicidal ideation. It was at the peak of my pain that I dived deeper into my spiritual path. Hopeless and lost, I was desperate for a radical shift. I had no idea that I would leave the Vipassana meditation retreat that I attended with a teaching that would change my life. The spiritual lessons that came through for me during my time sitting are the foundation of this book. Let me just say that Vipassana is not easy, nor is it a vacation. Instead, it is hard work that produces the fruits of one's own liberation.

After three days of sitting, my mind cracked. The sum total of my life seemed to sit around my neck like a chain. I had felt body hatred before, but this was something else entirely. What I felt could only be described as gender hatred. It had the feeling of sharp edges, like small knives that were driven into my body. Suddenly, it was clear that I resented being female. I rejected my female gender. While I can obviously understand why from an intellectual level, to feel the root of this old and deep hatred was both a release and a revelation. I had internalized within myself the anger, resentment, grief, and bitterness that I felt about being female. Regardless of what I had experienced and regardless of whether that narrative was true, I had internalized the hate within myself. Hate was stored in the memory of my body, in the very fabric of my subconscious mind, running like a perpetual riptide that would eventually always sabotage my best efforts to be happy, healthy, and free.

In yoga, we have a word for deeply held behavior patterns that live in the subconscious mind. These patterns are called *samskaras*. Well, gender hatred was the deepest and most powerful samskara that I have ever encountered. I consider myself a feminist, so to see how I hated femaleness was paradoxical in the way a non sequitur just doesn't make sense. I didn't see that I couldn't be a feminist while hating my femaleness—that is, until I sat with the feeling at the root of the knot within myself.

Even though I had rejected my gender, I viewed my experience from a place of immense privilege as an able-bodied, cisgender, white-passing, multiethnic person from an upper middle-class family, with the luxury of taking ten days off to sit in a silent meditation retreat. The intersection of my privilege has allowed me the time and space to dive deeply into my subconscious patterns.

Gender is an issue that strikes at the core of our being, both individually and globally. Untying whatever knots lie at the core of one's being, whether male, female, or nonbinary, has the power to set one's soul free. No matter the gender we identify with, learning to love and accept ourselves completely is the work of liberation. There is a moment when each of us is ready to learn what it means to love being who we are and to embrace our own power.

The journey of gender liberation holds value for all, regardless of whether a person identifies as female, male, or gender nonconforming. Just as the world puts femaleness in a box, so too does it put maleness and gender binaries in boxes. Love and respect for all beings begins with the acceptance of who we are. The action to affirm one's gender originates within one's own heart and is nothing short of a revolution.

Is Love Really Blind?

People often say that love is blind, but it's really lust that is blind. Love sees all and accepts all. Lust is driven by desire and spirals into possession and jealousy.

Jacob and Amelia appeared to be a happy couple, with two adorable children and two cute dogs. I met them when Jacob booked a private session for his wife, Amelia, as a surprise birthday present. They made the transition to being regular students and often came to practice together, sometimes even as a family. I didn't see through the perfect family image at first, but the shiny, happy appearance started to crack one day when Jacob stopped coming to class. At first, Amelia said that he was just taking a break, but after a few weeks, I had a sense that something else was going on. One day, Jacob asked if he could book a private session with me. I said yes, of course, just as I would for any serious student of mine.

When I arrived for our lesson, I found Jacob in tears, sitting on his mat. It appeared that perhaps he needed a counselor more than my yoga expertise, but I could show up and listen. His first words were, "I messed everything up." From there, I almost instinctively knew what would come out next. The feeling of shame hung in the air with a palpable sense. Jacob told me that he was terrified that his wife would find out about his secret pornography addiction. Jacob was so obsessively engaged in watching pornography that he no longer felt sexually attracted to his wife. To complicate matters, even though they were both relatively liberal and practicing yoga, Jacob had been raised in a traditional evangelical Christian family.

While he had never engaged in sexual intercourse with another woman during his marriage, the guilt he carried over his behavior stifled his ability to move forward. He felt he had cheated, and there was a part of himself that he rejected deeply and could not reconcile with the image he kept of himself as a family man of outstanding character. Due to the guilt and shame that Jacob carried, the conversation he should have had with his wife happened with his yoga teacher. I advised him to go home and tell

Amelia everything and to do the work that yoga recommends, which is to make yourself whole.

So many people, like Jacob, live with feelings of guilt and shame. Rather than understand that these are symptoms of a larger illness, we assume that we have done something that makes us unworthy of love. Operating in the world with a subconscious feeling of unworthiness, we reap the consequences of our low self-esteem. First, we engage in behaviors that reinforce what our subconscious minds think about ourselves. Despite our best efforts to break cycles of suffering and turn a new leaf, we find ourselves caught in the same old patterns. It feels like there is no escape. We could conclude, mistakenly, that there must be something wrong with us, or we could lash out at the world, blame God or the government, or even spew hate. But the truth, nevertheless, remains that our cycle of negativity begins in our own hearts.

Psychologist Timothy Jennings describes love as a law that, when broken, implodes and twists into internalized feelings of guilt. In *Could It Be This Simple?* he says,

> Breaking the law of love not only damages our faculty of reason and conscience, but also begins convicting us of wrongdoing. We experience such self-incrimination as fear, anxiety, and insecurity, causing us to lose the ability to think clearly. (Jennings 2021, 64)

We instinctively know that the truth about who we are cannot be that we are made of darkness. Even if the story that the subconscious mind tells about life is one of failure and selfishness, there is a place, somewhere within, that knows that the truth is more than that. It hurts so much to feel the pain of isolation and loneliness because the heart and soul never lose their connection to worthiness and love. There is always a place within that is seeking a passage back home. The assumption that one is unworthy to receive and give love because of past actions forces people to run away from the work that would bring atonement.

Rather than running away, the path to reconciliation begins with feeling all the pain, shame, and guilt. Once the coating that covers the heart's wounds dissolves, healing begins. Shame, guilt, fear, punishment, and retribution form a cycle that occlude the natural state of the soul. It is, however, possible to break the cycle. The first step begins with forgiveness. Forgiveness is not forgetting.

Guilt and Grief

Guilt and grief are two different things. Holding on to grudges toward others wedges bitterness into the fabric of the heart. Stubbornly choosing unforgiveness plants ticking time bombs in the emotional landscape that can detonate at the lightest touch. Anger and offense often come easily to those saddled with guilt.

Inappropriate guilt can get in the way of processing grief. The sickness that so many people take on as a private affair with pain is actually nothing more than the spiritual lesson that they are meant to face, heal, and transcend. There is nothing wrong with us. In fact, there is only something so right with us. All the actions, thoughts, behaviors, and experiences that have been a part of life, including the good and the bad, have been perfectly designed to bring each of us to an apex point of awakening. Without the pitfalls, struggles, and suffering, the crescendo of change and evolution would lack the momentum it needs to complete its process. This is true, both on an individual level and on a global level.

Seeing the world as fallen is not a judgment against it. Recognizing the pain manifest in the world is not an invalidation of its divine origin. Far from it, seeing the pleasure and the pain is part of the revelation of the world's purpose. Every being contains yin and yang, light and shadow. To assume that purity of spirit assures the end of one's suffering on earth is a reductionistic misstep that cheapens the very concept of heaven itself. To love is to love in whole, not in parts or conditionally. That which some would say taints us with an irredeemable scar is the very thing that liberates us.

Metabolizing Trauma and Shame

The Buddha teaches in the first of the Noble Truths that "Suffering is." An awakened heart does not avoid suffering, not one's own or the suffering of the world. Instead, the path of awakening is about growing your heart big enough to contain both light and shadow. Jesus gives the commandment to love our neighbors as we love ourselves. But if we cannot even love ourselves, what hope is there for loving our neighbors, let alone our enemies? If our love is conditional and rests on the judgment of our past, then we and everything in our world will be eternally damned.

Many people live in such a high state of self-rejection and selfishness that the idea of love has been warped into a two-dimensional postcard greeting. The best intentions of our modern self-help psychology lead to more confusion. We are advised to engage in acts of self-love. Yet most of these actions, rather than truly teaching us how to love, perpetuate selfishness. Using the mantle of self-love, we justify heinous acts of selfishness, declaring we are reclaiming our voices and power. Hiding under self-love, we stop giving to others and withdraw into a world of self-preservation. Shielded by a delusional self-love, we wield words of hate, claiming to simply stand in our truth. Love has so many meanings in the English language that finding true love amid a sea of counterfeits can be challenging. If we claim to love everything from motorcycles to pineapples to puppies, then it is highly likely that we truly love nothing.

We are told to follow our bliss, to trust ourselves above all others, to be our own gurus. But how is that possible when a virus has infected the very fabric of our being—when all the thoughts, which we think are unique thoughts, and all the feelings, which we think are signposts from the depths of our inner beings, are merely the repetitive cycles of the past?

To live in love is to be a wellspring of spontaneously flowing wisdom and compassion. To live in love is to be a Buddha; to walk in the footsteps of Jesus and become Christlike. Which one of us can claim to achieve such a high state? Yet that is the promise of our awakening; that is, that one day, we may live in such a state of love and harmony. What's more, the dream is not for us, personally and alone; the dream of a New Earth is a dream of a return to love, a restoration of the human spirit to its natural home.

Until that day, we must have the humility to admit that we are not there, that we are not walking Buddhas, and that our habituated feelings and flawed patterns of thoughts govern the operating system of the mind. This is where we are. To admit this first step is to be willing to take the medicine. To admit that we are lost in the jungle of the mind is the first step to finding the path that leads out. To wander aimlessly while claiming to know the way and even leading others on winding roads to nowhere is a further delusion. To fight, to stand one's ground, when the land upon which we stand is stolen is a hypocritical false statement of power. We will be at war with both the world and with ourselves.

Instead, the spiritual path begins in earnest on the day we realize that we and our whole world are in chains. Until that moment, we may be hedged into our beliefs too strongly to truly learn. We may be so satisfied with our own answers that we are unwilling to ask or be interested in the most important questions. We think we are free, but we are in chains. These chains are in the mind and have been passed down to us through generations. There are personal, familial bondages, as well as social, cultural, and universal chains that we have inherited.

The way out must begin with a turning of the mind inward, into a period of deep self-observation. We have to begin by looking bravely inside ourselves and searching for the truth. If we lie to ourselves, how can we ever hope to be honest with anyone else? Intimacy and connection in earnest begin with a feeling of wholeness within. We are only ever willing to meet people where they are to the extent that we have met ourselves. We spend so much time trying to prove ourselves to "the world," when we are the ones whose love and approval is hardest to get.

So much of life is wasted on feeling unworthy, thinking that we're less-than, wondering if we have what it takes, and doubting ourselves. To awaken is to walk the unsung hero's journey, privately conquering demons and winning wars without the hope of a big homecoming parade. To move beyond guilt and shame onto a path filled with love is to make the world a better place, starting with the world of our own minds and hearts.

1. Meditation and Reflection Points

Close your eyes; settle your mind on your breath for a few moments. Then, pose these questions to yourself: Am I ready to let go of the cycle of guilt and shame? Am I ready to move beyond a zero-sum paradigm, where I need someone (perhaps myself) to "pay" in order to forgive? If the answers are yes, then trust that your *yes* is enough to begin the untying of a deep knot. If the answers are no, then ask yourself why not. What do you think you gain from keeping that cycle alive, and what would you need in order to break free from the blame-and-shame loop?

✳

Chapter 10

Navigating Anxiety, Being Overwhelmed, and Fear

Love is what we were born with. Fear is what we have learned here. The spiritual journey is the relinquishment - or unlearning - of fear and the acceptance of love back into our hearts. Love is the essential existential fact. It is our ultimate reality and our purpose on earth. To be consciously aware of it, to experience love in ourselves and others, is the meaning of life.

—Marianne Williamson

Youth is often full of boundless optimism and unbridled idealism. Innocence is trusting and jubilant and full of life. Experience often breaks hearts and shatters dreams, bursting bubbles of positivity with cold, hard reality. Age can bring disillusionment, and a feeling of learned helplessness can take over. It can feel like the machinery of existence is just too big, the forces-that-be are just too powerful, and that nothing ever makes a substantive change. Even the things that once were joyful might one day feel hollow and empty. It can feel like the cards are stacked against our best efforts. When we think about all that has gone wrong and all that could go wrong, it is easy to feel full of anxiety.

Many people recognize themselves in these thoughts. I've been there too, perhaps more than anyone might think. In fact, I believe we all have faced periods of what could be called anxiety and learned helplessness. These dark nights bring up periods where joy disappears and fear creeps in.

Anxiety can come from every corner of life. It is tempting to think that the source of anxiety is outside of oneself, but the reality is that we perpetuate our own anxious states as much, if not more, than the world forces us to be anxious.

Negativity Bias

Negativity bias is the human tendency to exaggerate the negative and downplay the positive. Many people experience negativity bias as remembering only negative experiences and forgetting positive experience. This well-documented proclivity exists in each of us to varying degrees. Some people suggest we are the descendants of those humans whose negativity bias was strongest because they were the survivors. There was once an exceedingly useful need to accentuate the negative over the positive. In the times before civilization, the human population was subject to a potential onslaught of life-threatening situations on a daily basis. Seeing the sign of danger first played a critical role in determining dominance and survival. Then, the arrival of an imminent threat triggered the nervous system's fight-flight-freeze reaction. The faster and bigger the response, the more likely it was that the human survived. Natural selection assures us that our ancestors are the ones who survived, which means we have inherited the genetic predisposition toward negativity bias.

What worked well for the survival of the human species in those times no longer works. Lions, tigers, and other predatory animals have been culled. We now try to protect these large predators. Another way of saying it might be that human beings are now the most dangerous species on the planet, a threat to ourselves, to animals, and even to the earth itself. The negativity bias that once served to ensure the survival of the human species now threatens to harm the quality of human life, if not hasten the extinction of the species.

The sound of email, texts, and other notifications often triggers the fight-flight-freeze system in the human mind and nervous system. People find themselves in the grips of crippling anxiety, paralyzing fear, and desperate loneliness and are driven to unhealthy extremes with no way out. While the cradle of civilization has some benefits—indoor plumbing, air conditioning, travel, communication, and agriculture, just to name a few—that doesn't stop the mind from perceiving threats and catastrophizing. There is no end to the potential perceived threats that pervade contemporary society. Some organizations and individuals even consciously create misinformation for profit schemes that play off these dueling systems within the human being. Social media then exacerbates the apparent prevalence of threat, polarizing communities and weaponizing the biological features within our brains and bodies. Many people are left feeling anxious, helpless, alone, and fearful of the world. It could be argued that we are at a unique point in the evolution of humanity, in that we have the chance to consciously participate in a reprogramming of the human mind, nervous system, and body.

Proliferation of Thoughts

The stringent lockdown measures of the COVID-19 pandemic prevented Priestly from taking yoga classes, which were the only thing that kept his anxiety at bay. To make matters worse, his local yoga studio had closed due to the economic hardship of being shuttered and was not offering online classes. While he also worked with various self-soothing techniques, yoga was the thing that worked for him.

After trying a few of my videos online, Priestly decided to book a private session with me to help keep up his practice. We worked together on the yoga poses, but what he really wanted to do was talk about his anxiety. I'm not a trained therapist, but when a student starts talking, I always listen and then make referrals to trained professionals, when appropriate. Priestly told me that his anxiety was boiling over, and his thoughts screamed with fever-pitch intensity. Each news notification seemed to promise one sort of apocalyptic scenario or another, with no end in sight. There might have been good moments in each day, but he couldn't remember them or focus on them. There were only negative, only insolvable problems, only stress. It was usually in the final relaxation at the end of deep, sweaty practice that his mind would stop, and he would feel at peace. Online classes just weren't the same, and he hadn't felt a moment of true peace since before lockdown. During our session, he asked me how he could reconnect to that thoughtless place on his own.

One particular thought pattern that plagued Priestly is referred to in Sanskrit as *prapañca*, which means *proliferation*. It's sort of like negativity bias on steroids. While reading an email from the law firm where he worked, which indicated he would be put on furlough during the lockdown, Priestly had an anxiety attack. His mind cast thousands of disaster scenarios that all ended with him being homeless on the street in a matter of weeks. The reality is that, as a lawyer, he had earned a good living and had seven figures of savings. That, combined with being single and having low monthly expenses, meant that his fears were largely unfounded in reality. He told me that he sat at his computer, paralyzed, unable to move for what felt like an eternity. Truly, he did not know how much time had passed when he finally came out of that zombie-like state. Unable to function, Priestly did a search for "Yoga for Anxiety" and found one of my practice videos. He practiced that day for the first time since his local yoga studio shut down, and he felt like he could breathe again.

I'm happy to say that Priestly kept practicing with me during the pandemic. Once the lockdown lifted, he applied for and secured a job at a law firm where he now works. He even carried his passion for yoga to the corporate office and organized a weekly yoga class for all employees.

While threats may be very real, as in the case of COVID-19, job loss, or other sources of potential harm, the mental and emotional anguish only adds more weight to an already complex situation. Anxiety cannot help the problem. Spiraling thoughts cast a web of fear that incapacitates even the best of us from cohesive thinking and fruitful action. The spiritual path is about breaking free from negativity bias so that the mind can work optimally.

The Paradox of Choice

It's not always easy to know what you want. In fact, it is often almost impossible to choose from the endless options presented. The greater the number of possibilities, the harder it is to choose. This phenomenon is called the paradox of choice.

There's a sweet spot for the human mind when it comes to making decisions. If there's only one option to choose from, it's not really a choice. If there are one hundred options to choose from, there are too many to choose from to make a good choice. If, however, there are more than two and less than a dozen, it becomes possible to make a choice and feel good about it later. It's not so much about what's right or wrong. It's more about how the choice feels afterward.

Studies show that when the number of choices exceeds a certain threshold, the human mind does something very interesting. Each option has certain good and bad qualities that the other options don't have. By choosing one, you block your access to the good qualities of the options that you didn't choose and lock yourself into the bad qualities of the one you did. The mind plays a trick. Instead of settling on the option chosen, when the number of choices exceeds the magic dozen number, the mind amalgamates all the good qualities of all available choices into a mythical perfect option that doesn't exist. Then, no matter what option is chosen, the result is always dissatisfaction with the result. This is why it's called the paradox of choice.

People assume that having more options to choose from is better, but that's not always the case. Sometimes having more options to choose from just makes things more complicated. Having too little to choose from can be just as problematic for your emotional state. My husband, Tim, is from Denmark. The first time I visited him there was in the early 2000s. I went to the supermarket to buy groceries, and peanut butter was on my shopping list. Standing in the aisle, I looked down to find two options—salted and unsalted. I inspected both jars and deposited the salted option in my cart. Even though the salted peanut butter I bought was organic and tasted good, I was never really happy with my selection—I chalk this up to the paradox of choice. Since I didn't have enough to choose from, I didn't feel I had a choice at all and was unhappy with my selection.

When I recounted the story to Tim, he shared his first experience at a US grocery store with me, which, ironically, centered around peanut butter as well. Ten years before we met, my Danish husband, who grew up with the simple dichotomy of salted or unsalted, was in New York City, and his roommate asked him to pick up some peanut butter. When Tim arrived at the grocery superstore and located the peanut butter section, he stood in front of a wall of peanut butter options and brands, far more than the standard options available in his native country. He could choose from organic, non-GMO, conventional, salted, unsalted, creamy, chunky, sweetened, unsweetened, cinnamon, chocolate swirl, no-stir, coconut oil, palm oil, nut mixtures (including almonds, cashews, and macadamia), and all sorts of other things he had never heard of before. After reading numerous labels and reflecting on the benefits and disadvantages of each item, Tim closed his eyes, put his hand out, and just grabbed one. The lucky winner of the peanut butter lottery was Skippy. Unfortunately for him, this choice was not lauded by his roommate, nor was Tim proud of his selection. My husband's inability to choose from the wall of peanut butters is a perfect example of the paralyzing impact of the paradox of choice.

Peanut butter is a harmless and perhaps humorous example, which is why I chose to share it. But when the paradox of choice impacts all our decisions, from shopping online to job searching to choosing a life partner to voting, then the repercussions can be potentially dramatic and debilitating. It's no wonder that so many of us are filled with anxiety. In a world where we can have everything and anything, no one is happy.

Which Way Are We Looking?

The act of rehashing old stories of the past assures that they will repeat themselves. Reliving those moments locks the mind into a cycle of repetition. When we keep thinking about the past, then the past repeats itself. When the mind gets caught in a cycle of perpetuation, the future ends up looking just like the past. Years are sometimes lost in replaying old events and worrying that they might happen again. If we want the future to look like something different from the past, we have to shift our focus in the present.

Projecting into the future is powerful, and thoughts do impact what our lives are like. Worrying about an endless barrage of problems fills the mind and heart with images that can produce debilitating fear when that train of thinking cannot be stopped. While it is useful to make contingency plans for things that might go wrong, obsessing about too many details derails our path to happiness. Stepping out of the present and projecting into the future also brings up the wide-open landscape of the unknown. The present moment is the only vantage point around which we have power to impact change. When thoughts tell the story of tomorrow, anxiety, stress, depression, anger, or other destructive emotions appear and sometimes take over. Casting out worst-case-scenario disasters might be useful in some situations, but very often, the worrying is worse than the experience.

Jason was the father of a precocious teenage girl named Mary. They both loved yoga and would practice with me often. One day, I overheard them in the lobby after practice. Mary was only twelve, but she was already talking about what kind of car she wanted to drive one day. Dreaming of a sports car, she asked her father if he would get her a sleek sports car for her sixteenth birthday. Even though Jason had the financial means, it was clear that under no circumstance would he buy his precious daughter a sports car. If they could afford to buy her a car, he wanted something safe, first and foremost, which he shared with his little princess. Mary got emotional and looked almost like she was going to burst into tears at the thought of driving a large safe "tank" around town. Well, there's a happy ending to this story. This father/daughter duo kept coming to practice, and when Mary turned sixteen, she inherited her mother's old car, which happened to be both safe enough to please her father and small enough not to be considered a tank.

Projecting into the future, we can always see problems. But standing in the future, addressing those same problems, is often an entirely different scenario. What we think we can handle is often far less than what we can actually handle. What is acceptable in reality varies, sometimes dramatically, from what is acceptable theoretically. There is the expression that God only gives us what we can handle (and some people say that they wish God wouldn't think so much of them!). The lesson here is relatively simple: don't argue about what will happen in the distant future. Instead, focus on the present, and let the future arrive on its own. Have faith that when the future does arrive, it will be something you can handle.

But what if, in the present, everything appears to be wrong, and a flood of emotions drowns out any ability to execute a clear plan of action? In that case, the work begins with shifting the focal point of the present moment. Even in the midst of a bona fide catastrophe, there is no reason to add emotional distress to an already troubling situation. It is possible to choose how to regulate thoughts and emotions and make a qualitative difference right now, today, with no change in external circumstances. What matters most is the quality of focus and the direction in which one's gaze is pointing. Whenever the present seems like a burden, the roots of that problem are often stuck in the past or projected into the future. Dialing down the speed of the emotional roller coaster of life requires each of us to be conscious in where we are looking and to redirect our attention to the present, over and over again.

Emotional Self-Regulation

There is little training in emotional self-awareness, let alone emotional self-regulation. Most people have learned one technique or another to repress or hide their emotions from others and even from themselves. Instead of emotions being dirty little secrets, emotions are brilliant signposts from our inner world. By learning to navigate the world of emotions, we will gain access to an intelligence far beyond mere intellect.

Not only are emotions a good indication of where we are, but they are an indication of where we are going. More than that, we can craft our emotions by training our nervous systems to self-soothe and hold the state of how we want to feel. It might feel slightly facetious at first or like acting, but we can call up any emotional state at any time. Whether it's happiness or anxiety, emotions are not something that control the human experience, even though many people feel that way. Instead, by learning techniques of emotional self-regulation, everyone can understand what it means to be rooted in love, moment by moment.

When yoga practices work with the breath, this calms the nervous system in what is sometimes called bottom-up regulation. When we breathe deeply, the activity of the body calms the mind and down-regulates the fight-flight-freeze response. With a conscious choice, we can choose to reprogram our thoughts and change our emotional course. Anxiety and stress are practiced just like anything else. It might be hard to accept that happiness, peace, and love are available to everyone (including you and me), but that's the truth.

It is impossible to control external circumstances. How people respond to any given situation is up to them; it is not up to anyone else to manage other people's emotions. Each and every person is responsible for his or her own emotional well-being. Let's explore this more to be sure that this train of thought is not just a way to use spirituality to bypass the hard work of life and human interaction. Understanding that we are responsible for our own emotional well-being does not mean that we are free to harm other beings, emotionally, physically, or in any other manner. It simply means that we remove the burden from others for our ability to feel good. We no longer need to wait for the world or anyone in the world to comply with a set of standards in order to be happy. It's up to each of us to feel better for ourselves and to do so in a way that, as a minimum, does not harm others.

Love Over Fear

A Course in Miracles says that every action is either rooted in love or in fear. To find out what the true basis of any action really is requires deep digging. On a superficial level, something may seem like an action rooted in love, but it's actually rooted in fear. Only a calm, quiet mind and a relaxed nervous system sees clearly enough to ascertain the root cause. As we learned, the Sanskrit word karma is translated into English as action. The root of any action shows itself in the fruit of that action. In yoga terms, this is often referred to as karma, which can be understood as the fruits of any action. Actions rooted in love will always bear the fruits of more love. Actions rooted in fear will always bear the fruits of more fear.

Each and every human being is connected to the source of life and is on a journey of evolution and awakening. There is some intimation, even if only subconsciously felt, that already guides each of us toward a path of love. We instinctively gravitate away from the chains of fear and move toward the freedom of love. The intelligent guidance system within each of us is perfectly equipped to direct the journey of life. The work of the spiritual path isn't so much about getting some addition to who we are. The work of the spiritual path is more about learning how to listen to the messages that arise from within ourselves with more precision and confidence. Once we get the hang of dropping down and tuning in to our inner navigation, then life flows with much more grace. Love is our natural state. We are here not to find love outside ourselves but to wake up to the love that is already inherent within.

Meditation

Come to a comfortable seated position. Close your eyes, and center yourself for a few moments by bringing your attention to your breath. Be aware of the natural breath, and gently encourage the breath to deepen. Stay with the steady pace of inhalation and exhalation for a few moments. Once the mind has calmed down, drop your attention into your heart center. Call up the vibration of happiness and love within you. If it's hard for you to tap into the raw emotional state, then recall a time in your life when you were filled with love and truly happy. Or envision yourself in the future, filled with love and beaming with happiness. If you're working with memories or visions of the future, don't get caught up in the details. Instead, focus on the feeling. After your mind, heart, and soul become present to the feelings of love and happiness, bring in the vibration and feeling of happiness to your body. Observe the breath and the sensations in your body. Steep in what you feel. Practice anchoring the state of love and happiness within you every day. Practice in times of ease so that you are well established. Practice in difficult times as well, and find a place within yourself that is beyond the inevitable vicissitudes of life.

Chapter 11

The Awakened Activist

The quieting of our mind is a political act. The world does not need more oil or energy or food. It needs less greed, less hatred, less ignorance. Even if we have inwardly taken on the political bitterness or cynicism that exists externally, we can stop and begin to heal our own suffering, our own fear, with compassion.

—Jack Kornfield (2009, 358)

If you have come here to help me, you are wasting your time. But if you have come because your liberation is bound up with mine, then let us work together.

—Lilla Watson, an aboriginal woman

Yoga is a space to make change and take right action. It is a space where body acceptance can be realized, and it's also a platform that has the potential to pioneer true equity; that is, if the deeper spiritual realization that is the heart of yoga can be fully utilized. As any yoga practitioner knows, that is not easy. Practicing yoga strengthens our hearts so we can put in the real work of changing our lives and, ultimately, changing the world. But within the broader scope of the wellness community, we cannot talk about yoga without touching on the uncomfortable things that many people would rather not discuss. Things like racism, classism, sexism, capitalism, and colonialism exist within yoga, meditation, and wellness, especially in the Western world. Even though many spiritual seekers turn to these ancient practices to "disconnect," in a sense, we cannot actually disconnect these social issues from our practice. The real work of social awakening has to move beyond the mat and off the meditation cushion. The tools of yoga and meditation give every practitioner the tools to deconstruct the way these conscious and unconscious biases live within the mind. As long as the limiting factors of division are at work, no one individual or any society will live up to its full potential.

These are hard conversations that need to be had within the community of yoga practitioners, teachers, and enthusiasts. The way that yoga is packaged and delivered today, especially in the Western Hemisphere, can have a big impact on personal and individual connections to the lineage. There is a strong movement within the Desi community of the Indian diaspora, led by teachers like Anusha Wijeyakumar and Susanna Barkataki, to decolonize yoga and reclaim yoga's traditional Indian roots. Asana is just one part of the long lineage of yoga. Decolonizing yoga is not just the next wellness buzzword. Instead, the historical implications of colonization and how that manifests in the contemporary wellness world has the potential to do real harm to real people and real communities—the very people and communities whose ancestors safeguarded and practiced the yoga and meditation techniques from which so many benefit today. We can use our spiritual practice as a tool to dismantle and decolonize our minds. We can platform minority voices, refrain from acts of cultural appropriation, and break down unconscious barriers in our own minds that could translate into our practice, our teaching, and our lives.

It isn't only the wellness community in which the work of decolonization must happen if real equity and inclusion is to be actualized. We start our discussion here because the broader teaching of this book happens within the framework of yoga and meditation, two traditions with knowledge bases that come from India. It is necessary to clean out one's own house before embarking on a larger quest. The same patterns of racism, sexism, capitalism, and colonialism are at work in almost every corner of society. At any given moment, tuning in to the flow of urgent causes that seem to require active protest can feel overwhelming. In truth, if you tune in to the suffering of the world, there is great need for active protest, and there is an abundance of urgent causes that could be aided by your attention. But the means by which you seek to engage and the root of your emotional state matter nearly as much as the mere fact that you choose to act.

The year 2020 rocked the world to its core. To many, this year was a fiery crescendo of crises. COVID-19 impacted the world with infection and considerable loss of life. The virus laid bare the inequities of peak capitalism and laid the foundation for a global shift in awareness. George Floyd spoke the words, "I can't breathe," as he was dying at the hands of police officers. His death sparked a wave of activism against systemic racism. Protesters took to the streets to voice legitimate frustration over the failure to reform police practices in the US. Small minorities of people from all sides of the political spectrum committed acts of violence, including looting and even murdering their political opponents. A historic hurricane season pummeled the Atlantic, while wildfires raged in the western United States, while the most contentious presidential election in history threatened to corrode the core of American democracy. The feeling was ominous and overwhelming.

Internal conflicts mirrored the tumultuous times of the world. Unhappiness, anger, and irresolution sit inside, like a tinderbox waiting for the spark to ignite the conflagration. Once burning, the emotional flames threaten to consume all and leave only devastation. But what is unseen in the moment of tension is the need for destruction in any cycle of regeneration. It wasn't all for nothing; there was meaning in the suffering.

When a forest fire rages, it's easy to see only the devastation. When a volcano erupts and lava spews, the fascination is often with the flow of lava. But there's something else at work in times of great conflict. Both the charred ashes that lie on the ground and the cooled lava play a vital role in the birth of something new. To move forward, sometimes you have to burn the old to the ground. While I would not wish pain and suffering on anyone, there is a particular state of growth that can only be achieved by going through suffering.

Could these larger social trends be a period of post-traumatic growth, a kind of spiritual awakening for the world? It's too early to tell, but I hope that once we see these series of events in the rearview mirror that we will be able to say that there was a palpable shift in values, relationships, personal strength, social resilience, and spiritual change. Core beliefs need to shift in order to impact change. Social scientists often say that as little as a 2 percent change in opinion has the power to elicit a turn in direction of public policy. Perhaps the same cycles of personal growth and evolution happen on societal and global levels as well. We will only see in hindsight what the lessons were during the darkest of nights. The lessons learned take time to work themselves out, like new seeds sprouting from the charred remains of the past.

Spiritual Bypassing

Most people have some cursory knowledge of yoga, at least that it exists. Even more people have taken a yoga class. However, the image presented in yoga videos or in most yoga classes is most likely rooted in an understanding of yoga culture that is quite far from its roots as a spiritual practice from India. Think about yoga, and you may associate it with a certain soft, delicate, and breathy voice, with long pauses between the words. The head is tilted slightly toward the side, with dreamy eyes and a subtle smile. Crystals and eco-conscious clothes help with good vibes, high frequency, and raising the vibration. Hands might rest in prayer position under flowing, natural-fiber organic clothes. Music with the sounds of Sanskrit set to modern beats might fill the air. This iconic image of a yoga teacher is just that—an image produced both in our minds and by the culture around yoga in the West. Many yoga teachers, including me, have felt that they have to fit the mold in order to be accepted as a bona fide yoga teacher. Just as with any crafted image, however, it isn't real.

Hidden just beneath the love-and-light veneer lurks the unprocessed realms of the subconscious mind. We cannot talk about activism in the wellness world without talking about spiritual bypassing. Many people turn to a spiritual tradition or framework for the tools to calm the unconscious mind. Some even try to whip the subconscious mind into shape in an attitude similar to that taken in exercise. The mind is yet another realm that needs "fixing," and well-intended spiritual aspirants hedge their well-being on the grounds of mental purification and inner detox. Seeking these tools can truly help pave the way toward helpful change and self-study, but it can also present a dangerous and deceptive "out." When people proclaim "good vibes only," it can be used as a tacit rejection of anything deemed "low vibe." Most interactions that challenge deeply held beliefs and biases are confrontational and difficult and easily are labeled as low vibe. While managing your thoughts is exactly what I'm suggesting you do, sometimes we all need to dive head-first into the darkness before we find the light. Whether you consider yourself a yoga practitioner, a Buddhist meditator, a devout Christian, or a follower of any religious faith, it is likely that your faith-based values contain the potential of a spiritual bypass.

Every spiritual seeker should get familiar with the important term spiritual bypassing. Understanding this concept is integral to the journey because it can potentially be what holds back spiritual growth in yoga—or other paths. The term *spiritual bypassing* is a concept that was originally introduced by John Welwood in the 1980s to describe when certain aspects of the yogi's spiritual path are co-opted and used for avoidance, repression, and other negative coping mechanisms. All of the concepts that we learn about in yoga—patience, acceptance, enlightenment—can be bypassed by our behavioral routines without our even realizing it. Activist Rachel Cargle states, "Spiritual bypass is a defense mechanism. Although the defense looks a lot prettier than other defenses, it serves the same purpose." The purpose of a spiritual bypass is to shield the dominant group from the truth and allow them to disconnect from the bigger picture. She says, "It is more about checking out than checking in."

We all think negative thoughts sometimes. We can't have the light without the dark. Under the pressure to "be positive," many spiritual seekers feel guilty or embarrassed by their negative thoughts. If we feel guilty about our shadow, it is very likely the result of a spiritual bypass. It is hard enough to accept your shadow self as it is, let alone under the presumption that spiritual seekers should emit only love and light. In the moments when insecurity, frustration, or even jealousy appear, it can be hard to reconcile some of the metaphysical and spiritual concepts with one's current state. Statements like "everything is fine" and "just breathe" can feel disingenuous, even flippant. We can't pretend that problems don't exist, but we can take control of the way we react to those problems. We can change how we treat ourselves when a cycle of negative thinking begins. We can learn how to respond with compassion and wisdom when adversity arises.

Spiritual tools are meant to give us the confidence to go into the deepest darkness of our shadow selves with the understanding that nothing is permanent. I share the ways these tools work for me and how we can all implement them into our own yoga routines and our daily lives. This way, when a spiritual bypass tries to say that nothing matters, the practice itself will reveal the truth and lead the way between the bypass and the spiritual path. The middle ground between the spiritual bypass and the path to enlightenment is not easy to find. There are still days when I get on my yoga mat and feel angry and insecure about my poses or my body. There are still times when I feel ashamed of my depression, anxiety, anger, and other "dark" emotions. But it helps me to recognize when I am bypassing my emotions and pretending to be in love and light. As soon as I realize which cycle is at play, I can shift the paradigm and sit with whatever emotions are present within myself.

Spiritual bypassing is when the lofty language and high ideals of a bona fide path of spiritual realization are used to avoid confronting the often murky, ugly, twisted, contorted, painful realities of the present. Cargle states,

> When confronted with the ways they have offended a marginalized group with their words or actions, they immediately start to demand unity and peace; painting those harmed as aggressive, mean or divisive.

In yoga, when fellow yogis are angry or upset about something, they are often told to just breathe. When Buddhists voice angst and outrage, their fellow meditators often advise them to remain equanimous. Christians are held up to the standard of whether their behavior is Christlike enough. It's a trope that stems from the very real feeling of transcendent peace that happens when the mind grows large enough to see the picture of both agony and ecstasy as one. On some instinctive level, we all want to be at peace and for the world to be at peace with us. When we read the words of an enlightened master such as the Buddha, who has transcended anger, we try to take on that persona for ourselves. But the reality is that we are not the Buddha (at least, I am not yet at that level). It is well intended and delusional at the same time to think that "negative" emotions have no place in the spiritual community.

The unfortunate and unintended side effect of the spiritual bypass is to deny the fundamental truth about one's reality. None of us chooses when or if we are triggered. We cannot deny what we feel, especially when what we feel is as powerful as anger. Denial creates the perfect scenario for internal and external stagnation. If we deny anger, it will be repressed and eventually explode or implode. More importantly, if we deny anger, we will not be able to listen to its wisdom or integrate the deep life lessons that it has to teach us.

The Importance of Anger and Outrage in Spiritual Work

Anger and outrage often have a message to tell about boundaries, especially when those boundaries are violated. Most of the spiritual practitioners of the world are not enlightened masters living in a nondual world, where all is love and light. We are just human beings deeply motivated to live better lives. That means that in order to take any substantial step forward, we will have to be willing to look deeply at all the places inside of ourselves that make us uncomfortable. For many yogis and meditators, that means looking at anger. If the language of the spiritual path is used to silence voices of outrage that bring up much-needed issues regarding equity and justice, then the spiritual community will fail at its goal of liberation before it even begins.

In the case of the spiritual bypass, the danger is that the dominant groups, who often control the narrative of popular culture, seize and co-opt the words of a spiritual leader like Buddha or Christ and then deploy those words to protect their positions of power in larger societal structures. Most of this is done unconsciously, but some of it is done consciously. Further harm happens when a member of a dominant group deploys the spiritual bypass. The usage of moral language perpetuates a sense of superiority over the marginalized voice that is seen as loud and angry and not spiritually evolved. Think about how often we see on social media that those who voice genuine concern for harm being done are told that they are being negative. Unfortunately, this tone-policing happens all too often.

Each time a person is driven to become an activist, it is often because of the experience of unacceptable violation of personal liberty at the hands of the dominant group in power. The anger felt is righteous and valid. The dominant group benefits from the silence and compliance of the marginalized group. The absence of marginalized voices in positions of power normalizes the power imbalance and keeps the dominant group in a position of dominance. When a member of a marginalized group wakes up and speaks out against the violation of personal liberty, the first reaction from the dominant group often is to resist, defend, and deny. In the spiritual community, one of the biggest tools of defense is the spiritual bypass. The only way we can get beyond this is to understand how vital a component anger and other so-called negative emotions really are to the fullness of life.

Spiritual practitioners need to accept that anger is an appropriate emotional response to injustice, even if anger sometimes rages like a mighty conflagration that destroys what is in its path. Destruction is a part of the cycle of growth too. Unprocessed, repressed anger is perhaps the most dangerous because it is unspoken, unfelt, and unconscious. Anger can be a part of both action and love if the tools of the spiritual part are deeply understood, but it isn't easy.

Anger is 100 percent justifiable when heinous acts of injustice are committed. What we do with that anger is a choice that each of us must make. Anger is not hate. Hate is part of the cycle of violence that each of us will have to face within ourselves. The foundation of a new paradigm of living has to include a way to work with the intense emotions that arise when confronted with injustice. When anger and hate arise, we need tools to help us do the work required, both internally and externally; otherwise, our spiritual practice ends up being a big, fluffy spiritual bypass.

I do not consider myself an activist, yet I care intensely about the suffering of every being—human and nonhuman, young and old, every color, every size, every religion. I believe that every being has value and worthiness. Spiritual practitioners are being called out of the comfort zones of pure practice. It's not enough anymore to simply be a good person. It's not enough to simply share outrage on social media. There is work needed on the path of awakening to wake up the slumber of delusion. The promise of the spiritual path is to break the cycle of suffering and to become an awakened activist and an enlightened agent of change. We cannot work to end the suffering of others while disregarding our own suffering. And we cannot diligently work to end our own suffering while ignoring the suffering of others. If we are all one, then each one of us matters. What we do to another we do to ourselves. Cargle says, "I don't want your love and light if it doesn't come with solidarity and action."

Yoga, meditation, and the spiritual path are more than pretty pictures and fun-looking poses. The spiritual path promises full liberation. As long as violence lives in any of us, the cycle of suffering will continue. Members of the dominant group of any society are especially responsible for doing the work to weed out the dormant seeds, the sprouting trees, and the full fruits of violence from their own hearts. People in positions of power must unpack the chains of their own limited beliefs and work to actively dismantle systems that support violence. When we sit silently by and do nothing, we tacitly participate in a culture of violence. We become a cog in the wheel of systemic hate. Whether or not we ourselves are the perpetrators, our belonging to that culture means we share in the guilt. I do not write this to shame anyone. I'm part of that culture too. We all are.

Love and light must be backed up by concrete actions; otherwise, it's just words and fluff. Neither can we let our rage and anger go unchecked and unprocessed and fuel destructive cycles of yet more violence. There is a calling to break the cycle that all spiritual practitioners are called to answer. Awakening is a personal revolution that begins with oneself. But it cannot stop there. Only by breaking the cycle of systemic violence itself can we seek to be free of it as a society. As long as we live in a society that tacitly condones or outright embraces violence, we are all bound to suffering. When enough of us wake up and do the work to shift the paradigm, both within ourselves and in our world, then change happens. We have to break the cycle, both within ourselves and within our world. It matters, more than we might think, that we each continue to practice. And it matters even more that we take the lessons of our yoga practice off the mat and into our lives even more. There can be no true love in life while deep knots of self-hatred or gender hatred remain unprocessed and repressed. The only way to truly move into a fully thriving life is to go through the anger, welcome it, and get to the root of it.

Just as we are advised to sit with our pain in our practice, we are advised to sit with the pain of others in our lives. Our hearts must grow big enough to embrace all the suffering and loss of the world.

Addicted to Outrage

Anger and rage are addictive, both in person and virtually. Venting raw, unprocessed emotion is a behavior that gets easier when practiced. Once the adrenaline rush associated with the highs of outrage courses through the body, it is easy to give in to the rage and further sow the seeds of division. The moment a fellow human being is labeled as evil and unworthy of love, forgiveness, or compassion, the cycle of violence gets permission to keep spinning.

A few years ago, I engaged in an online campaign to affect behavior change of a large billion-dollar company. In my mind, I was fighting what

I thought was the "good fight," aligned against "evil" people in positions of power, whom I had defined as villains who were incapable of doing good. When I first started sharing my story, it felt cathartic, and, on some level, giving in to the rush of anger was intoxicating. But after a few weeks, the toll on my nervous system started to show. Using anger as fuel burned me out, and I realized that the moment I allowed myself to hate my opponent, I had already lost myself.

So many people are driven by the same hunger for antagonism. There is a yearning to burn the house down, which anger often sparks. While there is a time when old institutions that no longer serve current needs must be destroyed, much like a forest fire clears the ground for new growth, human interests are not always as impersonal as a forest fire. People cheer from the sidelines with no stake in the game. Fascination with the abomination of hate is much like watching a car crash or a boxing match. As two gladiators fight in the auditorium, crowds demand blood. But once the fight is over, the cheering crowds are nowhere to be found. The fighters tend their wounds in solitude, and few are there with them while they heal. The winner too is cherished only as long as the winning streak is maintained. Those who claim to be the greatest supporters in a war are often feeding their own addiction to suffering. Their allyship often does not extend to moments of loss, depression, and evolution. Participating in social movements in which the dominant force is hate ties everyone into a destructive and unsustainable cycle. This is true whether that movement is aligned with conservative, liberal, or any other ideology. In fact, one could argue that the extremes of both sides of any political or religious landscape are often mirror images.

Now, I am not saying that outrage itself is invalid, nor am I seeking to neutralize the heinous wrongs that many social movements seek to discuss. I am proposing that we, as spiritual seekers, do better. Imagine what changes to the world can be done by using love as fuel for the movement. Endeavoring to build a fortress springs from insecurity. A barricaded society is closed off from compassion and connection.

Finding problems and picking others apart is actually quite easy. Building up what works is much harder. When members of any community engage in what is called a "circular firing squad," they tear themselves apart. When like-minded people, who are close to each other in terms of value, fight among themselves instead of aligning for large social change, the power of community is diluted. What ends up happening is often a perpetuation of the status quo. Differences among very similar people are meaningful, but no one is perfect. If everyone who says one wrong thing is canceled, called out, and humiliated, there is no hope for positive growth or unity. As standards of perfection eliminate the possibility for people within a community to make mistakes and fail up, the circular firing squad casts its stream of bullets at anyone who messes up, even if they learn from their mistakes. The unfortunate result is the misdirection of angst toward one's allies, the result of which only seeks to empower true opposites. If aligned interests remain divided over small details, while larger and more powerful opposing forces remain united, it will render the impact of any social-change movement inert. This incapacitation only helps the dominant group. Divide and conquer is an age-old colonial strategy and works only to keep the marginalized out of power.

Learning to act in love when it comes to activism is an antidote to the circular-firing-squad mentality. There has to be room for members of a community and allies of a given community to learn and make mistakes along the way. People come to the spiritual path to be awakened. If they were already awake and perfect, they wouldn't be here. We need to make room for people to wake up and to forgive them for the places where they may not yet have awakened. Of course, we need to allow ourselves that same space.

This is not about not being angry. Anger is intimately connected to joy and love, so when anger gets repressed, so does love. Actions taken under false love are merely a ruse of the ego, designed to make the ego feel better about itself. If we can learn to listen to the intelligence contained within anger when it arises, especially in the case of activism, which can unlock great moments of awakening. Yet anger, while valid and sometimes appropriate, is not a sustainable fuel for the long haul. A weathering happens when the stress of being angry and outraged is sustained for long periods of time.

Not only will the mind be set up to seek the next situation to get angry about, but there will be a craving or addiction to the high of anger left in the physical body. Anger creates a veneer of power, but it fades the moment the chemicals of anger wear off. Then the body is left feeling down and worn out, and it will naturally seek out the next high. This cycle is simply not sustainable.

When the Dalai Lama was asked how he was able to remain calm and happy and not let his anger at the situation in Tibet color everything amid the struggles of losing his country, he responded by saying that the Chinese took his country and that he wouldn't let them take his happiness. Of course, one could argue that his activism has been ineffective, such that the Chinese still occupy Tibet. In a world of illusion and show, it can be helpful to judge the root of action by its fruits. In the Dhammapada, the Buddha says,

> 'He abused me and beat me, he threw me down and robbed me.' Repeat these thoughts and you will live in hate. 'He abused me and beat me, he threw me down and robbed me.' Abandon these thoughts and live in love. In this world, hatred never ceases by hatred, but by love alone is healed. This is the ancient and eternal law.

The words of the Buddha have been used as a spiritual bypass for people in positions of power to continue their acts of aggression against marginalized groups. This is simply a perversion of the teaching. Rather than a call for the sins of the past to be wiped away, I take the Buddha's direction as part of a paradigm of freedom. The "work" of antiracism and dismantling systems of oppression can be done with a heart full of love or a heart full of hate. It's like treating an illness in the body or going on a fitness regimen. If the paradigm is hatred, then every action is centered on hate. Even what appears to be a victory can end up feeding the cycle of aggression. To change the paradigm entirely requires a heart full of love.

When I raged against a corporate giant that I deemed to be a perpetrator of evil in the world, anger clouded my vision and led me to normalize hateful actions. I failed myself and my spiritual path for a good while. That is, until, amid hate, anger, and victimhood, I changed the dialogue in my mind to love, forgiveness, and compassion. While I certainly didn't end up as the winner in the war, I left the experience with valuable firsthand knowledge on the toxicity of anger and its delusive yet seductive quality. I grew immensely from the experience of cultivating love amid hate.

It is my intention to provide support for the inner work of activism. Just as contemporary activists seek to dismantle the systems of oppression at the intersections of race, gender, and class, I seek to dismantle the systems of oppression that are latent in the subconscious mind. This book or my teaching is not to be used as spiritual bypassing or a cover for the offended to deploy the love-and-light barrier. Far from it, my hope is to provide another front for the battle of liberation and freedom for all. Make no mistake. We are at war, and, like any good wartime strategy, we need to fight the battle on all available fronts. While it may be easy to see outward signs of activism, such as protests, marches, and other forms of social awareness, as agitators, let's reframe our views. They are doing the outward work that all seekers of liberation must do internally. It is my hope that the spiritual path laid out in this book will provide sustenance and healing for all activists and will inspire all persons to truly embody the change that they seek in the world in the inner regions of the mind.

The inner and outer work go hand in hand. Without a significant change in the operating system of the individual and the collective mind, no amount of societal change will produce lasting results. Much like the power of the subconscious mind to sabotage our personal relationships, without a change in the inner workings of the deeply held power structures that govern our thinking internally, change on a social level will be only superficial and temporary. Even a few steps forward will be met with such a fierce backlash that the reactionary recidivism will pull us, as a whole, back to a place of more brokenness than where we started. The only way for social change to stay in effect is to update the operating system in the mind. For that to happen, we must be committed to dismantling systems of oppression that govern our thinking, both conscious and unconscious.

Without sounding cliché, this is where love is truly the answer. Throughout the course of this book, I have shared techniques that help break the toxic cycle that is at work in our minds, challenged the framework of thinking that we have absorbed through osmosis, just from being alive, and suggested updates to the operating system that sabotages all our dreams of success and happiness. When we install this upgrade to the mind, a totally new paradigm of thought opens a portal to a radical way of living. Have no doubt; we will change the world when we change ourselves.

Not everyone is meant to be a vocal activist. Some of our work is about changing our own inner worlds. We also need to live out our values and beliefs in our lives. If we claim to be a feminist, we must live out our feminism in actions. There are many ways to be active in the world and to go beyond our own inner awakening; rather, to put our inner awakening to use for the greater good. Do not doubt that your awakening is a vital and crucial part of the planet's evolution. It is. You matter. Your happiness matters.

Small Acts of Love

We are often told that we should do things, but the conversation is perhaps most effective when presented as things that we can do—what we *could* do for an issue, rather than what we *can* do for someone. It is really easy to feel overwhelmed with all the issues out there and easy to feel a sense of shame that we aren't doing enough. But as yogis, we are called to action. As it says in the Gita 3:8, "Perform your duty, for action is indeed better than no action."

There are untold acts of bravery that shift the balance of power in even the most insufferable conflicts. A man known as the "Cellist of Sarajevo," named Vedran Smailovic, engaged in an act of resistance amid the three-year siege of Sarajevo. Despite the ravages of war, Smailovic would get dressed in his performance tuxedo and play Albinoni's Adagio in G Minor in ruined buildings, at funerals, and under sniper fire. Once, he played for twenty-two days straight in a Sarajevo marketplace after twenty-two people were killed by a mortar while waiting for food. He did this to give the people, himself included, hope.

We each have some music to give to the world. It is through our innate connection to all beings that we can make a difference. Of course, we have to get our own houses in order first.

Spiritual teacher Ram Dass says,

> Remember, we are all affecting the world every moment, whether we mean to or not. Our actions and states of mind matter, because we are so deeply interconnected with one another. Working on our own consciousness is the most important thing that we are doing at any moment, and being love is a supreme creative act.
> (Dass 2021)

I believe it is possible to work toward a positive resolution without bypassing the much-needed work of recognizing the pain of the present. To have hope, even amid what can feel like a hopeless place, is what drives us to act and evolve. Scenes of love that emerged during the George Floyd protests deeply inspired me. An African American woman crossed over the lines to hug a police officer. The embrace lasted for over one minute and diffused what was a tense situation. In Miami, police officers apologized to protesters, took a knee, and prayed with them in a peaceful protest. These acts of courage, bravery, leadership, and love will win the tide. Love may look different, depending on what vantage point you hold in society. Members of the dominant group may show love by lifting up, listening to, and protecting marginalized groups. Members of marginalized groups may show love by speaking up and demanding that their voices be heard.

To be clear, it is up to each of us to nurture the seeds of change in our own hearts and in the world in which we live. These anecdotes of goodness do not erase the scars of hurt, but they can help till the soils of the heart to receive the seed of healing

We all sit at the intersection of differing identities. We may find ourselves as a member of the dominant culture in one context, only to find ourselves as an outsider in another. Cisgender allows many to sit well within the heteronormative majority. But within that group, there may be a female person of color who also finds herself in the minority. It is important to contextualize one's identity. We often foreground our outsider status and downplay our insider status. This is due to trauma. When we exist within the dominant group, that privilege affords us the bliss of ignorance. We have no concept of what it feels like to be outside the majority because the status quo is the norm. When we fall outside the boundaries of the standard, we are hit with the glaring reality of our difference. Places where we feel different seem to be larger and more powerful than places where we are the same. In this way, we all have some privileges and some disadvantages. Ideally, the shifting lines of intersectionality allow each of us to embrace the unique concerns of presence and love from both the dominant and the minority viewpoint.

To act in love as a member of a subordinate minority may very well be met with active resistance from the dominant group. Love can seem like a violent act. It is self-affirming and works to reclaim lost identity and power. Love is a revolution and a challenge to the status quo. To affirm one's own minority identity as worthy against the message received from the dominant group is a radical act of resistance and love incarnate.

To act in love as a member of the dominant group means something different than it does to act in love as a member of the subordinate minority. Dominance is not always defined by being the majority. Sometimes dominance is formed in relationship to power and control. Minority groups are not necessarily lower in number. Apartheid makes that crystal clear. Additionally, people of color actually comprise the majority of the human population, while the white culture remains dominant. Realizing one's place within the power hierarchy of the world creates the space for each person to embody love differently, moment to moment, as his or her shifting identities account for. A member of a dominant group, acting in love, is not interested in defense or reclaiming lost ground. Nor is it loving for a dominant group to—well, continue dominating. Love means opening your heart to compassion and welcoming the otherness of those in the minority. Power is only love when it is used to equalize and not entrench. Sometimes listening is enough. Sometimes more is needed from those in power, such as lifting up the voices and causes of the marginalized.

A positive example of the way that members of a dominant group can use the privilege to act in love is when white people use their privilege to protect black bodies from harm. While it doesn't happen often, there are certain cases where a white person or group of white people have stood between a black activist and the authorities. As is the case of white-privileged action, the authorities do not touch the white people; instead, they reach out to try to subdue the black body. When the white allies surround the black person who is speaking, they act in love to both elevate and protect the marginalized voice.

Members of the dominant group cannot merely do what their hearts tell them. Privilege is subconscious and systemic. It is like a virus that impacts every decision and action, coloring good deeds with the stigma of racism, classism, and exclusionary logic. We must each consider where we are members of intersections of power in the world. Perhaps we benefit from economic privilege, gender privilege, race privilege, educational privilege.

When members of the dominant groups of society seek to help, that too presents a problem. Unless the paradigm is changed within one's own mind, then even the most well-intended action can further cause suffering. Violence is sometimes subtle, and it's sometimes the most subtle forms of violence that do the most harm because they go unnoticed.

An unawakened activist runs the risk of taking personal psychodrama to the public stage. Often, our own knots of irresolution trigger us the most. If we act and protest every situation that triggers us, without doing the inner work of awakening, one unfortunate consequence may be the accentuation and spreading of an unevolved state. Instead of actual social change, we may merely trade one for the oppression of another. Once given power, after having been oppressed, we may not be the just, equitable leader for all that we think we are.

We all have biases. To think we don't is to lie to ourselves. The danger lies not in admitting our bias but in leaving those biases unchecked and operating without supervision in the subconscious mind. To do the work of activism requires doing the work of inner awakening in equal parts. Awakening the heart is twofold—first, as a personal journey of enlightenment, and second, as a collective evolution of justice. Both are equally important, and one cannot be done without the other. Otherwise, the potential to merely play out one's own personal drama triangle on a larger, macro level is just too great.

Changing the way we think requires us to install a totally new software on the hard drives of the mind and heart. If we want the world to move beyond the old rules of a drama triangle, we have to be willing to do it ourselves.

Step Out of the Echo Chamber

It is tempting to think that keyboard activism is sufficient to be an agent of change in the world, but the work of creating a better society is done in the real world, offline, as much as—if not more than—it is done online. While posts can certainly spark a dialogue, if that dialogue does not initiate a change of behavior in people offline, then it is limited in scope. Discussions that occur in the realm of the online world can sometimes happen in a controlled environment that blocks divergent views in what is called an *echo chamber*. What appears as dialogue in echo chambers risks fostering extremism, rather than understanding and connection.

Social media is not organic. What you see is structured, based on algorithms written by coders. These are people who have bias, just like you and me. These algorithms are owned by multinational billion-dollar companies, whose interest is capitalistic, not altruistic. Multinational corporations are rarely founded with the intention of making the world a better place for all. Their interests more often revolve around maximization of profit, even at the great expense of devouring the human connections that found a healthy society. Before I paint the corporate behemoths as yet another villain, let me say that it is only natural that money and power amplify what is at the heart of every human being—a quest for happiness and love. When that search is defined by external standards and actions, then the endless need to achieve more and do more defines all actions. We are no better than the leaders of these corporate giants. It is just that our sphere of misery is limited and, therefore, not as destructive. Let us not think we are better than the corporate leaders of the world, but with practice and a shift in consciousness, we can be. And so can every human being on the planet, even the leaders of the most powerful corporate behemoths. Who knows? Maybe people in a position of real power will read this book, and a shift will happen in their consciousness that ricochets down through the vast network they control.

But for now, let's try to understand what the danger of an algorithm, designed to highlight engagement, means for our minds. Scrolling on social media is designed to enhance outrage. Beyond fluffy animals, food porn, and selfies, something else is happening. Hidden between what we trust as an innocuous feed of images from friends are social-political posts, highlighted due to the outrage they generated. The algorithms on which the apps are built play upon our negativity bias. We are drawn to controversy in the same way that we are drawn to gawk at a car accident. While it is untrue, negativity bias highlights the negative and makes them seem bigger than everything else, even though there are always more positive things in any given day than negative. Negativity bias is a limbic-system-alert response that can do real damage to the fabric of society when exploited by algorithms of attention.

Algorithms create echo chambers, where people who express interest in a particular subject by engaging with it through comments or "likes" get shown more of the same type of content. Like a bubble or a world within a world, if we click on Labradors, for example, the algorithm shows more

Labradors. If we click on a yogi, we will be flooded with lots of yogis. In an organic skim of all content posted across the whole world, there is natural diversity. In an algorithmically created universe, there is sameness. Now, there may, at first, be no apparent problem with this—if we love Labradors, why not just see Labradors all day? Studies show that when an echo chamber is created, people's views get more polarized and extreme. People who are exposed to only similar beliefs get more rigid and dogmatic in their views. People who are exposed to divergent views tend to be more compassionate, accepting of difference, and willing to compromise. If it's just Labradors, that's not a big deal, but when it's political, economic, and social views, it gets dangerous.

Viewing the world through the algorithm filter can be destructive. Outrage-generating posts appear on our feeds, while the opposing view is silenced. When we unfollow people who espouse a different belief than we have, we feed the algorithm's tendency to create a virtual wall from difference. People pass judgment with the click of a finger and follow and unfollow with an astounding rapidity. The basis of these quick judgments is often rooted in the engagement-driven algorithm and not the reality of deeply connecting with other human beings who are worthy of respect and love, even if their views are diametrically opposed to ours. Sometimes media bubbles facilitate a broad scale denial of reality. Buddhist teacher Jack Kornfield says,

> Denial can also function collectively. Buddhist psychology describes how whole societies can be manipulated into a violent people by ignorance, racism, and fear mongering. The consumer advertising and television propaganda around us can deliberately foster anxiety and reinforce our political and economic delusions. Collective delusions can operate for years before we awaken to the cost. (Kornfield 2009, 228)

If we are going to awaken, it requires practice and effort. In order to cultivate real offline connections with people who fall outside the realm of our echo chamber, we will have to learn how to listen and perceive innocently, without the help of a coded search filter. In doing so, we will work to shift the collective patterns of subconscious thought as an attractor point for our social creation. There is both individual and collective accountability in each of our actions. While we are each individually responsible for our own private attraction point, we are also responsible, even if through quiet complicity, for the collective attraction point. If we do nothing to shift the patterns of discourse, then, despite our best intentions, the patterns will repeat. Simply living your life under the assumption that you're a good person isn't enough. Every action must be intentional in order to dismantle the systems of power that keep a privileged few at the top of a hierarchy built of exploitation and discrimination.

A New Hero

Maybe each of us has a deeply held knot in our souls that governs many aspects of our lives from the hidden layers of the subconscious mind. The thing is, we can be free of it if we are willing to dive down to a previously unknown depth. There, at the center of ourselves, we will meet every broken shard of our hearts and get the chance to pick up those pieces and glue them back together with unbreakable, pure, golden light. The work of the spiritual path is more than the next trend. We are embarking on an age-old tool to start a revolution in our minds, one that has the power to fully liberate us all. The path is there for all who are called, so all that is needed is to start. To the degree to which we have untied knots within ourselves, we live in the free space of an open heart, which is filled with joy and love.

Too often, we throw people out because they've made a mistake; because they didn't get it right. Too often, we judge ourselves harshly for not getting it right the first time; for not being perfect on the path. But there is no dress rehearsal for life; it's all happening now, in real time. We don't get a practice run or a do-over. If we are at risk of being canceled for every mistake we make, sooner or later we will all be canceled. Human beings aren't single-use plastic containers that serve their purpose and get tossed out. We are each valuable beings, here to learn and grow. Each of our evolutions matter, but we won't get there if we don't make space for mistakes, for stumbles, for faults and flaws and scars. Instead of hiding, being a plastic, perfect veneer, perhaps what we need to see is the beauty of imperfection in ourselves and in our world. There is no "us and them"; there is only us—human beings, doing the best we can.

In every culture, there is a mythology of leadership and heroism. Joseph Campbell first documented the similarities of the hero's journey in what he described as a "Monomyth." Regardless of cultural origin, the hero's journey embodies an archetypical act of love that follows a winding path through trials and tribulations, which ultimately end with a world-changing boon bestowed upon the hero for the benefit of the world. Campbell's book *The Hero with a Thousand Faces* is the story of a global quest for love and a yearning to rewrite the story of senseless loss and enduring hardship from the paradigm of growth and understanding. Somewhere in our collective hearts, we measure our leaders to the standard of the hero myth. Whether our personal hero is Lord Rama, Gandalf from *Lord of the Rings*, or T'Challa of Wakanda, each of these individuals stands out for being willing to sacrifice themselves for the benefits of a greater cause. Our heroes are who they are because their stories tell the story of love, written large on a societal scale.

We live in such times of disillusionment because this promise has long been broken. Our heroes have shown themselves to be all too human, perhaps no better than we are, with our stumbling, fumbling ways. In a fallen world, power corrupts, and absolute power corrupts absolutely. Power rooted in love is inviolable and just. The power of love is freedom. We need to look no farther than the vast inequalities of wealth in our global society to see the destructive nature of those in positions of power. Yet we cannot look back to a time when things were better. We must look forward to the promise of restoration. We cannot blame these leaders because they, just like us, suffer from the same disease of selfishness. Would we truly be able to resist the temptations presented by holding positions of power in the world? Would we truly be selfless leaders, or would we fall into the same (but perhaps smaller) traps as our fallen heroes?

There are countless beings in the world today—billions of people, trillions of animals. There are stories of suffering and joy in every day and in every moment. To walk the spiritual path with the intention of awakening is to take on the mantle of liberation, not just for yourself but for every being on the planet and in the universe. Some say that social justice has no place in the world of spiritual awakening; that it's too "divisive" and that identity politics take away from the experience of oneness. Well, in my experience, this is a statement of immense privilege, one that can be spoken only from a place of dominance. In our culture, there are many forms of dominance, just as there are many forms of oppression. It is the unspoken voice of nondominant cultures—people whose lives are at stake at the intersection of class, race, gender, size, ability, and age—that often is unheard, unaccounted for, undocumented, uncared for. Enlightenment is the dispelling of darkness and hate. It may start out as a pursuit rooted in individualism, but it has to evolve beyond that if it is to truly spread love and light to the whole world.

One person's awakening has the power to change the world. When one person starts meditating and awakening, they vibrate at a different frequency. Their very presence imparts change and plants seeds in the lives of those around them. They can do this without ever saying a word. Truth cannot be expressed in words as well as it can be embodied. When our very presence embodies love, then we are a revolution, a force of change in the lives around us.

Lifelong activist, sociology and gender/women's studies professor, and cofounder of the Yoga and Body Image Coalition, Melanie Klein recently discussed the positive changes she sees that are afoot in the wellness industry. The changes, while intended as the goal, seemed far off in the distance when she began bringing intersectional critical theory to the yoga community and wellness spaces in 2010, as the yoga blogosphere and social media took hold. Klein says that current conversations in the mainstream media related to diversity and inclusion were off the radar just a few years ago; these conversations were initially met with resistance and backlash, not only by the mainstream but by the yoga community and wellness spaces. There is now, at least, some attempt at diversity, inclusion, and representation in most magazines today or on the shopping pages of most fitness brands—and in some cases, successful paradigm shifts, as well as new and emerging media platforms and companies building their brands on the foundation of these core values. While it's true in some cases that acts of performative allyship or tokenization take center stage, overall, there is a massive shift in a new direction, one that is inclusive, diverse, and equitable. The key, Klein states, is not to be lulled by progress and confuse it for equity but to continue toward the horizon line, where this becomes the new norm.

While we still have a long way to go toward creating real equity in the world, it's important to celebrate the small steps forward in real life, just as we would do on the yoga mat. When people start living in a new way, that is when the world will change. When love is the basic motivator of every action, word, and thought, then we will live in a new world. It starts with the only vantage any of us can truly control—ourselves.

Meditation and Reflection Point

Do you think you can only be an effective agent of change when you let anger or hate be your fuel? Do you think it is OK to hate someone else as long as the cause is valid? Is it possible to maintain a heart full of love while working for social change? Evaluate the efficacy of using anger as fuel and assess whether the same course of action could be more or less effective with or without anger or hate. Look for an example in your own life where hate as fuel has been successful and an example where it has failed. Look for an example, perhaps in your own life, where love was used as the fuel for action, and evaluate whether that was as successful or perhaps even more successful.

✻

Chapter 12

For the Love of God

Religious and spiritual contemplation changes your brain in a profoundly different way because it strengthens a unique neural circuit that specifically enhances social awareness and empathy while subduing destructive feelings and emotions.

—Andrew B. Newberg

I was not raised with any religion. My grandfather was Buddhist. Both my parents belong to the secular but spiritual segment, affiliated with no religion. Perhaps because of this spiritual gap, I was drawn to find my own answers to the question of faith. I found my relationship with God through the practice of yoga.

From the time I can remember, I have always had an almost visceral antagonism to organized religion of any kind. I associated religion with the source of everything that has gone wrong in history, from the Crusades to misogyny to the normalization of the slave trade to culture wars. In my youth, I harbored an anger toward the God of a culture that two millennia of formal religion seemed to codify.

When I finally decided to search for a spiritual path, I turned to yoga. I practiced yoga and found deep peace, if only in the moment immediately after practice. Yet I was still searching. After the dust of daily practice settled, there was still a subconscious yearning that drove me forward, like a subtext to each action that told the hidden story of a quest for the deepest knowledge about God, the universe, and beingness. I was still a seeker on the timeless journey to eternity. That really is what yoga is all about, after all—the desire to know directly the answer to some of life's most difficult questions. Who am I? Where did I come from? Where will I go when this life is over?

My yoga teacher said that when you practice yoga, you should think about God in nearly every class. He often clarified and said "your God," but I never knew who God was. I entered Hindu temples and felt the holy space of worship. I meditated in Buddhist temples and fell into a trance of peace. I practiced yoga and immersed myself in the infinite. I let the sun's rays cascade over my body in the early morning hours as a blessing, felt the intelligence of trees teach me about life, drifted off to a flow led by the ocean's waves, and let the sugary sweetness of fruit be a testament to the kindness of life. God, for me, was everywhere—everywhere and nowhere, specifically. When asked to use the word *God*, I often balked and preferred statements like "the love of the universe" or "divine oneness." When I closed my eyes and asked for God to show up, I expected to see the Buddha or Krishna or some other deity, but I didn't. Mostly what I felt when I tuned into the vibration of divinity was the tune of a kind of eternality, a timeless presence of immovable peace, infinite compassion, all-knowingness, gentle wisdom, awe-inspiring beauty, and miraculous wonder. I always thought that was enough for me.

Then, one day, everything changed. I was sitting on an airplane on the way to Dallas to teach a yoga workshop. My tablet was opened, and I was about to put my headphones on to watch a silly TV program and zone out. Then, something happened that I can only describe as a direct, personal, and revelatory experience of God. My vision turned white, and the world literally disappeared. All I could see was a wash of impenetrable brightness. In the blinding light, the outline of clouds appeared to form a kind of gateway. The fluffy, cotton-ball clouds with friendly round edges began moving and shifting to reveal a kind of golden tunnel of yet even more light. It felt like I had entered a sphere of what a child would draw as heaven. To my great surprise, I saw a figure descend from the clouds, moving toward me. This being was unlike any I had ever met, a light without shadow. I was on my knees in a gesture of respect and surrender that was familiar to me from my student's work in yoga. My eyes looked up to see Jesus Christ standing before me.

My initial reaction was not excitement. To be honest, I was confused. I wasn't looking for Jesus. I had never read the Bible. I was a spiritual seeker on a quest to know God, but I had never once considered the Christian God as part of my search. And then Jesus simply showed up for me. What happened next is hard to describe in words. I felt the hands of Jesus on my head and, with the sensation of touch, a light entered me, physically and spiritually, penetrating the depth of my being. It felt like a wave washed over the very fabric of my existence. Stillness overtook me while the concurrent feeling of ecstasy rose up. My eyes rolled toward the back of my head, and my body grew weak and faint. After some time, Jesus removed his hands, and I returned to the world.

The airplane had taxied, taken off, and flown for some time. I had no sense of how long I was lost in this vision. It felt timeless. But I can estimate, based on what I remember before and after, that I was in an other-world space for about an hour. This experience changed me and shook my foundation to the core. This is what Christians call *testimony*. This is what yogis call *Guru diksha*, or *śaktipāt*, which is the bestowing of divine grace through the hands of the true teacher in an experience that leaves you forever changed. I now sat with an answer to a question about God that blew the doors off my mind's preconceptions about what is and isn't true. My heart and soul were open from the yogi's quest and when the guru arrived, I knew what to do.

But now, the work to be done was to integrate the teaching, and I had no idea where to start or how to make sense of this. I knew that I had been touched by a being of pure love and light, unlike any other, and I knew I had been forever changed by that meeting.

Nothing to Fear in Yoga

Yoga traces its lineage and roots to India, and it is inherently tied to the history of the Hindu religion. Many yoga students in the West start practicing yoga without any idea that the class they're joining has an origin story in a culture from South Asia. Some devout Christian students box with the idea that the practice they love is born from the deities of another faith. When I've shared my story of meeting Jesus with some evangelical Christians, they have stared at me with disbelief. There are even fundamentalist Christian religious leaders who claim that yoga opens people up to acts of heresy and even demonic possession. I'd always wondered why Christians fear yoga, and I got to understand intimately what that's about, thanks to a student of mine.

Ronnie was a tall, blonde, and cheerful student who walked into my class one day. She said she had found me on YouTube and wanted to learn how to do a handstand like I did. Many students start yoga with a desire to be upside down. It's the seed of inspiration that begins what is sometimes a lifelong journey of spiritual awakening. Most don't intend for more than a little shoulder and core strength, and then the magic of yoga happens through them. Well, Ronnie started practicing diligently and fell in love with how she felt after practicing yoga. Soon, she was practicing daily and found relief from the chronic debilitating pain, stemming from fibromyalgia and migraines. All was going smoothly until one day, when she told her Christian pastor about her yoga practice. Immediately, the pastor instructed her to stop practicing yoga or else she would open herself up to demonic possession. After a lengthy conversation with her pastor, she left in a crisis of faith. Ronnie's experience in yoga told her that when she practiced, she felt better in her body and mind. More than that, Ronnie felt like yoga made her a better Christian, with more compassion, love, and forgiveness in her heart. But the pastor's words wouldn't go away. At an impasse, Ronnie invited me to meet her pastor so that we could discuss the apparent conflict between yoga and her Christian faith.

As I drove up to the church grounds and walked into the back-room office to meet with the pastor, I wasn't sure what was going to happen.

The pastor introduced himself as Pastor Larry and asked if we could begin the session with prayer. To be honest, I wasn't sure if Pastor Larry thought I was the devil or if he was going to try to exorcise me, but I agreed to the prayer. While it contained verbiage the likes of which I had never heard before, his intention seemed truly congenial. We spoke at length about the spiritual intention of yoga, the interrelationship between yoga and Hinduism, and what, if any, pitfalls I could see for Christians who practiced yoga. The question about demonic possession was the elephant in the room. The unspoken fear seemed to be the demon itself, if there was one at all. After a long time, Pastor Larry came out and said, "Yoga opens practitioners up to demonic possession, so we advise Christians not to practice yoga."

I really didn't have a response, other than sharing my own experience. There is no yoga text that talks about demonic possession. Yoga talks about spiritual awakening and the process of breaking free of destructive habit patterns. In some ways, yoga is a kind of spiritual psychology that uses the body as a means to encourage more inner work.

All I could do was share my story with Pastor Larry, just as I shared it with you. After I finished, Pastor Larry's eyes grew large, and he asked, with slow deliberation in his words, "Are you telling me that you met the Lord, our Savior, Jesus Christ himself?"

"Yes," I said, "I did."

He paused in a long silence. Then he turned toward Ronnie and said that he gave her his approval to continue taking yoga classes with me. I am happy to say that Ronnie is still practicing yoga with me to this day.

This happy story is not true for every Christian or person of deep faith. I've had deeply religious students from a non-Hindu faith stop practicing yoga because their rabbi, imam, or priest told them yoga was against their religion. A Catholic priest disseminated a letter to their parish, explaining that practicing yoga amounted to cheating on Jesus. An orthodox rabbi told his congregation that the chanting done in yoga violated the precepts of Judaism. A council of Malaysian Muslim clerics issued a fatwa against yoga, declaring it *haram*, or forbidden by Islamic law. Buddhist meditation sometimes suffers the same fate in religious circles as yoga. Meditation too has been proclaimed by religious leaders to open practitioners up for demonic possession and other outlandish claims. Attempts to present yoga and meditation as separate from their origins leads to co-opting ancient teachings for an industrious aim, one that has sometimes been called "McMindfulness." Not only is this harmful to the cultures of origin, but it is also misguided and untruthful.

Simply put, we cannot divorce yoga from its Hindu roots, nor meditation from its Buddhist roots. The vilification and fear-based mentality of religious leaders in the face of what is a truly liberating personal practice is unfounded. Yoga and meditation are paths of truth. The goal of the contemplative practices of the East is to give people a practice and a method to realize the truth about themselves, the world, and, ultimately, about God. The search for truth starts off with the body and the mind through the vehicle of yoga and other mindfulness-based practices. Then, the heightened powers of awareness cultivated through yoga and meditation are directed toward the deeper realms of reality. Ultimately, the spiritual path asks students to answer the question of God for themselves through direct experience. For whoever truly believes that God is the most powerful force in the universe, it would be a logical conclusion to trust that true spiritual seekers will find the one true God through the path of yoga.

Yoga and meditation do not make anyone change religion. In fact, my teachers in India advised against my trying to become Hindu. Their direction indicated that yoga makes students more established in their personal relationship to the God they know directly and personally. Some people try to make yoga appear more palatable to others by editing out all the unsettling elements of the practice, like unkempt sadhus, dreadlocked rishis, and nomadic renunciants. Some even attempt to say that yoga is just stretching, and they ban the usage of Sanskrit. Recently in the US, state legislatures that once banned yoga approved the practice again, while banning Sanskrit and the sound *OM*. Washing out the Hindu origins of yoga and the Buddhist history of meditation is a disservice to the reality of the practices' roots. Burying the true origins of any practice is an act of cultural appropriation. Instead, I believe it is possible to humbly learn from the intelligence of both yoga and meditation, no matter which religion one follows, while maintaining the authenticity of the practice as a rich spiritual tradition of India. At least, I can say that I have personally strove to straddle multiple spiritual worlds while honoring all.

If God is in our hearts, true spiritual practice will reveal that. Similarly, if anger, hatred, and other repressed shadow emotions are in our hearts, the practice will reveal those too, not as an end but as a part to bring about our ultimate liberation. Yoga and meditation are paths of a direct, personal revelatory experience of all that is, including the divine, beginning with the cultivation of the tools of self-observation. The spiritual path aims to reveal the truth about oneself and the world. We only need to fear the truth if what we believe is an illusion.

But What about Suffering?

If God is love, and God created the world, why is there so much suffering?

Misidentifying the source and cause of suffering and shirking personal responsibility is a path that only leads to more suffering. If religious beliefs protect us from admitting faults and encourage us to perpetrate harmful actions on others, then those religious beliefs may be an impediment to our spiritual liberation.

Patañjali states that ignorance is the root of all suffering. Called *Avidya* in Sanskrit, the root ignorance is centered around our inability to recognize the truth about who we really are. Accordingly, we would not be able to see the truth about the universal laws because our truth is not only built on the laws but is an expression of these laws. We are not separate from the universal laws; we are one with the laws of the universe; one with love and liberty.

It might be helpful to revisit the notion that God created the world. Whether you believe that the world was created in seven days, according to Genesis, or that the big bang started everything doesn't matter right now. Both perspectives agree that there is an intelligence that guides the creation of life. If we take the idea that a loving force is behind the architecture of the universe, then we could say that God (or whatever term best describes the generative force behind life) created the universe. Rules govern this universe, and as subjects living within this realm, we are subject to the spiritual laws, just as we are subject to the law of gravity. We are not victims of an angry, wrathful deity. If we are subject to the spiritual laws that govern the universe, we have to find out what those laws are in order to live at peace with them. Instead of a being on the other side of the veil, judging and punishing us, imagine if there was a stream of well-being created for us by a benevolent force. When we play by the rules, we act in love, and the world is a paradise. But when we act in fear, we break the rules and live in our own personal hell.

It's easy to say that God created this world, but the truth is that we are the ones who have created our personal realities. The lived experiences of our lives are just that—ours. We each play a far bigger role in the creation of our lives than we realize. Rethinking our concept of God requires us to update our spiritual paradigm to include personal responsibility and individual agency. We are co-creators in this world. This is our world. The things we experience are a byproduct of our state of being. The light and the shadow that we see in the world are nothing more than our light and shadow, vibrating and reflecting back to us.

We are born free and then choose, with our actions and thoughts, which path our lives will take. The root word of *sin* means "missing the target." And the target is always love; to stay in alignment with God's will means to act in love, every single time. Each time we act in fear, we miss the target of our highest potential. Each time we act in love, we hit closer to the target of our highest potential. We are made to love. We are born in freedom. Love researcher Barbara Fredrickson says, "Love is our supreme emotion. It governs all that you feel, think, do and become. It lifts you toward the higher spiritual altitudes of oceanic oneness" (Fredrickson 2013, 194).

In the current state of the world, true love is revolutionary. We have been conditioned so that the human race does not naturally operate in love. While there are certainly moments of love, these are the peak experiences of our lives and the greatest achievements of humanity. They are powerful breakthrough moments. Without changing the operating system and addressing the deepest fundamental issue at the core of the human being, that's all those moments will be—momentary breaks in the storm, not the total healing that we seek. The ego's desires of selfishness, preservation, and narcissism are antagonistic to love.

The desire to return to a bygone era where things are better is a kind of desire to return to the Garden of Eden—a soulful yearning that can only be described as a desire to return to love. All human beings carry the promise of love within themselves. A human life has the potential to be a restoration of the path of love. Each and every sentient being is good at its core. The work that we have to do here is about removing all the obstacles that are in the way of the revelation of the highest and ultimate truth; that is, the truth about who we really are. Like all truth, in order for it to be truly real, we must experience it firsthand. No feeling and no intellectual thought process can substitute for a direct, personal revelatory experience of our true nature.

To cure the disease of the mind, we have to first understand that we are not the disease, no matter how much we are identified with it. Then, we have to find the root or cause of the disease. The thought of separation, the notion of I, what we call the ego, is part of the disease. Selfishness seeks to erect towers of protection and build walls to keep enemies out. But in the heart, there are no enemies. There is only connection, intimacy, and love. We have to update our fundamental thoughts about God if we want to be restored to our true nature, the nature of love.

Rewiring Our Thoughts about God

If we think of God as a wrathful deity whose anger will judge the world, which makes an impact on how we live our lives. If, on the other hand, we think of God as an embodiment of love, which will lead us to live radically different lives. Even if people consider themselves as agnostic or atheist, decisions about how they see the universe will impact the way they live their lives just the same. If it's a story we are telling ourselves, let us be sure that we are telling a good story, one that is beneficial for us and will lead to a happy, peaceful life.

If we see God as the grand architect of the world, whose masterful intelligence sets up every law of the universe from gravity to karma, then a God of love means that the world is based on love. Casting God as wrathful changes the social contract of life itself to something terrifying and insecure. It is our ignorance about the universal laws that leads to suffering.

The God of my heart is not angry and wrathful. We have given ourselves over to patterns of anger, hate, resentment, bitterness, and other cycles of self-inflicted harm. When I met Jesus, I could only describe him as the ultimate manifestation of love. Seeing God as unforgiving or requiring appeasement divorces the Father from the Son, according to traditional Christian terms. If Christ is merciful and willing to die for our sins, while God is angry and judgmental, there is an illogical disconnect in the presentation of divinity. Many people have instinctively rejected this theory because of an innate understanding that God is love, but it's not only a feeling. There is textual evidence of this paradigm in the New Testament. First John 4:16 (NIV) says, "God is love. Whoever lives in love lives in God, and God in them."

If God is love, then love is changeless and eternal. The nature of love cannot be changed. When we are not in love, who is out of alignment? Is it us, or is it God who needs to come back into alignment? We are the ones who need restoration. It is our minds that have separated us from the stream of well-being that is the true nature of the world and our birthright.

Psychologist Timothy Jennings states, "The process of reasoning out the evidence and discovering the truth for ourselves dispels lies from our minds and transforms us back to Christlikeness" (Jennings 2012, 147).

Many Westerners who come to yoga are in search of something, just like I was. In a materialistic society—where consumer capitalism defines every action and reduces everything to the bottom line, and beings are commodified—there is a hollowness that pervades almost everything. Chasing the American dream has left so many people sitting with a broken, empty, and unfulfilled promise. Instead of the idyllic image of happiness, many people feel alienated and disconnected. We have lost our sense of belonging and have traded true intimacy for digital anonymity. Our religious institutions have become politicized and sullied from social media tirades. I believe that many of us have essentially lost the foundation of a personal, direct, and revelatory relationship with God. Without that direct connection, in many ways, we have lost ourselves.

Enter the practice of yoga. Yoga is a path to know God, personally and directly. The very reason yoga works is because it has the power to democratize the epiphany moment of knowing God. No one needs to gain access to an exclusive club or subsect. No one needs to follow any particular faith. All anyone needs to practice is a sincere desire to practice. It is said, ask, and it will be given. But we have to be sure of what we are asking for. How can we pray to a being we have never met? How can we have faith in something we don't directly know ourselves? To take such a leap into an illogical darkness goes against the grain of intelligence and critical thinking. There has to be a way to plunge into the depths of the universe and discover not only mind and matter but also what lies beyond in the realm of spirit.

God is of the spirit and not of this world. If this world is working for us, then we may make the fatal mistake of thinking that the path to peace lies in achievement or that our spiritual worthiness is defined by our ability to manifest the life of our dreams. Jesus said, "Whoever finds their life will lose it, and whoever loses their life for my sake will find it" (Matthew 10:39 NIV).

God is working in ways that we cannot imagine. There is a perspective of spiritual learning on the level of the soul and spirit that supersedes any material success or failure. To understand this gives a much-needed perspective on the transitory sufferings of the material world. Nothing is perfect here, yet everything is perfect in the spirit. We suffer because we do not and cannot see things from the grand perspective of the universe. We are all God's children. Some of us are more lost than others, but rest assured that we are all loved. Our mistakes are not failures but lessons.

To me, God is love, and that is why I will end this book with a discussion about God as love. Love, as we have seen, is a commonly used term by many. We like to say that we are love, which the fabric of the universe is love, and love is the most powerful force in the universe. Some people even say that love is their religion. But as we have seen throughout the course of this discussion, defining love and how to act in love requires a deep dive into the operating system of the mind. And the question "What is God?" has eluded humankind since time immemorial.

No one can absolutely define God, no matter how much they try. God is infinite and undefinable. Language defines how we think about things and codifies certain thoughts in words. It can be used as a tool of liberation or bondage. No name of God will ever be good enough to fully express the grandness that God is. That is something many people instinctively feel when asked to use the term *God*. In yoga, we are encouraged to find our personal relationship with God. After years of practice and searching, I have found God at the beating heart of the universe, the mighty power that is bigger and grander than all others. Learning, evolution, growth, and life lessons all happen under the watchful eye of God, but God is not in the business of shame, blame, and punishment. God loves all things, including our mistakes and our failures. God is not the judge that we so often hear in our heads; that voice of judgment is actually our own voices. We judge ourselves, while God loves us, forgives us, and leads us. Most of all, God loves us and carries us when we feel unlovable, broken, and discarded by the world. Yes, to me, God is love. And yes, love is the most powerful force in the universe and truly is all things. Everyone is worthy of love, just as they are, complete with all their mistakes, faults, and misery. At least, that's how I see things.

Not everyone agrees with me, and that's OK. I am not trying to convert anyone. It's up to each of us to figure out what we think about God and the origin of life and to make sense of where we fit into it. What I'd like to unpack here are some of the harmful tropes that can get entrenched about God. There was once a paradigm in religious institutions of sin-punishment-atonement, where great sacrifice was demanded to right the wrongs of our actions. We could also think of it as the manifestation or structure of karma. We could think of this as a cycle, where human beings, being flawed and imperfect, fail constantly at walking in perfect union with God. When human beings committed a sin, that act of sin kept them separate from God, and they needed to atone for the sin with a sacrifice before things were set right. The cycle of sin-punishment-atonement was an eternal loop that humans had little chance of escaping simply by happenstance. In Judeo-Christian terminology, this may sound like the covenant of the Old Testament, but one could easily replace the word *sin* with *samskara*, and think of this cycle in a similar manner. A samskara is a behavior pattern that obscures the free and clear flow of consciousness and blocks union with God, revelation of truth, and final freedom. We are born with samskaras that are said to be carried over from previous incarnations, which one could read as "being born in sin." Yoga says that we spend our lives either generating new samskaras or working to remove and burn away our existing ones. Through great effort, called *tapas*, the yogi seeks to willingly submit to suffering and to purify the body and mind in a heroic effort to remove all samskaras. Traditional yoga philosophy also says that through total devotion and surrender to God, the samskaras can be removed through what could be called an act of grace and love.

Grace is a new covenant that supersedes the law of cause and effect. In my experience, we are not ready for grace until we are in true need of it. Until all our effort fails, and we sit with the disaster of our lives in our hands with no way to put the pieces back together, the option of choosing grace might not be too appealing. But at a crucial moment in our lives, when no other options are available, the miracle of grace happens. The spiritual contract of retribution gets replaced with the paradigm of grace. Instead of the burden of earning worthiness being placed on the individual actions of each person, worthiness is redefined as an inherent quality of being. In other words, the miraculous act of grace supersedes all other paradigms. Forgiveness replaces punishment, command replaces control, and all beings are worthy of love exactly as they are, with all their flaws, mistakes, and imperfections.

I believe that we each need to make that shift in our hearts to experience the miracle of grace in our lives. I also believe that path is through surrender. The bigger and grander our failures and flaws and the darker our lows, the greater the depth of our surrender will be. It is because I make an endless stream of mistakes that I need grace. No matter how hard I try, I'll simply never be perfect. I am not the most powerful force in the universe, and I am not in control of it all. I realize that I need a power that is bigger and grander than I am step in and take the reins of my life. It's not on my shoulders. That, in and of itself, is a relief.

Nothing is outside God. All is held within the body of God. Love is the heartbeat of the universe, and God is love. Quite simply, when we act in love, we are in alignment with God's will. When we act in fear, we are out of alignment with God's will. To worship God, we must make everything an act of love. Even our failures are an act of love, and our shortcomings are a way to demonstrate our relentless devotion.

Pour your heart and soul into every single thing you do, with no agenda. Do not judge; just give and give of who you are not to gain anything but because the act of giving is your song of praise to God. No need to follow the rules of worship or speak particular phrases or visit particular institutions. Be fresh and new, and discover the truth—the timeless, eternal truth within. The heart is a temple, a portal that leads directly into the God realization.

Born Again in Love

Love is a paradigm of listening and learning. It is a devotion, not a critical, intellectual fight. The Bible says, "Be still and know that I am God." The goal of yoga is the state of stillness—*Nirodah*, in Sanskrit. Meditation seeks to reveal the true nature of all things. Perhaps God has already spoken in moments of stillness, in the gift of silence.

Love, we learned, happens between beings. This might be a stretch, but imagine a world where love could happen not just between two human beings but between all beings and, ultimately, also with the universal being that is God. The typical signifiers of love are usually defined within human interpersonal actions, like smiles, gestures, nods, body positioning, tone of voice, and facial mirroring. I believe that love and positivity resonance exists not only between humans but also between human and nonhuman beings. Those with cherished pets will confirm that they have felt an exchange of love between themselves and their animal companions. There are sounds, movements, and expressions that make the presence of love evident.

But what about God and the universe? So many people don't know what to believe about God and the divine because they have not felt the kind of confirmation of a loving presence that comes from synchronicity, or, as Fredrickson calls it, *positivity resonance* with any being other than a close-knit circle of humans. But if every action is an act of love, not just the actions that are done toward those humans in one's inner circle, then it opens up the possibility to connect deeply with all beings, human and nonhuman, and inclusive the great, grand presence of the being of God.

While it may appear naive or unrealistic, I believe that we each have the innate potential to feel the love of the universe, to be present with intimate detail in the mind of God, and to recognize our connection to all things, all beings, and every atom in the whole world. The grand intelligence of infinity is expressed in a participatory universe that speaks to us through a universal language of alignment. The basic premise that I have presented throughout this book is simple: we have the power to free our minds. Think a thought, and it becomes real. Repeat the thought, and it becomes automatic and programmed. How we think about things matters immensely. A small shift in perspective can produce miraculous changes. The process of waking up is about being a conscious co-creator with the most powerful force in the universe. We are co-creating every moment of every day. The question is not whether we are powerful enough. The question is, how will we use the power vested within us?

It is possible to tap into a flow of happiness so deep and true that it infuses every fiber of the body with pure magic. It happens as a small shift in the heart and soul. Life itself can become a great artwork of expression; a tapestry of the spirit, woven into matter. This is our potential. We are here to realize who we really are.

It might sound like a fairy tale, but it's one in which I am willing to believe. If the unseen presence of the divine could be made manifest in the world and reflected back to us in our hearts, we would see the world as a place of immense blessing (and maybe it is). To act in love could then be simply a choice to tune in and listen to the connection between beings.

But how does God or the universe smile, gesture, lean, and nod toward all beings? Could it be that there is a language of love that speaks to us all when we are finally tuned in to it? Maybe love is not only a romantic notion but also a transcendent path of ecstasy and splendor, a path of liberation, and a way out of suffering to true peace. Radically reprogramming the mind and reclaiming the vibrant seat of power is being reborn in the language of love.

The spiritual seeker must be reborn again, for that is the fulfillment of a quest of the soul. What does it mean to be born again? It may be a surprise for many Christians to learn that traditional Hinduism contains the concepts of the Dvija (Sanskrit: द्विज), or the "twice-born." The premise, referred to in chapter 15 of the Bhagavad Gita, is based on the premise that a person is first born physically and then later undergoes rites of passage and initiation for spiritual study and development. Whatever outer signifier is used to denote this rite of passage is based in history, culture, and religion, but the inner journey of the human being is universal. A declaration of faith combined with an outward ceremony is not enough to safeguard one's soul. A ritual may hold deep symbolic meaning, but in order to be truly born again, the entire operating system of the mind must be wiped out. The old patterns have to be unlearned, and one must truly see the world as a newborn child. This resetting of the habit pattern of the mind and the subsequent installing of a new paradigm of thought is the hidden message of the call to be born again. Without the inner work of spiritual evolution, rituals are devoid of the actual transformation that they call upon.

The initiation to the spiritual journey happens in the heart. It is a choice made by the true seeker to change the paradigm of fear to the paradigm of love. Jennings says,

> The law of love is the law of life—the principle upon which all life and the universe is best. As God himself is love, he designed everything that he created to operate in harmony with this law of love, this circle of beneficence in which all things give freely to others. (Jennings 2012, 60)

Waking up to this truth is spiritual liberation.

We do not need to be affiliated with any religion, or go through any formal rites of passage, or be ordained in any formal sense. What we need is to ready our hearts for the wild ride that is a life in love. The spiritual path opens in true depth when we are ready to wager everything we have ever known and jump to a place of the unknown. When we are ready to trade the fear of the world—the existing paradigm of smallness, scarcity, and ego—for the new paradigm of love, infinity, and God, that is when we begin our own hero's journey. It is not an easy task, but once it begins, there is no turning back.

In order to discover within our being that which is indestructible, we will need to be exposed to total annihilation, over and over again. It is not an easy task, but it is one that sets us free. We must truly discover that we are not our thoughts, emotions, job, or skin color. This shift can only happen when we catch a glimpse of a timeless presence that is intimately connected to all things and is simultaneously no thing. When we not only see love and strive to act in love but also see that who we are is love, the shift happens. We are finally free, born again in the eyes of spirit. This step is taken in innocence and cannot be manipulated or bought with anything other than an open heart.

Many people have never thought of themselves as initiated into a spiritual lineage. Reading this book could be considered as an initiation to the universal religion of love. We could say that the process has begun; the seed within has been activated.

There is a question in every human being's heart that can only be answered by a total immersion in timelessness; in manifest, universal truth. There is no logical construct that can account for the grand being that is the heartbeat of the universe. Until we each have personally experienced that timelessness ourselves, we may always wonder whether or not it's true, whether or not God exists, and whether or not we have a place in the vastness of the universe. But once we have even a moment of total surrender and immersion to that which is beyond the field of mind and matter, everything in life changes. There is simply no going back to the old ways of being. We are born again into a new life. This spiritual rebirth is where we wake up to the answers of life's deepest questions—Who am I? What is this thing called life? Where will I go when it's over?—and find that the answer is love.

Waking Up to Eternal Love

The message of this book is simple: let everything you do be an act of love. Infused with the power of love, what was once ordinary can be extraordinary. We can reach out our hands and heal a small piece of this wounded universe. We can do it with a heart full of love. If we fill our hearts with innocence and wonder, our world will reflect back the purity and peace we carry within. No matter how small or trivial an action may seem, when done with love, every action carries the promise of grace.

The love we each carry in our hearts is always there. Yes, sometimes difficult experiences can make it feel like love is lost, but nothing can destroy our ability to give, receive, and be love in totality. As Paul says in 1 Corinthians 13:2 (NIV), "If I have absolute faith so as to move mountains, but have not love, I am nothing."

We do yoga poses, but what's really at the heart of the practice is the journey to the center of the self. We sit on the meditation cushion, but what we find is an immeasurable depth. Love is what is there when we look deeply enough—pure, timeless, eternal, all-encompassing love. Paul states in 1 Corinthians 13:4–8 (NIV),

> Love is patient, love is kind. It does not envy, it does not boast, it is not proud. It is not rude, it is not self-seeking, it is not easily angered, it keeps no account of wrongs. Love takes no pleasure in evil, but rejoices in the truth. It bears all things, believes all things, hopes all things, endures all things. Love never fails.

There is no truth deeper than love. There is no power greater than love. There is no greater agent of change than love. It's up to each of us to find love in full power, presence, and being.

Many spiritual practices have the potential to lead to an "awakening." Sometimes reading a book (maybe even this one) is the catalyst that sparks the beginning of a long journey home. Whether we do yoga, meditate, pray, chant, journal, sit in silence, commune with nature, do tai chi, or something else, if the reason we turn to that practice is to liberate the mind and find deeper truth, it is a spiritual path.

The truth about love is very simple. We are all worthy of love but not by the acts that we have done. We are worthy of love simply by the grace that's already in our hearts and souls. When we act in love, we act in alignment with who we really are.

Whenever we think that we are not worthy of love, we step away from our true selves. We are human. It is inevitable that sometimes we will wake up in a yucky mood, get angry, or do things that are less than ideal. Think again. Humanity is flawed, imperfect, and stumbling. Love cannot exist without the balance of its opposite. The shadow side makes us whole, and embracing the shadow self is a major part of spiritual practice. Just because we sometimes feel negative emotions does not disqualify us from sharing love, compassion, and kindness. To be love and live in love does not mean that anger, sadness, or hurt will never arise. To be love means that we are finally strong enough to let it all in without breaking.

Anger, anxiety, sadness, and other forms of woundedness are the moments that have the biggest potential to grow our capacity for compassion, love, and kindness. When everything is rosy and going according to plan, it's easy to be nice to everyone. But when we learn to maintain an open heart amid difficulty, struggle, and challenge, we know the practice is truly working for us. I'm not perfect. I get it wrong more times than I can count, each and every day. The purpose of learning to act in love is not to set up another perfect picture to measure against. Instead, it's about coming home.

Out of the billions of beings on the planet, each being is special. And what makes each of us special is intimately tied with our awakening and our own process of liberation. When we awaken, the gifts within us rise, and we reveal our greatness. Everyone is a seeker of some sort, or at least every being contains the seed of seeking within them. Once the seed of awakening is activated, we will embark upon the path.

Life is an eternally flowing stream. Life is bigger than any one person. Show up every day, and join the deep flow of limitless consciousness, a vast, expansive beating heart that fills the world with love.

I want you to know that I love you, just as I love myself; that my capacity for love knows only the limits I allow; and that the more I love myself, the more I love you too. We are one and the same. I am love. You are love. When we act in love, we bring the blessings of heaven to earth. Together, we are the love of the world.

Reflection

1. Stand outside in silence for a few moments. Open your heart and mind to the beauty and grandeur of the world. Listen for the still small voice of wisdom and love, and let yourself fall. How does the universe speak to you in the universal language of love?

References

Brach, Tara. *Radical Acceptance: Embracing Your Life with the Heart of a Buddha.* **New York, NY:** Random House Publishing Group, 2004.

Brown, Brené. *The Gifts of Imperfection: Let Go of Who You Think You're Supposed to Be and Embrace Who You Are.* Center City, Minnesota: Hazelden Publishing, 2010.

Carless, Monica. "The Power of Vulnerability: Brené Brown's TED Talk May be the Breakthrough You've Been Looking For." Elephant Journal. February 27, 2017. https://www.elephantjournal.com/2017/02/power-vulnerability-brene-browns-ted-talk-may-be-the-breakthrough-youve-been-looking-for.

Chrissy. "50 Body Confidence Quotes to Inspire Self-Love." Fun Loving Families. June 22, 2021. https://www.funlovingfamilies.com/body-confidence-quotes.

Dass, Ram. "Qualities of Conscious Love." Ram Dass. January 6, 2016. https://www.ramdass.org/qualities-of-conscious-love.

Dass, Ram. "Being Love." Ram Dass. May 26, 2021. https://www.ramdass.org/being-love.

Dispenza, Joe. *Breaking The Habit of Being Yourself: How to Lose Your Mind and Create a New One.* Carlsbad, California: Hay House Inc., 2013.

Fallis, Jordan. "The 9 Most Promising Psychobiotics for Anxiety." Optimal Living Dynamic. September 5, 2021. https://www.optimallivingdynamics.com/blog/?author=55832ca0e4b0fe87a727e7ed.

Fredrickson, Barbara. *Love 2.0.* New York, NY: Plume, 2013.

Grupo MContigo. "Subconscious Mind Conscious Mind." Exploring Your Mind. December, 2017. https://exploringyourmind.com/subconscious-mind-conscious-mind.

Hanh, Thich Nhat. *Cultivating the Mind of Love.* **Berkeley, California:** Parallax Press, 2004.

Hanson, Richard. *Hardwiring Happiness: The New Brain Science of Contentment, Calm, and Confidence.* New York, NY: Harmony, 2016.

Heyman, Jivana. *Yoga Revolution: Building A Practice of Courage & Compassion.* Boulder, CO: Shambhala, 2021.

Islamic Foundation UK. "Towards Understanding the Quran." Islamic Studies. January 27, 2021. https://www.islamicstudies.info/tafheem.php?sura=29&verse=2&to=3.

Jennings, Timothy. *Could It Be This Simple?* Hagerstown, MD: Lennox Publishing, 2012.

Karpman, Stephen. "Transactional Analysis articles." Karpman Drama Triangle. 2015. https://karpmandramatriangle.com.

Kornfield, Jack. *A Path with Heart: A Guide through the Perils and Promises of Spiritual Life.* New York, NY: Bantam, 1993.

Kornfield, Jack. *The Wise Heart: A Guide to the Universal Teachings of Buddhist Psychology.* New York, NY: Bantam, 2009.

Kornfield, Jack. "Suffering and Letting Go." Jack Kornfield. March 16, 2021. https://jackkornfield.com/suffering-and-letting-go.

Longfellow, Henry Wadsworth. *The Complete Works of Henry Wadsworth Longfellow: Paul Revere's Ride, The Song of Hiawatha, Evangeline, Christus: A Mystery, The Masque of Pandora and More.* Kindle Edition, 2014.

National Council for Behavioral Health. "How to Manage Trauma." The National Council. November 2020. https://www.thenationalcouncil.org/wp-content/uploads/2013/05/Trauma-infographic.pdf?daf=375ateTbd56.

Newberg, Andrew B. *How God Changes Your Brain: Breakthrough Findings from a Leading Neuroscientist.* New York, NY: Ballantine Books, 2010.

Paramahansa Yogananda. "Excerpts from God Talks with Arjuna: The Bhagavad Gita—Chapter 2." February 12, 2021. http://yogananda.com.au/gita/gita0200.html.

Riggs, Benjamin. *Finding God in the Body.* USA: Benjamin Riggs, 2016.

Sad Gurujv Quotes. "Life Experience Suffering." October 2020. https://sadhgurujvquotes.com/quote/2530.

Tolle, Eckhart. *Stillness Speaks.* Novato, CA: New World Library, 2003.

Van der Kolk, Bessel. *The Body Keeps the Score: Brain, Mind, and Body in the Healing of Trauma.* New York, NY: Penguin Publishing Group, 2015.

Wikipedia the Free Encyclopedia. "Lilla Watson." Wikipedia. December 2020. https://en.wikipedia.org/wiki/Lilla_Watson.

Williamson, Marianne. *A Return to Love: Reflections on the Principles of "A Course in Miracles."* New York, NY: HarperOne, 1996.

Zimberoff, Diane. *Breaking Free from the Victim Trap: Reclaiming Your Personal Power.* San Francisco, CA: Wellness Press, 2011.

Lightning Source UK Ltd.
Milton Keynes UK
UKHW011236281122
412977UK00001B/51